NORMAN MAILER

The Self-Appointed Messiah

Gwendolyn Chabrier

Orchid Press

Gwendolyn Chabrier
NORMAN MAILER: The Self-Appointed Messiah

ORCHID PRESS
GPO Box 13447,
General Post Office,
Hong Kong

www.orchidbooks.com

Copyright © Orchid Press 2008.

Protected by copyright under the terms of the International Copyright Union: all rights reserved. No part of this publication may be reproduced in any form or by any means, electronic or mechanical, including photocopying, recording, or by any information storage or retrieval system without prior permission in writing from the publisher.

Cover: Portrait of Norman Mailer, by Diane Bondareff / AP Photo.

ISBN: 978-988-97764-2-8

Praise for the French edition of
NORMAN MAILER: THE SELF-APPOINTED MESSIAH

Gwendolyn Simpson Chabrier delves into the life and work of one who undertook a mystic mission to be the prophet of his time and his country. A fascinating read.

Paris Match

A fascinating biographical essay on the 'unhappy conscience' of American literature.

Florence Noiville, *Le Monde*

Mailer can be found in all of his facets in this work of Gwendolyn Simpson Chabrier devoted to him (*Norman Mailer, un prophete americain*); simultaneously monster and genius.

Eric Neuhoff, *Le Figero*

Gwendolyn Simpson Chabrier enters Mailer's life through the influences of New York-Jewish literature, those of his mother, his wives, Women's lib, anti-Semitism, racism… subjects among many which Norman Mailer explored with passion and sometimes despair.

Le Quotidien des Livres

More than a biography of a man of many battles, not the least of which was the one he waged against itself, this book discusses the life and work of the writer through the large themes he has addressed.

Carol Binder, *Actualité Juive*

In her work, the author seeks to engage all facets of this complex writer, torn between his consuming passions and despair over American stagnation.

Cortay Philippe, *Le Dauphiné*

This book is a fascinating plunge into the world of the prophet Norman Mailer, legendary author of 20th century America. Read to understand America of the 21st century!

Claude Kibler Andreotti, *La Marseillaise*

CONTENTS

INTRODUCTION 1

    Chapter I   : Mailer and American Literature 5

    Chapter II : Mailer: The Jewish Prince 29

    Chapter III : Mailer and the Weaker Sex 65

    Chapter IV : Mailer: The Jeremiah 92

    Chapter V   : Mailer: Politics and Anti-Semitism 118

    Chapter VI : Mailer and the Negro 141

EPILOGUE 163

CONCLUSION 167

ENDNOTES 171

GENERAL BIBLIOGRAPHY 194

ABOUT THE AUTHOR 214

INTRODUCTION

Norman Mailer is one of the most emblematic literary figures of our time. And the charge, which is his, cannot be dissociated from the quasi-religious mission he had consciously undertaken since the beginning of his career: to become a prophet, a self-appointed messiah, of his times and of his country.

After a shielded childhood and adolescence, Mailer's first experience of anti-Semitism was his integration at Harvard when he was sixteen. At the time, Harvard was the elitist, WASP bastion of American society. He had barely graduated when the success of *The Naked and the Dead* in 1948 propelled him to the fore of the American literary scene. In the years that followed, his would be an endless quest for an identity, torn between his middleclass Jewish origins and the rigorous Protestant world he had discovered at Harvard. Despite this enduring conflict, Mailer seems with age more reconciled to and involved with his Jewish background. This is best illustrated by his latest novel, *The Castle in the Forest*, a fictitious account of Adolf Hitler's youth. Was not Mailer's pre-occupation with this Machiavellian demagogue ultimately a manifestation of his growing identification with the six million victims of the Holocaust? Was the author's choice of Hitler not an indirect avowal that late in life he was driven to affirm himself as a Jew? When he died, in his mid eighties, Norman Mailer had become a citizen of the world. Yet, having fled the Brooklyn of his childhood, he also admitted that "the nest's the place he wanted to go back to in moments of crisis"[1]; his oasis free of anti-Semitism.

The American prophet had become a retired patriarch. He had eight biological children, one adopted child and ten grandchildren. Mailer's work, *The Big Empty*, published in 2006, is even a series of dialogues on politics, sex, God, boxing, morality, myth, poker and bad conscience in America with his youngest son, John Buffalo. Despite his age, he had continued to write; the radicalism of his former years still existent but tempered. He wanted to make the news. True to his reputation as a protestor, he criticized George W. Bush vehemently. In a way, he was back at the starting block: at the age of twenty-five, *The Naked and the Dead* and the Second World War had inaugurated his career. The Holocaust and Vietnam have haunted his novels. The war against Iraq, launched by an American-led coalition, sharpened his critical verve. To Mailer, Bush was a Conservative using the Christian crusade against an axis of evil as an excuse for economic and imperialistic imperatives.

As a younger man, impatient and ultraistic, stimulated by alcohol and drugs, Mailer would harangue the crowds. By 2007, he had moderated his approach. Tortured by arthritis, he likened himself to an aging football player: "An elderly man who's been around for years, for forever nearly, measures his chances by his physical resistance. A back player, if allowed to choose his post, will perhaps say to himself, 'no, I won't try to catch that pass, because the last time I tried, I got licked'. As a professional, he always calculates the possibilities. It's the same when one writes, one calculates what one is or is not able to do."[2] He seemed to be observing himself with cynical detachment. Despite his two Pulitzer Prizes and National Book Awards, he believed he had failed—as have all the other American writers of his generation—to write 'The Great American Novel', that Tolstoyan epic spawned by the decadence and conformity of his country, which would have augured its moral, political and social rebirth; the œuvre that might have prevented George W. Bush and the American right to embark on their insane quest for an American Empire, the Roman Empire of the twenty-first century. Notwithstanding his reservations, Mailer chose still to be a contestant. Even if *The Castle in the Forest* never achieves the literary impact to which he aspired, his choice of Hitler exemplifies the blind inhumanity and boundless injustice which the author continued to address and combat as an individual, as a writer and as a Jew. Is not *The Castle in the Forest* another of the prophet's admonitions to the American public of the dangers of totalitarianism? Did Mailer not envision that America is also a potential candidate for its own genocide, should it not address its current decline and elect scrupulously leaders, unlike Bush, who will force the nation to recognize its decadence and endeavor to surpass it?

Although his mother, Fan, would have underwrote that Norman was destined for the Nobel Prize, he believed instead that "Certain authors are so vast they cannot be ignored. I don't belong to that category. Will I be able to last?"[3] We have to belie his doubts. He does indeed belong to the lineage of major authors who cannot be ignored. His recent death will prove, posthumously, that Normal Mailer belongs to the lineage of major authors whose work will transcend time.

CHAPTER I

Mailer and American Literature

"The Egyptians, the Babylonians, and the Persians rose, filled the planet with sound and fury; then faded to dream-stuff and passed away" wrote Mark Twain in 1897. "The Greeks and Romans followed and made a vast noise, and they are gone; other peoples have sprung up and held their torch for a time but it burned out, and they sit in twilight now, or have vanished... All things are mortal but the Jew; all other forces pass, but he remains."[4] Twain defines the persistence of the Jew in retaining his collective and individual identity while confronted with political and social adversity. Not only have Mailer and other Jews survived through this adversity, they have excelled.

Between 1654 and 1825, the Sephardic or Spanish-Portuguese Jews immigrated to the United States predominately during the colonial period. They were the descendants of the Jews who held established positions in Spain, Portugal and Brazil, and they sought asylum in America from the Inquisition. During this period, the Jews expressed themselves mainly through their religious writings, and Hebrew poetry. In the beginning of the nineteenth century, Mordecai M. Noah wrote his first play, *The Fortress of Sorrento*, in 1808, while the first Jewish–American poet to be recognized for her English verse was Emma Lazarus, the daughter of Sephardic and German-Jewish parents, writing in the latter half of the nineteenth century. Generally, the life of the early Jews in America was recorded through their diaries, letters and documents.

The German Jews were the next migration from Europe, between 1825 and 1894. By 1895, they were only five thousand. However, between 1820 and 1870, two to four hundred thousand Jews came to the United States from Central Europe, predominantly from

Germany, following the aborted German 1848 Revolution. These Jews were instrumental in contributing to America's institutional and economic life; however, they were not focused on promoting the country's literary and artistic community, as the later Jews from Eastern Europe would be.

In fact, between 1881 and 1924, two million Jews—one third of the Eastern European population—immigrated to the New World. They fled Eastern Europe due to the czarist-encouraged pogroms and mob-violence, which followed the assassination of Alexander II in 1881. These Russian Jews were to make the most significant contribution to the artistic and literary life of the country. This was clearly anticipated by the editor of *Harper's Weekly*, who stated in 1916 that "It is from the Russian Jews, who are the mass of poor Jews in America, that the real contribution to American life is likely to come, because their aspirations are spiritual, their imagination alive."[5] This group from czarist Russia was Yiddish-speaking and came from the *shtetls*, the country's Jewish ghetto communities. About ninety percent of the Jews in America belonged to this group, many of whom were Yiddish and Hebrew writers, some becoming bilingual, others continuing to write in their native tongues. A significant number of Eastern European Jews immigrated to the United States, Norman Mailer's family included, before the restrictive immigration laws of 1922 and 1924 were passed. Most importantly, it was at this time that the center of Jewish culture also immigrated. "Civilization never dies, it only changes its address." By 1920, "Vilna moved to New York, Grodno to Philadelphia, and Minsk to Boston."[6]

From 1880, until the eve of the First World War, during the largest wave of European-Jewish immigration to the United States, the prose and poetry of Jewish-American authors such as Joseph Bovshover, David Edelstadt, Morris Vinchevsky and Morris Rosenfeld exposed the difficulties of the immigrant and his family. Immigrants were faced with economic and cultural adaptation, and were maltreated as working men, peddlers or employees of the sweatshop system. No longer were they the revered rabbis and scholars of the Old World, and these authors frequently described the nostalgia felt by the Eastern European Jew for the ideals of piety, learning and family, as well as the sense of humanity and kinship characteristic of the *shtetl's* communal life. In *The Uprooted*, Oscar Handlin discussed the struggle of the Jewish immigrant, concluding that his existence constituted a "history of alienation and its consequences."[7] Their disillusionment was often so great that, as early as 1882, twenty-nine percent of Jewish immigrants had returned to Europe.[8]

However, for those who remained, assimilation was a major preoccupation. In 1904, the fiasco of the Russian Revolution and the new surge of pogroms reinforced this need to conform. Yet, unlike the earlier wave, this group of immigrants was comprised mostly of political and communal leaders, literati and members of the educated classes who were to make a more significant contribution to Jewish-American literature. Through their novels, short stories and theater, such authors as Scholem Asch, David Pinsky, Sholem Aleichem, Leon Kobrin, Joseph Opatoshu, or David Ignatev portrayed in Yiddish the travails of the Jewish immigrant. Despite the prevalence of Yiddish in literature, by the second decade of the twentieth century, English began to replace Yiddish as the literary language of the immigrant writers as well as having become the vernacular of the ghetto. As Leslie Fiedler observes, it was the manifestation, "that there is an American Jew... and he feels at home!"[9] At this time, numerous novels, mostly autobiographical, appeared in English, such as *The Promised Land*, by Anzia Yezierska, or the most distinguished Jewish-American novel written before the 1930s, *The Rise of David Levinsky*, by Abraham Cahan, editor of the Jewish Daily Forward, published in 1917.

Many of these novels focused on the conflict between life in the Jewish ghetto and the expectations and aspirations of the immigrant in his American Zion. Davis Levinsky, the Talmudist scholar who becomes a lonely garment millionaire, expresses his initial exuberance, as other protagonists had done: "The United States lured me not merely as a land of milk and honey, but also, and perhaps chiefly, as one of mystery, of fantastic experience, of marvelous transformations. To leave my native place and to seek my fortune in that distant weird world seemed to me just the kind of sensational adventure my heart was hankering for."[10] However, like so many Jewish immigrants, although David Levinsky manages to escape the miseries of ghetto life, he is still faced with the reality that, "Cultural baggage cannot be checked at Ellis Island."[11] In his case, the loneliness of his boyhood in Antomir maintains its prior hold: "I can never forget the days of my misery. I cannot escape from my old self. My past and my present do not comport well. David, the poor lad swinging over a Talmud volume at the Preacher's Synagogue seems to have more in common with my inner identity than David Levinsky, the well-known cloak manufacturer."[12]

Assimilation was a major issue in Jewish-American literature between 1880 and 1930. If the pre-war novels tended to celebrate the Jews' integration, later works, such as, *The Rise of David Levinsky*, were centered on the disillusionment provoked by this process. According to David Martin Fine, the second wave, "stilled the shriller messianic assimilationist voices of the pre-war immigrant."[13] Leslie Fiedler adds that the novels of this period reflect the intimate relation between the Jewish male's sexual conquest of the revered Gentile female and his capacity for assimilation. He portrays the Jew's quest for acculturation as a romantic encounter between the Jewish Don Juan and the *shiksa*: "The approach to and retreat from the Gentile community, the proffering of himself and the shying away out of fear of acceptance or rejection, becomes in the imagination of the Jewish writer a "kind of wooing," an act of timid and virginal love."[14]

This is well illustrated in Ben Hecht's, *A Jew in Love*, where the Jewish womanizer, Abe Nussbaum, juggles between his wife, his mistress, a whore who he really loves in his own manner, and the wife of an alleged good friend. Although he lacks any real desire for these women, the one to whom he is the most attached, not surprisingly, is the *shiksa*; he crudely explains this as, "the niggerish delight of the Jew in the blond"[15], who is representative of the Gentile world to which he cannot gain access.

Concurrently, this early Jewish-American literature, aptly described by Mailer as, "a counter-literature, whose roots were found in poverty, industrial society and the emergence of a new class,"[16] began to awaken the fears of the existing literary upper-class establishment. As early as 1907 in, "The American Scene", Henry James vituperated against, "the Hebrew Conquest of New York"[17] which he feared was threatening the purity of the English language. Similarly, in 1922, Theodore Dreiser, in a letter to H.L. Menken, wrote: "New York to me is a scream—a Kyke's dream of a Ghetto, the lost tribe has taken the island."[18]

In order to protect themselves from what they considered the Jewish literary threat, the Anglo-Saxon authors prolonged the European image of Shylock, the sinister Jew, in their writings. With the exception of certain writers such as William Dean Howells or Mark Twain, they almost systematically denigrated the Jew. Despite the literary ascension of the American-Jewish author, this negative stereotype prevailed in American letters as late as the 1930s, the WASP representing the Jew more willingly then the Jews themselves. Paradoxically, Hemingway, Mailer's literary hero, is renown for his caricature of the Jew, the middleweight boxing protagonist from Princeton, Robert Cohn in, *The Sun Also Rises*. Other Anglo-Saxon writers were equally as unmerciful in their treatment of the Jew. In, "Gerontian", T.S. Eliot:

And the Jew scats on the windowsill, the owner,
Spawned in some estaminet of Antwerp,
Blistered in Brussels, patched and peeled in London.[19]

Ezra Pound in, *The Pisan Cantos*:

The yidd is a stimulant, and the goyim are cattle
In great
Proportion and go to saleable slaughter
With the maximum of docility.[20]

Or F. Scott Fitzgerald in, *The Great Gatsby*: "A small flat-nosed Jew raised his large head and regarded me with two fine growths of hair, which luxuriated in either nostril. After a moment, I discovered his tiny eyes."[21] The Jew was presented as the symbol of modern social disintegration, the nemesis of Anglo-Saxon culture.

The 1920s were still very much dominated by the likes of Fitzgerald, Hemingway and Faulkner, those referred to by Lewis H. Lapham in, *Money and Class in America*, as the "equestrian class"[22]. By 1930, they began to cede some turf to the Jewish-American author, who was entering into the literary mainstream.

Meanwhile, during this period, the Jewish-American author's preoccupation with integration was further accentuated with the appearance of the second generation Jew. While his parents still found comfort and security in their Jewishness, the children considered it an obstacle to their desegregation. The sociologist Marcus Hansen analyses this conflict in terms of alienation: "Whereas in the schoolroom they were too foreign, at home they were too American... How to inhabit two worlds at the same time was the problem of the second generation."[23]

This conflict of generations was a centrifugal theme in Jewish-American novels of the 1920s and 1930s. This is well illustrated by Myron Brinig in, *Singerman*, and its sequel, *This Man is My Brother*, published three years later; by David Pinsky in, *The Generations of Noah Edon*; and by Meyer Levin in, *The Old Bunch*—one of Mailer's favorite novels. Pinsky's protagonist, Noah Edon, immigrates to the United States with his wife and three sons in the 1880s. Like many immigrants, he is obliged to adapt himself to American society and its estranging materialistic values. Sociologists and social psychologists attribute much of the immigrant's uprootedness to the change which he underwent in moving from a simple community to a more complex urban society described as "anomie" (Durkheim), "primary group" relations (Cooley) or "*Gemeinschaft*" and "*Gesellschaft*" (*Community and Society*, Tonnies). This urbanization undergone by immigrant families such as the Edons resulted in what Nathan Glazer describes as, "the destruction of the cozy nest, the kinship group, in which men once lived out their lives and in which spontaneous personal relations were possible, [which] is at the root of the experience of alienation."[24] Although the virtuous Noah attempts to transmit the family's cherished religion and customs, his children reject their Jewish past, wishing alone to assimilate into the decadence of American society:

"He had brought up his sons to be pious, but as soon as they had grown up, they had cast off their father's Judaism like a garment which they had outgrown. Charles, out of principle, Murray, because religion was no business for him. Oscar attended a synagogue occasionally, for political reasons. Better he didn't!"[25] Analogously, in *The Old Bunch*, the younger generation rebels against what they consider their elders' "old-fashioned foolishness".[26]

The conflict between generations and the subsequent breakdown of the family were issues mainly confronted by the second generation immigrants, who felt marginal in American society. Will Herberg observes that their marginality found expression in a sense of rootlessness, in an inferiority complex sometimes, which could result in self-hatred and hatred of their own people.[27] Logically, Jewish self-hatred became a major preoccupation of the literature of this period, particularly in the thirties, when anti-Semitism reached its apex in the United States. At the time, over a hundred anti-Semitic groups were formed, many of these, supported by the Fascist régime in Italy, and the Nazi régime in Germany. Both the second-generation Jewish-American author and his protagonists came to internalize the humiliations and suffering incurred by anti-Semitism. Some of the most well known novels treating the subject of Jewish self-hatred were, *The Island Within*, by Ludwig Lewison, *A Jew in Love*, by Ben Hecht, *I Can Get It for You Wholesale*, by Jerome Weideman, and *What Makes Sammy Run?*, by Budd Schulberg. Protagonists such as Victor Goldman, the talented young architect who commits suicide in, *The Island Within*, were prone to the same self-hatred experienced by Mailer himself, and by some of his characters, such as Denise Gondolman, in "The Time of Her Time". In *The Island Within*, Joe Goldman describes the cause of his brother Victor's death: "From his infancy on, he was made to feel from the very air around him that to be happy and successful and acceptable in the world, he must be something that he wasn't, something that he didn't even clearly grasp or understand, namely, an Anglo-American gentleman. Well, he had no gift for mimicry. He was confused. He was maddened. He shouted. He began to hate himself and his own kind. You said yourself it was self-disgust."[28]

Ben Hecht's *A Jew in Love*, is also about another self-hating Jew, a publisher, who changes his name and obsessively seduces young women, most of whom, inevitably, are Gentile. *I Can Get It for You Wholesale* and *What Makes Sammy Run?* are both novels about Jewish embezzlers, one in the garment business, the other in the film industry. During this period, there were many works of lesser importance portraying Jews disparagingly as criminals or as exploiters. Thus, the caricature of the Jew created by the Anglo-American "tribal families" came ironically to be prolonged and reinforced by the Jewish authors themselves.

In the 1930s, this tendency toward a literature of Jewish self-loathing was also main-stayed by the Anglo-American publishing world, wary of publishing Jewish related material, not only because it wished to avoid the "foreign" invasion of its fiefdom, but also because the Gentiles who comprised the majority of the reading public might not be able to relate to Jewish topics. Consequently, some Jewish-American authors who had initially written spontaneously about their own backgrounds, either renounced writing, like Henry Roth, or adopted Anglo-Saxon names for themselves or their characters, in order to reassure their non-Jewish readers. The playwright Henry Miller explains the dilemma created by anti-Semitism, which the Jewish writer had to contend with: "I think I gave up the Jews as literary material because I was afraid that even an innocent allusion to individual wrong-doing of an individual Jew would be inflamed by the atmosphere, ignited by the hatred I was suddenly aware of, and my love would be twisted into a weapon of persecution against Jews. No good writer can approach material in that atmosphere."[29]

Karl Shapiro, the first Jewish-American poet to receive the Pulitzer Prize for poetry would later elaborate on the prejudices facing the Jewish author: "It is only in the last generation or two that an American Jew could write Jewishly and still be thought of as American. Many years ago, when I was beginning to write for publication, I wrote to an American poet whom I knew to be Jewish and asked him what obstacles one had to overcome to publish poems under a Jewish name. His reply was so ambiguous that I decided his own name wasn't very Jewish after all. I was not imagining things:

many years later, a non-Jewish poet said to me, "when I first read your poems I thought you had an impossible name for a poet."[30]

This equally explains why many Jewish writers at the time would only receive literary esteem posthumously. Such was the case for Nathaniel Wallenstein Weinstein, alias Nathaniel West, whose novels, *Miss Lonelyhearts* and *The Day of the Locust*, gained recognition after his death. Henry Roth's masterpiece, *Call it Sleep*, published in 1934, would be republished over twenty-five years later, in 1960, when it was rescued from oblivion. Roth's novel came to be considered as one of the most important Jewish American novels. Critics such as Leslie Fiedler have judged it to be, "the best single book by a Jew about Jewishness written by an American, certainly through the thirties and perhaps ever."[31]

By the 1930s, Jewish American authors, the sons of the ghetto, had not reached the literary acclaim of the Anglo-American writers from the "good families", but they nonetheless became the leading spokesmen for radicalism in the United States; among them were writers such as Isador Schneider, with his novel, *The Kingdom of Necessity*, the Communist, Joseph Freeman with his autobiography, *An American Testament, A Narrative of Rebels and Romantics*, or Michael Gold, the most renown of all, with his novel *Jews Without Money*, which was translated into fifteen languages within five years of its publication, and printed seventeen times within a decade. Clifford Odets, with his two famous plays, *Waiting for Lefty* and *Awake and Sing*, embraced the same radicalism in drama.

During this period, the Jews were impoverished by the Depression, and victimized by the persecutions and prejudices fatally magnified by social and economic upheavals. Discontented with American capitalism, Michael Gold vividly remembers his boyhood on the Lower East Side, and chastises America, which was, "rich and fat because it has eaten the tragedy of millions of immigrants."[32] Beginning in 1930 with the publication of *Jews Without Money*, until 1941, with the publication of Meyer Levin's novel, *Citizens*, the Proletarian Novel, or the novel of social protest, became the main vehicle by which the Jewish author expressed his dissent. Socialism, or communism in particular, was received as the response to the evils of capitalism. Michael Gold expresses this belief in concluding *Jews Without Money*:

A man on an East Side soap-box, one night proclaimed that out of the despair, melancholy and helpless rage of millions, a world movement had been born to abolish poverty.

I listened to him.

O workers' Revolution, you brought hope to me, a lonely suicidal boy.

You are the true Messiah. You will destroy the East Side when you come, and build there a garden for the human spirit.

O Revolution, that forced me to think, to struggle and to live.

O great beginning![33]

However, the proletarian novel was not only about the working-class; it was equally concerned with poor farmers, the lower middleclass and intellectuals, in particular those who identified with the oppressed, and gave their allegiance to Marxism or the Communist Party, the vanguards of the underdog.

Born to poverty, Itzok (later Irwin) Granich, alias Michael Gold, had contributed, until 1917, to such publications as the socialist *New York Call* and *Masses*. In the 1920s, he edited *Liberator* and became the editor of the *New Masses*, an organ of the Communist Party. Gold was a party activist and columnist for the *Daily Worker* and the *People's World* throughout his life. Like many Jewish radicals, Gold, a forerunner of Mailer, rebelled against Orthodox Judaism and sought a substitute faith. Social protest, for Gold as for Mailer, became a surrogate religion, a means of assuming his Jewish self-hatred, of effacing his Jewishness, of erasing what was foreign in order to become a fully integrated American. The difference these authors perceived between traditional Judaism and radicalism is summarized by Joseph Freeman in, *An American Testament; A Narrative of Rebels and Romantics*: "From my uncle Moishe, I heard about the revolution; from grandfather about God and the destiny of the Jewish race. No ideals could be more sharply at odds. Uncle wanted the whole of humanity to go forward; grandfather wanted his own people, a fragment of humanity, to go backward..."[34] Michael Gold, or later Mailer, concurred with Allen Guttmann's claim that the goal of the writer estranged from traditional Judaism must be the secularization of its historic purpose: "If the writer departed from the temple it is not to lose himself in the lonely crowd, he must labor to bring about the transformation of society. He must create the Zion in which exile ended."[35]

In a similar manner, Moses Richin describes the classic socialist or anarchist as a man who transferred his allegiance from "Moses to Marx"[36]. For the Jewish radical, the messianic element in traditional Judaism acted as a bridge between Judaism and Marxism, since Marx had also conceived of himself as a prophet. Michael Gold expresses this when he writes: "I believed the Messiah was coming, too. It was the one point in the Jewish religion I could understand clearly. We had no Santa Claus, but we had a Messiah."[37] By the 1930s, radicalism in its multiple forms became the awaited Messiah for many American Jews.

During the 1920s and 1930s, despite the Anglo-American literary establishment's attempts to thwart the Jew, he pursued and endured, not only in literature, but also in all the arts and sciences. In the theatre, Clifford Odets, Luther and Stella Adler and John Garfield made their mark, while Paul Muni, Edward G. Robinson and Irving Thalberg excelled in film. Meanwhile, only scientists of equal stature, such as Albert Einstein, rivaled painters like Marc Chagall. As a consequence of the *halacha* law against the representation of the human body, the Jews' true contribution to visual arts would come later. This prohibition had been strictly observed in the *shtetl*, and numerous painters followed Chagall and Soutine, emigrating to Paris, while others, such as Max Ernst, Larry Rivers, Helen Frankenhalter and Elbert Weinberg, immigrated to America, when the rigors of the *halacha* injunction had been tempered.

Jewish musicians, violinists mostly, came in great numbers, bringing with them the Russian custom of teaching the violin to young boys: Heifetz, Ellmann and Stein were among the violinists. As teachers of varied instruments, they produced pianists the likes of Horowitz, Rubenstein, Fleischer and Graffman, cellists like Pratigorsky and Freudmann, and opera singers such as Pearce, Tucker, Merrell, Resnick, Judith Raskin and Beverly Sills. Many important composers were equally Jewish, from Aaron Copland, through David Amram and George Gershwin, to Jerry Bock. Jewish creativity also played a considerable role in musical comedy, with Rogers and Hammerstein's *The Sound of Music*, being only one example.

However, the Jews would probably achieve the most prominence during this period in the field of entertainment, with performers such as Charlie Chaplin, the Marx Brothers, Eddie Cantor, George Jessel, Al Jolson and Fannie Brice, as well as many other directors, actors, and song-writers. The Jews in the creative arts seem also to have internalized the loathing directed against the Jew, portraying the *schlemiel*, the self-conscious clown, the outcast and victim, the prototype Jew that Mailer so feared and detested from his own background. In fact, it became a holding position: the Jew projected an image that could comfort the Anglo-Saxon, before his unexpected resurrection, especially in literature, after the Second World War.

During this pre-war period, the Jewish-American author was generally passive regarding the rise of Nazism and Fascism. Edward Dahlberg in *Those Who Perished*, and in his lecture to the first American Writers' Congress, "Fascism and Writers", Ludwig Lewisohn in *Trumpet of Jubilee*, and Martin Levin in *Citizens*, were among the exceptions. Even though the left-wing press voiced its discontent, the American-Jewish author was either not fully aware of the situation, or he preferred to occult the issue, all too aware of his own vulnerability confronted with the anti-Semitism in America. However, his situation would change radically with the cataclysmic effects of the Holocaust on world Jewry. After the Second World War, the American Jew, besought by guilt, would no longer write out of self-loathing, rejection and dissent; his voice was now one of self-affirmation and self-defense. In *The World of Our Fathers*, for which he obtained the National Book Award for non-fiction in 1977, Irving Howe describes the Jew's culpability: "We were living directly after the Holocaust of the Eastern Jews. We might scorn our origins; we might crush America with discoveries of ardor; we might change our names. But we knew that for an accident of geography we might also now be bars of soap. At least some of us could not help feeling that in our earlier claims to have shaken off all ethnic distinctiveness, there had been something false, something shaming. Our Jewishness might have no clear religious or national content, it might be helpless before the criticism of believers; but Jews we were, like it or not, and liked it or not."[38]

After the war, the American-Jewish writer was addressing the Holocaust, especially in non-fictional works. In *Barbary Shore*, as early as 1952, Mailer was one of the first Jewish authors to fictionalize the Holocaust. Although it is certainly not the main focus of the novel, Lannie's recollections of the cruelty and brutality of the concentration camp guards are a poignant rendering of the Jews' suffering. However, not until the 1960s was the Holocaust openly integrated into Jewish-American fiction, with Saul Bellow's *Arthur Sammler*, Edward Lewis' *The Pawnbroker*, I.B. Singer's *The Enemies* or Susan Fromberg Shaeffer's *Anya*. Unlike European novelists, the American-Jewish author did not focalize on *l'univers concentrationnaire*, and its horrors, but chose to scrutinize the Jewish past, its preservation and transmission.

Otherwise, there are many common traits between America with its Protestant foundation, and Judaism. As early as the seventeenth and eighteenth centuries, the New England Puritans identified themselves with the Jews. According to Stephen Birmingham in *Our Crowd*, the Puritans' literal interpretation of the Old Testament led to a sort of "neo-Judaism, a Judaism translated into Anglo-Saxon terms"[39]. "The Christian Church so-called", also declared John Stevens, "is only a continuation and an extension of the Jewish Church."[40]

Like the Jews, the Protestants considered that they had been chosen by God to transmit his word. Like the Jews, they studied the Old Testament in search of a personal, more direct connection with God. They associated their arrival in New England with the Jewish quest for the Promised Land. George III, the English king, had been their persecuting Pharaoh. The Protestants likened America to the land of Canaan, insisted on studying Hebrew at college and university, naming their children after the heroes and heroines of the Old Testament. New England preachers were forever referring to the 'God of Israel', to 'Jacob's God', to Zion and Jerusalem.

After the Second World War, the American Jew reasserted his Jewishness and condemned anti-Semitism. Before the war, he had been forced to confront in silence an insidious American anti-Semitism. Although considered a war novel, the bestseller, *The Naked and the Dead,* is a denunciation of anti-Semitism in the American army, portrayed through two characters, Roth and Goldstein, the Gentiles' scapegoats. Of Roth, Mailer writes: "Nothing he could do was right, nothing would please them. He seethed, but with more than self-pity now. He understood. He was the butt because there always had to be a butt. A Jew was a punching bag because they could not do without one."[41] The same year, Irwin Shaw published *The Young Lions*, a novel on the same theme, but treated more optimistically: Shaw argues that prejudice and hatred can be overcome by moral valor. In *Focus*, Arthur Miller mocks anti-Semitism through the unemployed, the 'gentile' districts and the hotel industry. Laura J. Hobson, in *Gentleman's Agreement*, her bestseller adapted to the screen, relates the story of a journalist who passes himself off as a Jew—which he is not—in order to write articles on anti-Semitism and who in turn becomes a victim of racial prejudice.

This turning point in the attitude of Jewish novelists deeply affected by the tragedy of the Holocaust was to radically modify the attitude of American intellectuals in general, and writers in particular. By 1950, anti-Semitism as an issue became a concern of the gentile author. Another bestseller, John Hersey's *The Wall*—later dramatized by Millard Campell—describes the heroism of the Jewish underground in the Warsaw Ghetto.

However, the wave of awareness aroused by the genocide in the United-States was not the only factor to play a major role in Jewish writing. The creation of the State of Israel in 1948 was a powerful inspiration, as evoked by Karl Shapiro in "Israel":

> When I see the name of Israel high in print
> The fences crumble in my flesh; I sink
> Deep in Western chair and rest my soul.
> I look the stranger clear to the blue depths
> Of his unclouded eye. I say my name
> Aloud for the first time unconsciously.[42]

After the Sinai campaign and the Suez Canal crisis in 1956, Leon Uris published *Exodus*, a eulogy to the creation of Israel and the heroism of its immigrants.

Between the two world wars, unlike those who either ignored or disdained the liberation of Palestine, the Jewish writer was to become increasingly engaged in the creation of the state of Israel. If, in the 1930s, Ben Hecht denied his Judaism, by the end of the forties, he was occupied with the struggle against the British anti-Jewish administration. The Holocaust having brought him back to his ethno-religious roots, he joined the IRGUN, an extreme Zionist group in Palestine. In the same way, Michael Blankfort who had reneged Judaism for Marxism until the 1940s also came to believe that, "In the Communism of Judaism, the identification with my people, my active affection for the land of Israel, my faltering efforts to live by the precepts of the prophets, I have found a peace of the spirit."[43] Following a visit to Israel he wrote *The Juggler*, which was made into a film, then *Behold the Fire*, a portrayal of the NILI, a small group of Palestinian Jews who liberated Israel from the Turks during the First World War, thus laying the foundation of the State of Israel.

The year 1945 was the starting point of a renewal, a vitality in American-Jewish literature. In their collection of critical essays, *Breakthrough: A Treasury of Contemporary American-Jewish Literature*, Irving Malin and Irwin Stark wrote: "For the first time in history a large and impressively gifted group of serious American-Jewish writers has broken through the psychic barriers of the past to become an important, a major reformative influence in American life and letters."[44] Norman Mailer was to be among the leading authors of this 'breakthrough'.

Although a minority of writers in the fifties had either rejected or were indifferent to their Judaism, most American-Jewish authors were still tied to their origins. Despite the fact that some Jewish writers considered Yiddish a "bastardized language,"[45] or that Edward Dahlberg, having grown up in both a Catholic and a Jewish orphanage, did not know where to find God, Arthur Koestler, by comparison, chose complete assimilation, while most of the other authors also endorsed their Judaism in one way or another. Mailer first expressed his faith through his radicalism and later, in the apocalyptic orgasm of "The White Negro"; later still, through his mysticism and his belief in reincarnation, present also in certain cabalistic strains of Judaism. Regardless of how it manifested itself, there was always an underlying element of political, religious or social dissent in his Jewishness. Others, like Meyer Levin, discovered theirs in Hasidism: "Godless though I profess myself, I have responded with more than warmth to the mystical elements of Hasidism. As a writer, I have considered that I accept the material as folklore. But in my soul, I know that I take more than this from these legends."[46] Edward Lewis Wallant expressed his through love for his fellow man and J.D. Salinger, through Zen Buddhism. Delmore Schwartz associated his origins with alienation; Leslie Fiedler, with dissidence and exile; Shapiro felt that to be a Jew was the consciousness of being a Jew. The triumvirate Bernard Malamud, Saul Bellow and Philip Roth understood and manifested their religion in their own personal ways. Malamud equated Jewishness with suffering, Bellow, with nostalgia, guilt and anxiety, Roth, with "a kind of sensibility if anything: the nervousness, the excitability, the arguing, the dramatizing, the indignation, the obsessiveness, the touchiness, the play-acting, above all the talking."[47]

By the post-war period, writers of fiction, particularly novelists, were not alone in voicing their ethno-religious identity. Critics such as Leslie Fiedler, Irving Howe, Maxwell Geismar were pivotal in promoting their compeers in literary reviews and other media.

The 1950s heralded the arrival of a third generation. "What the son wishes to forget", wrote Marcus Hansen, "the grandson wishes to remember."[48] This tendency is well described in *The Generations of Noah*

Eden, when Noah's grandson seeks his grandfather's guidance in order to surmount America's spiritual wasteland: "There is an emptiness in me. Often I am seized with despair. I don't know why I am living in this world... This emptiness and uselessness will lead to bad habits, to weakness and dissipation. I thought religion might help me."[49]

For most ethnic groups—Poles or Italians—identification with their origins had waned by the third generation. In *Protestant, Catholic, Jew*, Will Herberg explains how, if this generation seeks a return to religious roots, only the Jew desires the re-establishment of his ethnic ties: for the Jew, religion and culture are inseparable.[50]

Authors like Ben Hecht and Budd Schulberg exemplified this Jewish acknowledgment. While they had written self-derogatory novels in the 1930s, they became Judaism's staunchest advocates. Budd Schulberg rectified his earlier position by writing an apologia for the 1952 Modern Library edition of his novel, *What Makes Sammy Run?*: "While admitting the fear that bigots might be able to turn my book against my own people and the democratic ideal, I said this only could be done 'by wrenching characters out of their cultural sockets and paragraphs out of their continuity'."[51]

Philip Roth, viewed as the renegade of Jewish-American literature, also attempted to reconcile himself with his Jewishness. In his short story, "Eli the Fanatic"—deemed the best from his collection *Goodbye Columbus*, which received the National Book Award for fiction in 1960—he reproofs his Jewish characters for succumbing to the values of their gentile neighbors. Meanwhile, Malamud's protagonists were converting to Judaism—such as Frank Alpine in *The Assistant*, for which he also won the National Book Award for fiction.

Yet, the work which was considered the quintessential statement of Jewish pride and group consciousness was Charles Angoff's seven book saga, beginning with *Journey to the Dawn* published in 1951, and ending with *Memory of Autumn*, in 1968. It traces the story of the Polonsky family who emigrated from Russia to Boston at the turn of the century, relating their evolution into the 1960s. Angoff explained his indebtedness to his heritage in the following terms: "The people and the themes of *Journey to Dawn*, and *In the Morning Light*, selected the writer far more readily than he selected them. My distant past [...] is becoming more 'real' to me than my immediate past or present—and it was a past steeped in Jewishness."[52] Mailer's own Jewishness was also re-awakened during this period. Between 1962 and 1963, he wrote five articles for *Commentary*, in which he reviewed *Tales of the Hasidim*, recently re-edited by Martin Buber.

This post-war era also saw a radical change in the treatment of their protagonists by Jewish-American authors. Before the war, their fictional characters were Jewish anti-heroes, non-achievers worthy of pity and degradation. After the war, literature produced instead Jewish heroes as varied as Bellow's intellectual, Malamud's common man or Mailer's hipster. However, in *Strangers and Natives: The Evolution of the American Jew from 1921 to the Present*, Judd L. Teller traced the Jewish author's unwillingness to accept material success as a barometer of achievement in his justification of his 'unsuccessful' father or grandfather.[53]

As early as 1915, William Dean Howells had predicted the belated emergence of the Jewish writer, often a product of New York's slums: "Very possibly there may be a moment a Russian or Polish Jew, born or bred on our East Side, who shall burst from his parental Yiddish, and [...] slake our thirst of imaginative literature."[54] By 1920, "Vilnius moved to New York, Grodno to Philadelphia, and Minsk to Boston." With the exception of Saul Bellow, born in Montreal in 1915, most of the major Jewish writers of the second half of the twentieth century came from the Lower East Side or its surrounding districts and were born at roughly the same time. Norman Mailer was born in Long Branch, New Jersey and brought up in Brooklyn. For these authors, most of whom were native Americans, assimilation was not a problem; they had no need to become American, because they already were. Confident of belonging in a way their immigrant grandfathers never had, their religion was in no way an obstacle to their integration. This new Jewish generation had finally come to terms with itself.

The growing increase in mixed marriages was yet another proof of Jewish integration. This theme, evoked by Mailer in *An*

American Dream, would become important for other great Jewish writers such as Herbert Gold, Saul Bellow, Bernard Malamud and Philip Roth. The first to broach the subject, however, was Henry Harland, a Protestant passing himself off as a Jew named Sydney Luska. In his novel of 1886, *Mrs. Peixanda*, he advocates intermarriage, not only in the quest for personal fulfillment, but equally as a means of salvation for America.

At the turn of the century, a small percentage of Jews, smaller than the other immigrant communities, intermarried, because Jewish tradition forbade such practices. In an Orthodox Jewish family, if the son brought home a non-Jew, his relatives would sit *shiva*, assimilating intermarriage with death, and enter into an extended period of mourning. Less religious families threatened suicide.

Norman Mailer experienced this type of blackmail. Jack Maher, one of his Catholic Harvard friends, fell in love with his sister Bea. To mark her disapproval, his mother feigned a heart attack and refused to get up off the floor until her daughter swore she would never see Maher again. Yet, in Mailer's generation, eighteen percent of Jews intermarried. Today, over half the Jewish population—Mailer included—is married to non-Jews.

This improved assimilation was to have an effect on Mailer's international image. Although he had not yet reached the zenith of his literary notoriety in America, abroad he was regarded as what Fiedler dubbed the 'Imaginary American', the 'Terminal Jew'. While the Italian adolescent identified with Salinger's Holden Caulfield, his English counterpart fathomed American literature through Mailer[55].

Gradually, Jewish-American literature began to lose its political edge. "The American artist and intellectual no longer feels 'disinherited' as Henry James did, or 'astray' as Ezra Pound did in 1913...", esteemed Philip Rahv and William Philipps, founders of the *Partisan Review*.[56] As for Norman Mailer, although he remained true to his dissident creed, he tempered his protestations. Like many former radicals, he maintained "a sort of vestigial spiritual Trotskyism: an obligation to the attitudes of dissent, which survives the ideological grounds for dissent."[57]

These changes, which took place between 1945 and 1955, would be the premises of a powerful surge in Jewish-American literature. It would culminate in the 60s and 70s. In 1968, Mailer received the National Book Award, and in 1969, the Pulitzer Prize for *The Armies of the Night*. Still in 1969, short-listed for a second National Book Award in the historical and biographical category for *Miami and the Siege of Chicago*, he would lose to Winthrop D. Jordan, author of *White Over Black*. In 1980, the National Book Award and the Pulitzer Prize crowned him once again for *The Executioner's Song*.

The first Jewish-American writer to receive the Nobel Prize for Literature was Saul Bellow in 1976. Two years later, Isaac Bashevis Singer would become the first Yiddish novelist to obtain the same honor. "America's Jewish writers were the darlings of their generation", wrote Alvin Rosenfeld, "the new and major drive behind the renewal of American fiction in the decades following World War II."[58] The Jewish novelists humbled even the eminent Southern writers. As early as 1947, an anxious William Styron had anticipated this fatality: "Southern writing as a force is going to be over in a few years [...] running a pale tenth in the literary track race", eating "the dust of a pounding horde of Bellows and Schwartzes and Levys and Mandelbaums."[59] Yet, Anglo-American novelists chose to ignore this reality for many years, avidly hanging on to the vestiges of their former domination, eager to maintain their prejudices. The authoritative *Literary History of the United States*, published in 1963 still considered Jewish-American literature as an appendage, a side-stream apart from the American literary mainstream.

However, during the 70s, it became increasingly impossible for WASP writers—convinced they were the monarchs of the American literary kingdom—to dissimulate or harness the growing supremacy of Jewish authors. Essays on literary history, such as *Contemporary American Literature: 1945-1972*, published in 1973, had to concede a section—"The Jewish Novel"—on Jews, equivalent to "The Southern Novel" or "The Black Novel". The growing domination of Jewish literature distressed such Anglo-American patriarchs as Gore Vidal, John Updike or Truman Capote, and many more... Gore

Vidal wrote with consternation that, "Every year, there is a short list of O.K. writers. Today's list contains two Jews, two Negroes and a stage floating Goy of the old American Establishments (often of Mr. Wright Morris)."[60] In *Bech*, John Updike satirized the Jewish writer's literary celebrity, while Truman Capote, in a spout of anti-Semitic bile, openly attacked "the Jewish Mafia" in a 1968 edition of *Playboy*, complaining of: "A clique of New York-orientated writers and critics who control much of the literary scene through the influence of the quarterlies and intellectual magazines. All these publications are Jewish-dominated and this particular coterie employs them to make or break writers by advancing or withholding attention [...] Bernard Malamud, Saul Bellow, Philip Roth and Isaac Bashevis Singer are all fine writers but they are not the 'only' writers in the country as the Jewish Mafia would have us believe. I could give you a list of excellent writers [...] The odds are you haven't heard most of them for the simple reason that the Jewish Mafia has systematically frozen them out of the literary scene."[61]

Truman Capote expresses nothing more than his writer's narcissistic despair at this fully justified and uncontested literary dominion. The Jewish writer was the product of an intellectual civilization, in which prestige depended on culture and learning. Writing was a means by which the Jew remained faithful to his tradition. His cultural diversification opened wider intellectual perspectives, inevitably characterizing his victory over the literary endeavors of the more parochial, insular Anglo-Saxon. While Mailer returned to Egypt in *Ancient Evenings*, or Allen Ginsberg explored the intermingling of Asian and Jewish cultures, if the white Anglo-Protestant had bothered to raise his eyes beyond the lawn tennis court or the eighteenth hole of his elitist country club, he might have hoisted himself to the level of literary Zion.

Despite its indisputable importance, Jewish-American writing remained controversial in its essence. Frederick R. Karl, echoed by other critics, argued that Jewish-American writers, "are American writers, not Jewish writers, not members of a Jewish club, affiliated to each other not as Jews but as Americans."[62], deeming that their differences far outweighed their similarities. Concurring with him, Philip Rahv observed that Jewish-American writers did not form a literary faction or school: to claim so, "was a bad critical practice based on simplistic assumptions concerning the literary process as a whole as well as the nature of American Jewry, which all appearances to the contrary, is far from constituting a unitary group in its cultural manifestation."[63] During a discussion about the Jewish novel in America, in the same vein, W.B. Fleischmann claimed that, "Moses Herzog, Ph.D., could be Giorgio Esposito, Ph.D., Joe Malone, Ph.D., or Hermann Schmidt, Ph.D. He is the first generation American intellectual whom I have personally encountered in Irish, Italian and lower middle class Anglo-Saxon Protestant guise…"[64]

Saul Bellow and Philip Roth are two emblematic illustrations of the controversies and complexity surrounding the Jewish-American writer. Bellow was dubbed 'the crown prince' of Jewish-American writers. Not only did he obtain the Pulitzer Prize, but also he is the only writer to have received the National Book Award three times[*]. The most respected critics, such as Irving Howe and Alfred Kazin, consider him as the author who drew the most from his Jewish tradition. Inversely, despite his celebrity, Roth is seen as a defector among Jewish writers, and reproved by the likes of Howe for being "cut off from any Jewish tradition", denigrated as a "thin-lipped animus against Jewish woes, Jewish mothers, Jewish sentiments, Jewish aggrandizement."[65] The fact that Alexander Portnoy, the protagonist of Roth's *Portnoy's Complaint*, masturbated on a 109 bus was certainly difficult for puritanical America to digest.

Ironically, it is Bellow who does not wish to be perceived as a Jewish-American author, while Philip Roth advocates his allegiance to Judaism. Bellow esteems the label 'Jewish-American writer' intellectually vulgar and unnecessarily parochial: "I'm well aware of being Jewish and also of being American and of being a writer. But I'm a hockey fan, a fact, which nobody mentions."[66] Philip Roth,

---

[*] For *The Adventures of Augie March* in 1953, *Herzog* in 1964, and *Mister Sammler's Planet* in 1970…

paradoxical to the end, unreservedly criticizes the Jews and their "cringing deference, diplomacy, apprehension, alienation, self-pity, self-satire, self-mistrust, depression"[67], and a plethora of other faults, yet nonetheless affirms: "I have always been far more pleased by my good fortune in being born a Jew than my critics may begin to imagine."[68] The extent of his Jewish involvement was reflected in his publication of *The Other Europe*, a collection which introduced Milan Kundera, Tadeusz Borowski and Bruno Schultz to the American public. He also went to Jerusalem to interview the survivor and author, Aharon Appelfeld; visited Turin where he and Primo Levi, another concentration camp survivor and writer, "became mysteriously close friends."[69] In 1979, he published *The Ghost Writer*, in memory of Anna Frank, on the anniversary of what should have been her fiftieth birthday.

Differences between Jewish-American writers undeniably exist, but it would be an oversimplification to deny the existence of a common denominator among them. These authors have a common sensitivity, share a self-awareness, which results in part from a history of persecution, of being ostracized, in part from a many-faceted religion. With reason, Richard Fein thinks that Jewish writers are united by "the internalizing of a people's insecurity" that is, in Jewish literature, "this insecurity has been personalized, converted to a nervous psychological energy."[70]

In an interview with Robert Ebert in 1986, Norman Mailer sustains this concept and explains that his personality is fundamentally grounded in his Jewishness: "I'm not a Holocaust hustler, I'm not asking for pity, but every Jew alive feels his relationship to the world is somehow more tenuous than other people's, and so to affirm his own existence is somehow more important."[71] Fein goes further still, claiming that Jewishness is such a strong bond that Jewish writers are curiously transnational; "the works of Babel, Kafka, Singer and Malamud form a literature."[72]

Nonetheless, Mailer does not escape the difficulty of understanding "the uniqueness of the Jew and his writing", as insisted on by the critic Josephine Zadorsky Knopp[73]. Despite his fame, he is indisputably the most irreducible of American writers in his relation to Judaism. For many Americans, Norman Mailer was a major American writer whose ethno-religious background was and still is unknown. Mailer avoided restricting himself to any form of identity. Yet, in 1991, he still claimed emphatically: "I consider myself a Jew in every sentence I have ever written."[74] Unlike their treatment of Bellow or Roth, the critics who were conscious of his Jewish origins were unable to reach a consensus concerning Mailer. Some perceived him as a renegade who had renounced his Jewish legacy; others saw him as a modern-day Jeremiah. Donald Kaufmann claimed that Mailer "has shelved his Jewish heritage" and that "even in his literary criticism, the Jew in Mailer never shows."[75] Diana Trilling strikes the opposite chord, asserting that Mailer's "moral imagination is the imagination not of art but of theology, theology in action... His writer's role... is much more messianic than creative."[76]

Are not these contradictions a reflection of Mailer's own ambivalence? Did he not, on the one hand, constantly endeavor to erase the image of "the nice Jewish boy from Brooklyn", while seeking to play the role of the Jewish prophet, capable of transforming the consciousness of his time? Along with several other Jewish writers, Mailer symbolizes the evolution of the American literary scene over the secnd half of the twentieth century. Initially ostracized by the WASP establishment, the Jewish immigrant found solace in being one of the most fervent 'admirers' of the United-States. From there, he would come to own the American literary marketplace. Today, Jewishness has become "an eminently marketable commodity"[77]. In America, this amounts to unconditional social endorsement. Mailer is one of the most striking examples of success in the American melting pot....

CHAPTER II

Mailer: The Jewish Prince

Norman Mailer was born on January 31st 1923. Without a moment's hesitation, his mother Fan named him Nahum Malech—Norman King in Hebrew. "That's what he was, our king,"[78] Fan would later say. Nahum is one of the Torah's Minor Prophets; his mother named him after a prophet. Norman is his external name, for the Jewish child is given a Hebrew name for use within the intimate family circle, and an Anglo-Saxon name, for social use. With these two Jewish names, the mother expresses that her son has "a star on his forehead"—his will be a great and mystical destiny. Heeding the advice of relatives, Fan accepted to add a more appropriate middle name for his birth certificate: Kingsley.

Fan would become the incarnation of the stereotyped Jewish mother and her son's life would be indelibly marked by her all-encompassing adoration. In 1986, during his interview with Robert Ebert, Mailer declared that the two founding influences on his nature were Judaism and his mother: "…a mother who spoiled [him] out of sight, with all that's good and bad about that, so that [he] was accustomed to having attention paid to [him], and this probably is the key to [his] personality."[79] Later, the four years spent at Harvard where he was confronted for the first time with the anti-Semitism of a WASP realm were also to have a marked effect on his character, as he would confess: "I have often thought that the peculiar juxtaposition of a Brooklyn culture and a Harvard culture have had the most external importance I could name in making me wish to write."[80]

Like most Jewish families, the Mailers were close-knit, and resemble the Bosqueverdes in *Harlot's Ghost*, "If the daughter sneezes, the mother shivers."[81] As Alfred Kazin writes in his memoirs of a Jewish childhood in the 1930s, *A Walker in the City*, "the most terrible word was *alleyn*, alone"[82]. Isolation "is the ultimate Jewish nightmare."[83]

Bruno Bettelheim associates this feeling with a return "back to deep historical roots of which we're hardly ever aware. It has to do with the needs of the old ghetto, the mutual dependence in a totally alien world, the old anxiety that when the husband went to the next village with his pushcart he might not come back. All Jews have the memory of persecution in common, and Hitler reinforced it."[84] For the Jew, family ties were the best protection against alienation, what Heinrich Heine called the "portable homeland"[85], and Hannah Arendt, "the most potent and stubborn elements with which the Jewish people resisted assimilation and dissolution."[86] This was so true that surveys made at the time in several American cities showed that 98% of Jewish adults had been married at least once.[87]

Children were the pivots of family life. In the *shtetl*, a married couple who remained childless after ten years was often compelled to divorce. Outside of Hasidic and Orthodox families where birth control was prohibited, the ideal Jewish family was comprised of two children, in order that each child could receive the necessary care and attention. The Mailers had two children, Norman and Barbara. A Jewish mother's life revolved around her children, their wellbeing and their material success, especially the son's. This success legitimized the mother's life work, gave sense to an existence she had sacrificed to her offspring.[88] Fan Mailer toiled in the family oil business in order that Norman pursue his studies at Harvard and Barbara, hers at Radcliffe. Like many Jews, she knew that learning was the shortest path to a comfortable existence, and insisted her children "perform-or-else"[89]. Once more, Alfred Kazin in *A Walker in the City*, underlines this belief: "I walked on a hairline between triumph and catastrophe. Why the odds should always have felt so narrow, I understood only when I realized how little my parents thought of their own lives. It was not for myself alone that I was expected to shine, but for them—to redeem the constant anxiety of their existence. I was the first American child, their offering to the strange new God. I was to be the monument to their liberation from the shame of being what they were."[90]

Norman lived in Long Branch, New Jersey until the age of nine. His maternal grandfather, Chaim Yehudah, was the community's unofficial rabbi. A Russian immigrant respected for his piety and religious wisdom, Chaim Yehudah was schooled in one of Russia's best *yeshivas* and ordained at sixteen. Unlike the Catholic priest or the Protestant minister, the rabbi performs no sacramental functions. He is the most venerated member of the community, the most knowledgeable on the subtleties of Jewish law, the one expected to transmit to others the fruit of his Talmudic wisdom. Such was Chaim Yehudah. He gave advice to those seeking his help; counseled the rabbis who came from neighboring communities, soliciting his aid. Long Branch was too poor to afford a rabbi, so Chaim Yehudah offered his services gratuitously, living off the revenues of his butcher's shop and grocery store.

How far did Yehudah's orthodoxy influence his grandson? According to a childhood friend, Jason Epstein, Mailer declared himself an atheist. He refused to accept a religious identity that had been imposed upon him, one that he had neither chosen nor desired. As an adult, he confided to a journalist that he was "not a typical Jew", admitting that he had spent his youth "rejecting Jewishness at a great rate"[91]. He was much like Roth, the agnostic Jew in *The Naked and the Dead*, who considered that "God is a luxury that I don't give myself"[92], and his Jewishness as " an accident of birth"[93]...

Yet, Yehudah must have bequeathed to his grandson his inclination toward Jewish mysticism. Like Moshe Sefardnick, Goldstein's grandfather in *The Naked and the Dead*, "[drifted] in Talmudic halls of thought"[94], spending many sleepless nights studying the Torah. He was the paragon of the patriarch, the man his rebellious grandson respected the most, the one he most sought to please. He is deeply embedded in Mailer's imagination. Initially, in *Ancient Evenings*, Mailer had even planned to transpose the Russian origins of his family's saga. Beyond his work, was he not, with his eight progeny and one adopted child, very much a patriarch himself?

Other than his grandfather, Mailer's male role model was his cousin, Cy Rembar, eight years his senior. Cy was a winner Mailer would always sanction. To the young boy, "He was very much an older brother all through my childhood and I worshipped him (with enormous funds of love and envy) because he was a hero."[95] Above all, Cy triumphed over the innate pessimism of his Jewish surroundings: "He was the only figure I encountered in my childhood who seemed to believe it was more natural to win than to lose, and that life was therefore to be encouraged rather than decried."[96] Cy would be the only member of his family he would mention, years later, at Harvard. He personified the antithesis of the *schlemiel*, the opposite of Sam Slovada, the failed artist, hero of the short story "The Man Who Studied Yoga", a Jew, "through state of mind"[97] and "a man who is pleased to find others are as unhappy as he."[98] Is this not a confession of Mailer's own deepest fears? The critic Frederick Busch concurred by saying: "... it seems entirely possible that Mailer the writer is also psychoanalyzing himself, or at least studying himself, as he created a voice which might speak for him about Sam..."[99] Although Sam is only a quarter Jewish, Mailer compares him to the archetypal Jewish anti-hero, the *schlemiel*, those "*contrary-passive, timid, other-directed, pathetic, up to the nostrils in anguish, the world is stronger than they are; suicide calls.*"[100]

Through Chaim Yehudah, the Mailers were affiliated with Jewish orthodoxy. In 1930, they became members of the conservative synagogue and Fan would remain kosher until her parents' death, perpetuating the ritual with her sisters. Although his family had renounced their orthodoxy, Norman would have the traditional Bar Mitzvah at the age of thirteen. He "[hated] going through with [it]"[101], he confessed to Jason Epstein. To a Jewish mother, a religious education was not only a moral imperative, but also a means of transmitting her Jewish identity to her sons. To guarantee his passage through adolescence to manhood, Hebrew lessons which he "hated, hated, hated"[102], were imposed on the youth. His Bar Mitzvah was an opportunity for him to defy authority, scandalizing the reactionary circle of relatives and friends assembled in the temple on East Parkway. Influenced by his Hebrew teacher—a not so sleeping Communist— the teenage Mailer announced his desire to follow in the footsteps of such "great Jews like Maimonides and Karl Marx"[103]. He went on to laud Spinoza, philosopher, of course, but equally Portuguese Jew who had been expelled from the synagogue for his very unorthodox interpretations of the Scriptures. Isaac Bashevis Singer resumed Spinoza's philosophy in *Love and Exile: a Memoir*: "[He] believed that God is nature and nature is God. All men, all animals, even snakes and worms were part of the Godhead. The laws of nature are also God's laws. God does not regard the just and punish the evildoers. Many saints died young and in bitter poverty. Some of the wicked became rich and lived a hundred years. According to this philosopher, there was no Paradise, no Gehenna. The Messiah would never come, the dead would never rise from their graves. No cloud would ever carry away all the virtuous Jews to the land of Israel."[104]—a philosophy, which of course, Mailer adhered to completely…

There was Fan, the mother, Chaim, the grandfather, Cy, the cousin. There was also Barney, the father. Despite his filial affection, Norman could not ignore that his father was a failure: a drunken gambling womanizer who was most often without a job. His son would inherit his taste for women and booze, two very non-Jewish vices. Singer and Roth also portray many of their heroes as philanderers, which is paradoxical, because the family-orientated Jew is in principle a good husband. The Jew was also wary of excessive drinking, because it vilified his image and made him vulnerable in the eyes of the Gentiles. Sobriety was a means for him of "guarding his separateness, his way of maintaining the ghetto wall."[105]

To Carl Rollyson, one of his biographers, Mailer declared that his father was "an impoverished figure out of Chekhov […] a dapper gentleman in a bewildering world […]"[106]. Carole Mallory depicts him in *Flash*, a fictionalized account of her years with Mailer, as Sacha's father, as "the most elegant con man",[107] a gambler who "would walk into the room in his spats and charm the jewels off the wealthiest woman. Eventually he'd strip her of her riches."[108] Barney, Norman's father, may not have been a patriarch, but he did have panache, albeit he had very little influence over his family… "It was a nuclear family […] and my mother was the center of it and my father was one of the electrons […] I must say he was a most dapper electron."[109] Barney, a Lithuanian Jew who had lived in South Africa, was often unemployed and suffered from a lessened role in his family. Consequently, he often became "the angry but impotent patriarch"[110].

Rhoda Lazare Wolf, Barbara Mailer's best friend, described Barney as "just a shadow. The mother completely took over, nursed all of Norman's narcissism, and made him feel that whatever he did say was okay."[111] The father's weakness is illustrated in the short story Mailer wrote at the age of eighteen, in his third year at Harvard, "Maybe Next Year". Published in *The Advocate* and *Story Magazine*, it proves, on hindsight, to be an accurate description of the Mailer family: the hero constantly seeks role models to replace his inept father. Unable to find a suitable substitute, he has no choice but to submit to his mother's authority.

Barney, who had been an accountant in South Africa, did not bother to obtain a license in America. A quintessential dandy, he would leave the house to go job-hunting sporting a hat, an umbrella and spats, when he was only walking around the block. Like his son, he thrived on parties. He was "the kind of man hatcheck girls remembered and greeted"[112], said Cy Rembar, sensitive to his uncle's charm. Young Norman was also captivated. His father enabled him to escape the drabness and provincialism of his Brooklyn surroundings. When he died, Norman Mailer confessed to Buzz Farber that he had the impression "[…] of a pain that can never be filled. Not a day goes by that [I don't] think of [my] father."[113] Nevertheless we learn, on reading *Flash,* that Mailer disapproved of his father's dishonesty, conscious that, without Fan, the family would have been doomed. As proof of Mailer's subconscious ambivalent filial feelings, he systematically dedicated his works to different family members, but somehow never to his father. In Paris, in the summer of 2002, he maintained that he had dedicated *The Naked and the Dead* to Barney. When he was reminded that the dedication had been addressed to Fan and Bea alone, he seemed most upset: he hoped, he said, "that this had not hurt his father since he was really a nice guy"[114]. He went on to justify himself, claiming that Barney had probably not been alive at the time… But *The Naked and the Dead* was published in 1948, and Barney died twenty-four years later, in 1972.

In the early 1930s, when Norman was nine, Fan decided the family should move from Long Branch to Crown Heights, a Jewish middleclass area in Brooklyn. The stores were kosher and social life revolved around roughly twenty synagogues. Fan had wanted to remove her family from "the cheap goyism"[115] of Long Branch for more prestigious surroundings. Her wariness of goys, the Irish in particular, was common among Jews at the time. Although the Catholics and the Jews were both treated as minorities, and despite the fact that the Ku Klux Klan had persecuted them in the 20s (beyond the South, as far as New England and the Midwest), Jews were nonetheless convinced that Catholics were the most prejudiced of Christians. They associated them with the anti-Semitism of Father Coughlin and his Sunday night radio talks. The Jews also felt that the Catholic Church used its political clout to force its views on others. In a state like Connecticut, with its strong Catholic influence, both contraception and the propagation of information about contraception were illegal. The Jews were equally opposed to the Catholic Church's censorship of books they judged unsuitable... all these autocratic decisions only reminded them of their long history of persecution. Bruce Jay Friedman illustrated this deeply ingrained Jewish fear in a portrayal of the Catholic Church across the street from his childhood home as "a battlefield—a scary mysterious place"[116]. In *Studs Lonigan*, another of Mailer's favorite novels, James T. Farrell, an Irishman, violently satirizes Irish anti-Semitism: "Baseball's the only clean sport we got left", declares the bigoted Old Man O'Brian. "The Jews killed all the other games. The kikes dirty up everything. [...] Why they even killed their own God. [...] It used to be a good Irish neighborhood, but pretty soon, a man will be afraid to wear a shamrock on St. Patrick's Day, because there are so many noodle-soup drinkers around."[117]

In turn, Mailer would denounce this crass anti-Semitism characteristic of the Irish by transcribing it literally in *The Naked and the Dead*, when Gallagher and the other Irish boys he grew up with bully and humiliate an eleven-year-old "Yid" in Dorchester. As an adult in the army, Gallagher later tells his friend Red: "I see we got a couple of fuggin Yids in the platoon... I wouldn't trust a fuggin one of them."[118]

Despite the move to Crown Heights, Fan was increasingly dissatisfied with her marriage. Married at the age of twenty-eight, late for a woman of her generation, it would have been more natural for her to idealize her husband. Rhoda Lazare Wolfe insists that she considered him "a prince, a knight in armor..." and that she loved him, "even though very early the dream was destroyed."[119] Barney had many faults apart from his chronic unemployment, and impenitent gambling, but these were the fundamental issues of contention between Fan and her husband: "He'd go out looking for work and when he came home we'd throw our arms around him... and my mother would say, 'Ask Daddy if he got a job today.' He would shake his head sadly night after night."[120] In *Flash*, Sacha also describes the awful rows that took place between his parents when his father lost at gambling and the Mob came to collect. "Maybe Next Year" reveals Fan's resentment over Barney's ineffectualness as a breadwinner. The young hero also hears his mother's constant recriminations: "Why don't we have any money, we never have any money, what kind of man did I marry? [...] I never saw a man like you, they didn't make my father out of men like you."[121]

Fan was tempted to leave her husband, but stayed for her son's sake. As in the *shtetl* of her ancestors, she tended the house, supervised her children's education, and, for obvious reasons, provided financially for her family. Traditionally in Russia, as in Israel today among Orthodox Jews, the woman would alleviate her husband of his material obligations, in order for him to pursue his religious studies. She was the dominant figure in the family constellation. The more the husband fulfilled "the ideal picture of the man and scholar", according to Mark Zborowski and Elizabeth Herzog, "the more essential [was] the wife as realist and mediator between his ivory tower and the hurly burly of everyday life... The woman usually [stored] and [dispensed] cash and to a large extent [decided] how it shall be used. She [was] the chief counselor..."[122]

If, in general, the American family is matriarchal, the Jewish family is the epitome of matriarchy. The Jewish mother develops a strong personality as a defense mechanism. "Strong bonds of mutual love and dependency between mother and child are traditional among Jews. For most of their history, they have occupied the position of a beleaguered minority exposed to hostility... The responsibility of establishing the bulwark of [a] fortification was assigned to the mother, and the task began at birth of building a healthy body [and] a strong ego."[123]

Fortunately for Norman and Bea, Fan, like her three sisters, all first generation Americans, was very industrious and ambitious. From the age of sixteen, she had worked in her father's butchery, cutting the meat and making the deliveries herself. Later, she took over Barney's job in the family oil business, where she proved to be far more capable than her incompetent husband... Mailer, like Harry Hubbard in *Harlot's Ghost*, was, "the product of a marriage between two people so quintessentially incompatible that they might as well have come from separate planets."[124]

Yet unlike her forebears in the *shtetl* whose love was unconditional, Fan, a true American, expected her sacrifices to be rewarded by her children's good conduct—their success, above all. A Jewish mother's ambition was, according to Zena Blau Smith, "anything but modest. When her son began to make the first feeble sounds on his violin, the *Yiddishe Mameh* already envisioned another Elman or Heifetz. If he showed scientific proficiency, she foresaw another Einstein."[125] Fan did not think any differently: "I never questioned about Norman going to Harvard, I mean that was the place for my son."[126] Many years later, on Norman's fiftieth birthday, she spoke to Sally Quinn of her son's genius: "Norman was not an ordinary child. Other children always had that sameness about them, but not Norman. He was just different."[127]

Ambitious, castrating, over-possessive, tyrannical, but generous, positive, beneficial in her love, Fan symbolized the Jewish-American mother in all her splendid excesses. Mailer, says Germaine Greer, has forever been his mother's prisoner: "The concept of the worshipped feminine, which holds the Prisoner of Sex in thrall, is the Omnipotent Mother. To this day, Mailer's relationship with his mother is important; when he confesses that he has never been able to live without a woman, it is not just sex and company that he needs but nurture."[128]

In *The Prisoner of Sex*, Mailer names himself a "Prisoner of Wedlock", "for he had never been able to live alone"[129]. Are his frequent marriages and even more frequent affairs not ample proof of his dependence on women? Does he not reveal the same dependence through his heroes? In *The Deer Park*, Eitel cannot sleep without Elena: he drinks, panics, then rings her in the middle of the night. In short, she has become "a necessity"[130]. Sergius, in "The Time of Her Time" is also "one Don Juan who hated to sleep alone"[131]. Until the end of *The American Dream*, Rojack has never experienced solitude: when he suddenly finds himself lost in the desert, he telephones Cherry, although she is dead.

This dependence on women that Mailer transposes onto his heroes is inextricably tied to his relationship with his mother. Bea, his first wife, claimed that: "Norman would delight in teasing her like a lover"[132]. Adele, his second wife, believed that Fan was probably the only woman Mailer ever truly loved[133]. One day, when his parents were away, remembered Adele, Norman insisted on spending the night at their apartment, so as to make love in his mother's bed. He would also always seek his mother's traits in women. His six wives and Carole Mallory—the mistress with whom he was involved for nine years—all had strong personalities and resembled Fan.

Did Fan incarnate what Matthew Besidine calls "Jocasta mothering", whereby from his birth onward, a mother establishes with her son an amorous, intimate, exclusive relation in which he becomes the main object of her love?[134] One evening, Mailer improvised a rather unsavory scene while having dinner with his mother. He was at Harvard at the time. Instead of cutting the meat on his plate, he pretended to slice off his penis. Need we explain the symbol? By castrating himself, he was depriving his adoring domineering mother the power to do it in his place.

She overprotected him. When the family moved, she forbade him to play in the street with neighboring children, for fear he would hurt himself. Crown Heights was a district of Russian Jews. The children played ball to escape their families' worries. Each street had its team and when a boy did not take part in this masculine ritual, he was totally excluded. At a most critical age for young men to bond, sports would surely have been helpful to Mailer, already a victim of a domineering mother and an effete father.

Norman was as spoiled as he was protected. He had more money and more clothes than children of his age; he was the only one on his block to own a chemistry set, the first leather baseball glove, and a clarinet the day he expressed an interest in music. Fan would coddle him until her death. She often traveled to Boston when he was at Harvard. She would arrive laden with Jewish delicacies, his favorite dishes—matzo ball soup, herring in sour cream, chopped liver and pot roast. He would sequester her in his room, while she would mend his clothes, since she made him uncomfortable. Many years later, when he married Norris, Fan, for a period of time, moved in with the couple, in order, most probably, to dote on her beloved son all the more and satisfy his every whim.

This "Jocasta mothering" was not only negative. It implied a dialogue of love between mother and son that encouraged the child's intellectual and creative development—a classical pattern, which shaped such outstanding geniuses as Michelangelo, Gandhi[135] or... Mailer. In *The Prisoner of Sex*, he develops this theme when describing D.H. Lawrence, as—like him—a writer, "arrogant with mother love"[136], whose mind was "Possessed of that intolerable masculine pressure to command which develops in sons outrageously beloved by their mothers—to be the equals of a woman at twelve or six or any early age which reaches equilibrium between the will of the son and the will of the mother, strong love to strong love, is all but to guarantee a future tyrant, for the sense of where to find one's inner health had been generated by the early years of that equilibrium—its substitute will not be easy to replace in maturity. What can then be large enough to serve as proper balance to a man who was equal to a strong woman in emotional confidence at the age of eight? Hitler's development of such balance derived from imbalance, and great generals and great novelists..."[137]

Fan turned Mailer into "the tot of destiny"[138], a term coined by Robert Lindner to describe the psychopath's overbearing mother who instills her child with an inflated image of himself. She encouraged his passion for literature. Endowed with an IQ of 165, he was an avid reader since his early childhood. When he was nine, Fan gave him notebooks in which, each day, he consigned the fruits of his imagination. At this young age, he had already finished a two hundred and fifty-page "novel" called "The Invasion of Mars", whose plot unfolded far from his native Brooklyn, which was "not the center of anything"[139]. His mother collected these notebooks with love and pride. While other boys were out playing ball, Norman was made to stay indoors, studying. Her vigilance was relentless. Dismayed by one of his results in third grade and convinced of her son's superiority, she insisted his teachers change one of his grades.

Like the protagonist in "The Language of Men", Norman would grow up to become "the sort of guy who was accustomed to the attention and protection of women"[140]. According to Freudian postulates, one endlessly repeats as an adult the patterns established during childhood. It was not astonishing, therefore, that Mailer's exhibitionism would be clearly noted by Jason Epstein, chief editor at Random House: "Norman can't leave the camera... He likes to be on stage. He's a personage always attracting attention. Somehow that's his natural state. You wouldn't say a herring likes to be in the water. That's where he is. The stage is where Mailer is."[141] Adele would be more precise: "It didn't matter what type of publicity it was so long as he was center stage... 'Me, me, me, everybody look at me. Attention must be paid to my brilliance, my audacious intellectual concepts.' His convoluted rationalization was simple. 'Praise me and damn me, but for God's sake, don't ignore me."[142]

Curiously, at high school, he diverted his interests to mathematics and the sciences. Ignoring the school's literary magazine, he became editor of the student journal, *Physical Science*, before entering Harvard at the age of sixteen, to study aeronautical engineering. Much like Joey Goldstein in *The Naked and the Dead*, he had "ambitions [and] impossible dreams about college, or being an engineer or a scientist."[143] This in no way countered his mother's ambitions: what she wanted for her son was a lucrative and stable career, one that would be worthy of him. Fan's focusing thus on his education was an inherent part of the history of the Jewish Diaspora. In czarist Russia, where they were treated as second class citizens, like the Moujiks, the Jews were forbidden to own land. Their study of the Talmud helped them to develop their rational capacities, necessary in dealing with the concrete transactions of everyday life. Although they were also banned from universities, as early as the Middle Ages, their continuous reading of the Torah cultivated their intellectual rather than their manual faculties. They usually went into commerce and banking. Since the first century AD, they had at their disposal a system of education rivaled only by the Catholic clergy's. Traditionally, the most intelligent Jewish boys studied the Torah, while the others became tradesmen. Other than Hebrew, they spoke and wrote several languages, which they used in business. Mailer strongly felt this priority of the mind over the body. Roth, one of his heroes, declares, "I can see it here in the Army, all they know is that I can't do as much manual labor as they can so they look down on me. They don't know what goes on inside my head, they don't care. What are finer thoughts to them, intellect?"[144]

If Fan's behavior was emblematic of the Jewish mother, other Jewish writers also portrayed theirs. Sholem Asch in *The Mother*, Henry Roth in *Call it Sleep*, Michael Gold in *Jews Without Money*, or Alfred Kazin in *Walker in the City*. In Gold's paean to his "little East-Side mother", he stated that: "She was proud of the fact that she could work hard... She had a strong sense of reality... How can I ever forget this dark little woman with bright eyes... busy from morn to midnight in the tenement struggle for life. She would have stolen or killed for us. She would have let a railroad train run over her body if it could have helped us. She loved us with the fierce painful love of a mother-wolf. Mother! Momma!... I cannot forget you. I must remain faithful to the poor because I cannot be faithless to you!... The world must be made gracious for the poor! Momma, you taught me that!"[145]. First-generation Jewish women in Brooklyn were what Alfred Kazin called "the priestesses of an ancient cult"[146], and he went to glorify his own mother: "Year by year, as I began to take in her fantastic capacity for labor and her anxious zeal, I realized it was ourselves she kept stitched together."[147]

It was not until the 1950s—when Mailer was in his thirties—that the American mother, be she goy or Jewish, was accused of "maternal excess" and denounced as overbearing. She would become what Erica Jong in her bestseller *Fear of Flying* defined as, " a real literary property"[148]. Bruce G. Friedman, Dan Greenberg and Philip Roth also used this negative stereotype and even magnified it. Alexander Portnoy confesses to his psychiatrist in *Portnoy's Complaint*: " I am the son in the Jewish joke—only it ain't no joke! Please, who [...] made us so morbid and hysterical and weak? Why, why, why are they screaming still, 'Watch out! Don't do it! Alex—no!' Doctor, what do you call this sickness I have? Is this the Jewish suffering [that] has come down to me from the pogroms and the persecution? [...] Doctor, I can't stand any more being frightened like this [...] Make me brave! Make me strong! Bless me with manhood!"[149]

Was "the clinging mother the great emotional menace of American psychology, the counterpart to the heavy domineering father in England and on the Continent"?[150] Charlotte Baum believes that the Jewish mother is perceived as increasingly authoritative, although her strength and competence are unchanged. Only the context in which she evolves is different: "The very protectiveness of the ghetto mother may no longer be necessary, its vestige in contemporary Jewish mothering is no spontaneous eruption, but a holdover from a culture in which it was necessary and acceptable—indeed highly regarded. This mothering now appears to be exaggerated because the Jewish woman has lost most of her other social functions, and because it does not fit in with American notions about mothers… The "Jewish Mother" stereotype was created by third generation writers who felt comfortably Americanized enough to be able to shrug off the heavy emotional clothing of the ghetto."[151]

MAILER: THE JEWISH PRINCE

Is Norman Mailer typical of Charlotte Baum's analysis? With the exception of Harry Hubbard's mother who was only a quarter Jewish, the other mothers in his work, like most of the other characters, are Gentiles. In fact, whether it be Beverly Guinivere in *Barbary Shore* or Hallie Jethroe in *Why Are We In Vietnam?*, the mother in Mailer's work is a narcissistic *femme fatale*, the very opposite of Fan, and in no way inclined to being maternal. Jessica Hubbard is the epitome of the Jewish American Princess, like Philip Roth's Brenda Patimkin. Spoiled, materialistic, egocentric, haughty, she did not know the difference, says her son, "between the Torah and the Talmud. She brought me up to be ignorant of every Jewish subject but one: the names of prominent New York banking houses with Semitic roots. I think my mother thought of Salomon Brothers and Lehman Brothers as ports of call in some future storm."[152]

As the Jewish son feels more gratitude toward his mother than most other men, his feelings of guilt are also proportionally stronger, claims the literary critic Beverly Gray Bienstock. It is not surprising therefore that the Jewish-American author transforms his mother into a comic monster, comparable to Sophie Portnoy. Confronted with his material success, given his origins, this caricature becomes a means for him to assuage his feelings of guilt and alienation.[153] Mailer does not escape this logic: if—except on rare occasions—he is unable to transform the Jewish mother into a work of fiction, it may well be his manner of denying Fan's existence and appeasing some of his own remorse.

His love for his mother was, in fact, deeply equivocal; he resented and feared her crushing hold over him. In *Genius and Lust*, his portrayal of Henry Miller is equally an act of self-assessment. The power of Miller's mother, he writes, "*was beyond measure*", adding: "*... the earliest etchings of memory go back to that woman between whose legs they were conceived, nurtured and near strangled in the hours of birth*."[154] He had already expressed this overpowering, almost suffocating sensation in *No Percentage*, his first, as yet unpublished novel written at the age of eighteen. Larry Weiss, who read the novel a year after it was written, depicted it as the story of a middleclass Jewish family, in which the mother smothers with her love and attention a son whom she considers a child prodigy.[155]

Despite the ambivalence of his relationship with Fan, or maybe because of this ambiguity, his incestuous emotions towards her are instilled in his writing. Mailer's heroes are "engaged in an unending pursuit of the mother"[156], observes Howard Silverstein. The regression to the womb is one of his recurrent themes. Sam, in "The Man Who Studied Yoga" seeks refuge in "the womb of middleclass life"[157]. Rojack, in the original version of *An American Dream*, explains to Cherry: "I was a breech birth... They had to go with forceps and pull me out. It must be that my preference then was to die in the womb rather than enter life. I must have been more attached to where I had been before than to where I was going now."[158]

Homosexuality is another obsession, which has haunted Mailer throughout his life. He writes that he was born into "the classic stuff out of which homosexuals are made"[159]—the homosexual being the logical product of a strong mother and a weak and absent father, as typified by his parents. Although he accepted that we are all a combination of yin and yang, that the most virile of men is "probably 60 percent male and 40 percent female"[160], Mailer remained vehemently opposed to homosexuality, judging it much like the rabbis as *to'evah*—an abomination. He believed in the "intrinsic relation between homosexuality and evil"[161]. At the time, other American authors, especially Jewish ones, were of the same viewpoint. In *Mr. Sammler's Planet*, Saul Bellow vehemently states: "I don't think homosexuality is simply a different way of being human... I actually think it's a disease."[162]

In 1955 however, Mailer accepted to write an article for a homosexual review and read Ronald Corey's *The Homosexual in America*, which led him to reconsider his opinions. He finally had to admit that: "*homosexuals are people too*"[163]. Corey's work had a deep influence on him: "... I can think of few books, which cut so radically at my prejudices and altered my ideas so profoundly. I resisted it, I argued its points as I read, I was often annoyed, but what I could not avoid was my growing depression that I had been acting as a bigot in this matter, and 'bigot' was one word I did not enjoy applying to myself. With that came the realization that I had been closing myself off from a very large part of my life. This thought is very disturbing to a writer."[164]

Despite this acceptance of homosexuality, Mailer continued to view it as a weakness. He also believed that virility was necessary to the country's survival. There were too few heroes and too many homosexuals: "I think that there may be more homosexuals than fifty years ago. If so, the basic reason might have to do with a general loss of faith in the country, faith in the beginnings of one's work, faith in the notion of oneself as a man. When a man can't find dignity in his work, he loses virility. Masculinity is not something given to you, something you're born with, but something you acquire. There is very little honor left in American life. There is a certain tendency to destroy masculinity in America."[165]

Fears concerning his homosexual inclinations are latent in his work. In "The Homosexual Villain", he even confesses that they "stifle his creative reflexes"[166]. If he was able to find comfort in Sartre's definition of "the homosexual as a man who practices homosexuality"[167], he was aware of Kate Millet's analysis in *Sexual Politics*, which argued that male sexuality was permanently under threat and could at any time be "defeated by the lurking treachery of Freudian bisexuality, the feminine in a man giving out like a trick knee at a track meet."[168] For Germaine Greer, Mailer's latent homosexuality was the most powerful spur to his anti-feminism. According to her, his anger directed at the feminists was a means for Mailer to reaffirm his masculinity: "He wanted to be an object of that rage and he courted it because it made him feel more masculine. It's the same reason he [went] to dockside cafés and [got] beaten up."[169]

Although intoxicated when he stabbed his wife Adele, it was importantly at a moment when she had undermined his fragile masculinity by provoking him: "Come on you little faggot, where's your *cojones*, did your ugly whore cut them off, you son of a bitch!"[170] Two days after the stabbing, Mailer went on the Mike Wallace Show, reiterating remarks he had already made at a Brown University appearance on the subject of juvenile delinquency and masculinity: "You see, the sword's his word, his manhood."[171] It took him several days to part with the knife he had used in the near fatal assault on Adele...

Sexually vulnerable himself, he did not have many homosexual friends. James Baldwin was one of the few, yet Mailer's attitude toward him was equivocal. He considered Baldwin "too charming a writer to be major"; his style, "sprayed with perfume". If Baldwin "ever [climbed] the mountain and really [told] it, wrote Mailer, we will have a testament, and not a noble toilet water."[172] The repetition of such words as 'charming', 'perfume' and 'toilet water' only too blatantly reflect Mailer's unease concerning homosexuality. To him, it was not a balanced, equal relationship between two men, but rather a situation in which a man uses his partner as though he were a woman. To become a woman, believes Mailer, is the essence of homosexual desire. Repressed homosexuality, like all suppressed sexual urges, is apt to transform itself into violence, and violence into war. He illustrates this tendency in *Cannibals and Christians:* "being half-excited and half-frustrated leads to violence. Whenever one is aroused sexually and doesn't find a consummation [Tex and D.J.'s condition precisely] the sex in one's veins literally turns to violence. D.J. and Tex's violence [sprung] directly from their 'stifled homosexuality'."[173] Similarly, the Paret-Griffith prizefight illustrates the same pent up homosexuality: "Now at the weigh-in this morning, Paret had insulted Griffith irrevocably, touching him on the buttocks, while making a few more remarks about his manhood. They almost had their fight on the scales."[174] Ultimately, one would have to question the underlying motives behind Mailer's striking a six-month pregnant wife, or his later stabbing of her. Could he have been using this violence as a personal outlet for his pent-up homosexuality?

Mailer's sexual ambiguity is equally reflected in his quest for 'communion' with men that he respects, by seducing their wives or mistresses. In his biography of Picasso, *Portrait of Picasso as a Young Man: An Interpretive Biography*, he relates an episode, which took place in 1901, when Casagemas, Picasso's close friend, committed suicide.

Deeply distressed, the painter became the lover of Germaine, his dead friend's mistress. "Picasso, writes Mailer, was immersed now in homosexual preoccupations. He had to have carnal knowledge, at no matter what emotional costs, of the nominal widow of Casagemas. Even as he would copy other painters... as one means of entering their mentality, so did he absorb the loss of his friend by searching for Casagemas's presence in the body of the woman he had chosen for marriage."[175] Mailer almost invariably chose women who had 'belonged' to famous men. Adele had been with Jack Kerouac, Jeanne with the media mogul Henry Luce, Beverly, with Orson Bean, Eddie Fisher, Andy Griffith and, above all, Miles Davies, Norris, with Bill Clinton. As for Carole Mallory, she had had a series of tumultuous love affairs with such celebrities as Warren Beatty, Robert De Niro, Richard Gere, Matt Dillon, Peter Sellers, Rip Torn, and had married Claude Picasso, Pablo's son... As she would recount in *Flash*, Mailer liked to play the role of lover-shrink, questioning her endlessly on her sexual relations with other men. By communicating with masculine celebrities through these pillow-talk confessions, Mailer was appeasing his fears and convincing himself that he was their equal on the sexual battlefield.

If Mailer's dread of homosexuality was provoked by his relationship with his mother, his four year sojourn at Harvard would further kindle what he called his social complex. Like Sergius in *The Deer Park*, Mailer dreamed of projecting himself as a "rich man's boy", although entering the Eastern university had also "put a crown to his parents' ambition".[176]

At the time, the quota of Jewish students at Harvard was as low as ten percent. University files indicated whether a student was Jewish, or A & E—Andover and Exeter, the exclusive preparatory schools. Jewish students were relegated to special dormitories, a segregation reminiscent of the ghetto. During his freshman year, Mailer had few contacts with Gentiles. Yet this first year would be a watershed for his career. He was consigned to English A, a course designed to compensate the deficiencies of those students who had not attended private schools. Surprisingly, on entering Harvard,

Mailer was not well read. He even went so far as to falsify a list of books, which he had allegedly read, including *The Rise of Silas Lapham*, among other well-known classics...

His freshman course would initiate him to the great American masters, such as James T. Farrell, John Dos Passos, Ernest Hemingway and John Steinbeck. If Hemingway was later to become his literary model, James T. Farrell was the first to truly influence him. It was on reading *Studs Lonigan USA* that he discovered his writer's vocation. Through Farrell's provincialism (he was from Chicago), Mailer realized the literary potential of his own suburban roots. Farrell, an Irish Catholic, provided him with such reassurance that, within two years, he had already written his first, as yet unpublished novel on Brooklyn Jews, *No Percentage*.

Despite the innate antagonism, which existed between the Irish and the Jews, Farrell's fiction fascinated Mailer to such a degree that he would eventually come to identify with the Irish in his own fiction. While he criticized the Jews as "intellectual machines"[177], and as those *schlemiels* he so despised, he respected the vitality, the toughness and virility of the Irish, so essential to surviving at Harvard. He also admired their collective strength, one similar to the Jews and esteemed their, "*great bravura, a style, an elegance*".[178] According to Arthur Schlesinger Jr., Mailer perceived the Irish as "honorary Jews"[179], for they too were theatrical, oppressed and demonstrative.

If Farrell and Joyce stimulated him during his early Harvard years, it was only later, in 1946-1947, that this would express itself fully. At the time, he had sought refuge in garrets to concentrate on writing. It was there that he met Charles Devlin, a dark, Celtic "black Irish" and aspiring author like himself. He would develop an Irish alter-ego completely opposed to his Jewish roots, which, he later claimed in *The Armies of the Night*, gave him "the pride and arrogance and the confidence and the egocentricity he had acquired over the years."[180] He would give these 'qualities' to Sergius, a blond, blue-eyed swaggering hard-drinking stud, as well as to Xavier Pope, the Irish policeman in his film *Beyond the Law*. In fact, the movie would allow him to erase that "fatal taint, a last remaining speck of one personality he found absolutely insupportable—the nice Jewish boy from Brooklyn."[181]

At Harvard, he forged his new identity. By the end of his freshman year, he had already completed fourteen short stories. His great disappointment came from his inability to make crew, because his arms were simply too short to row in a team formation. Sports had never held much interest for him. Jews, according to Ernest Van Den Haag in, *The Jewish Mystique*, had never accepted the Greek cult of physical beauty and grace, or the German cult of strength, or the Roman cult of sex and cruelty... To the Jews, these pagan ideals were incompatible with their own intellectual and moral ethos. Long denied their political independence, and—in several countries— forbidden from bearing arms, Jews valued intellectual and cultural jousts over physical exploits.[182] Their true virility expressed itself in the synagogue, not on the battlefield. "I had been raised to be fearful and contemptuous of violence as a means of settling disputes or venting anger—my idea of manliness had little to do with dishing out physical punishment or being able to absorb it. Nor was I ashamed that I could do neither", confesses Tarnopal, Philip Roth's hero in, *My Life as a Man*.[183]

This Jewish code of non-violence was diametrically opposed to the machismo ethics dominant at Harvard. Mailer would quickly understand that, within its WASP cultural microcosm, the sporting spirit was identified with virility, and he would have to comply with this system of values. At Harvard, as in other Ivy League universities, sports were considered almost on a par with studies, and certain scholarships were even allotted on the basis of athletic achievements. Mailer also understood that sports were a means, for foreign or Jewish students, to befriend WASPs. Seen from this perspective, it becomes easier to comprehend his sudden enthusiasm for athletics and his new code of virility, which Saul Bellow treated with irony: "Today, the code of the athlete, of the tough boy—an American inheritance, I believe from the English gentleman—that curious mixture of striving asceticism, and rigor, the origins of which some trace back to Alexander the Great—is stronger than ever. Do you have feelings? There are correct and incorrect ways of indicating them. Do you have an inner life? It's nobody's business but your own. Do you have emotions? Strangle them. To a degree, everybody obeys this code. And it does admit of a limited kind of candor, a close-mouthed straightforwardness. But on the truest candor, it has an inhibitory effect. Most serious matters are closed to the hard-boiled. They are unpracticed in introspection, and therefore badly equipped to deal with opponents whom they cannot shoot like big game or outdo in daring."[184]

Diametrically opposed to Protestant culture, the Jewish background in which Mailer was brought up encouraged modesty and gentleness in men, strength and efficiency in women. In her short story, "The Genial Host", Mary McCarthy evokes the difference between Jewish and Gentile conceptions of masculinity, by alluding once more to the importance of the Jewish mother's influence: "Most Jewish men were more feminine than Gentile men of similar social background. You had noticed and supposed, vaguely, that it was the mark matriarchy had left on them…"[185] Soon after attending Harvard, in a reaction of self-defense, Mailer not only masked his more feminine traits but became openly, brazenly defensive. Allen Guttmann remarked with perspicacity that Mailer countered Jewish meekness by being overtly assertive and defiant.[186]

By his sophomore year, much to his elation, he made the class football team and became impassioned with sports. He practiced passes in his room unrelentingly, to the great chagrin of his dorm master who was living next door, and in the halls or the Harvard Yard, would apply football passes to those unfortunate enough to cross his path. He began to play squash, an upper-class game he had hitherto decried, which now opened him the doors to the inner sanctum of Harvard Waspdom. During his senior year, one of his short stories, "A Calculus at Heaven", was published in Edward Seater's anthology *Cross-Section*, where a Jewboy Wexter was "the biggest toughest blond Jewboy ever to play football for Freehold High"[187]. He actually satirizes the Jewish jock, who like himself, is so consumed by his passion for athletics that the Second World War is transformed into a football game. Mailer, now well integrated at Harvard, cannot help but identify with the short story's WASP protagonist, Brown Hillard; Mailer felt that it was "more attractive to conceive oneself as (and to write about) a hero who [was] tall, strong and excruciatingly wounded."[188] The writer had distanced himself from the Jewish jock he had been two years earlier, playing football in the university's corridors.

Yet the jock dimension Mailer had acquired during those Harvard years would remain an intrinsic part of his character, explaining his enthusiasm for Hemingway's machismo and his fascination with boxing. During his marriage with Adele, he had a workout room fitted in his barn in Connecticut, so that he could continue training. Later, he would befriend Jim Torres, the mid-weight world champion. In exchange for boxing lessons, he prefaced and practically rewrote Torres's book on Mohamed Ali, *Sting Like a Bee*. He proposed ninety thousand dollars to the same Torres to help sponsor the 1965 championship. Several of his novels describe fights: Patterson versus Liston, Paret versus Emile Griffith, Mohamed Ali versus George Foreman...

Beside his athletic accomplishments, during his second year Mailer was admitted to Harvard's *The Advocate*, one of the university's most prestigious literary magazines. It was the first time he was exposed to often wealthy, well-bred WASPs and his presence in the magazine was a subject of controversy. Some found him charismatic, others disapproved of his constant flouting of traditional values. In the Harvard literary world of those years, appearance was all-important, and the way one expressed oneself, paramount. Not only did Mailer not wear the traditional tweed jacket, but his striped trousers, sneakers or saddle shoes underlined the inelegance of his humble origins.

His Brooklyn accent was so pronounced that he was encouraged to take elocution lessons. Bowden Broadwater, known as an elegant esthete, remembered that Mailer's, "very black, oiled wavy hair", and his "shiny green gabardine jacket", made him resemble a "preppy Frank Sinatra"[189]. The son of modest immigrants, Mailer did not live in the prestigious students' halls, like the other members of *The Advocate*: Adams for the intellectuals; Eliot, for the social elite; Winthrop, for the jocks and preppies. No... He lived in the far less fashionable Dunster House; there he took to placing a bottle of gin on the mantle-piece in his lodgings, as a sign of allegiance to his literary mentor, Hemingway, who, ironically, was the perfect combination of the intellectual, well-bred young jock—a synthesis of the attributes of Adams, Eliot and Winthrop lodgers. In short, Mailer had nothing in common with the typical *Advocate* collaborator, and it is obvious that he was a victim of class prejudice. Not that the students were necessarily anti-Semitic; some of them simply, like Arturo de la Guardia, "detested all lower-class types"[190].

Mailer would occult much of the anti-Semitism and elitism he had suffered at Harvard, making countless efforts to transcend his lower middleclass Jewish roots in order to be accepted into Waspdom. Yet, he would never escape his origins, just as he would never escape himself, because he would never come to terms with his modest background. "He hated this because modesty was an old family relative, he had been born to a modest family, had been a modest boy, a modest young man, and he hated that…"[191], writes Mailer in *The Armies of the Night*, only to add that, "His deepest detestation was often reserved for the nicest of liberal academics, as if their lives were his own life but a step escaped."[192]

This fear of being himself would lead him to strike the most ostentatious, arrogant, provocative poses. In the room he shared with other students in his freshman year, he had plastered posters of nude pinups on the wall above his bed, which shocked his Jewish roommates. They refused to follow him to Dunster House the following year. His first contribution to *The Advocate* inaugurated his intellectual liaison with Hemingway. With his friend George W. Goethals, he wrote a parody of *For Whom the Bell Tolls*, renamed, "For Whom Your Balls Squall". Although today, this would seem quite tame, at Harvard in the thirties, this was not the case: "I don't think people realize how rigid and elegant and scary the atmosphere in Cambridge before the war was, Kingsley Ervin would later write. Very eighteenth-century, a mixture of Boston Brahmin and the literary faculty's elegance."[193] The need for social recognition was reflected in its sophisticated club system. Although tempered by the varnish of democratic values, this culture unto itself based on exclusion still exists today. Before the war, most of these clubs—the Hasty Pudding, the eating club, or the very socially elitist final clubs such as the Porcellian, A.D. or the Fly— were almost without exception barred to Negroes and Jews. Mailer joined the Signet, the only arts club at Harvard whose membership was based on merit rather than birth. Although he denied it, Mailer was vulnerable to the Harvard social hierarchy, which ruled the students' everyday life: there were the final clubs to which ten and twenty percent of the student body belonged, and then there were the others. He alludes to this power structure in *The Naked and the Dead*, when Hearn, one of his Midwest WASP protagonists, who had not attended an Eastern preparatory school, faces the obstacle of entering a final club: "If I knew then what I know now, I would have come east to Exeter or Andover, although they're not nearly good enough that's what I've been learning, but if we can get to meet the right fellows, we ought to make Speakers anyway, that's not so hard, and we can certainly make Hasty Pudding, but to get into a final club, that's the trick, although I've heard they're getting more democratic lately."[194]

Myron Kaufmann, a classmate of Mailer's, would evoke social barriers and virulent anti-Semitism prevalent at Harvard when they were students in *Remember Me to God*—not surprisingly Mailer's favorite novel. Its hero, Richard Amsterdam, is a social-climbing Jew who, like Mailer, must learn how to become a gentleman: "It's a snap for a guy to be cultured when his mother can remember William Dean Howells coming to visit in her childhood; you necessarily start from a different place when your mother never heard of William Dean Howells. Bill doesn't know what it's like not to be born and bred a gentleman, and to have to make yourself one, the hard way. Scrounging around, teaching yourself everything, keeping alert every minute, having constantly to fight your old habits like raising your voice and bickering with everybody. And stumbling and having relapses all the time. It's pretty discouraging. And there's no rest. And your parents, instead of being the ones that should help you and guide you, you have to take them and lead them by the hand."[195]

Yet, having to confront the social prejudices of Harvard life developed Mailer's talents as an agitator. At the time, this bigotry went hand in hand with a violent anti-Semitism and Mailer's provocations often projected the very image he wanted to efface. While he dreamed of being accepted by the elite, many students perceived him as, "blatantly and abrasively Jewish"[196]. George W. Goethals interprets Mailer's outspoken Jewishness at Harvard as a defense mechanism, "since by saying it straight out—'I'm Jewish, I'm Jewish'—he created a kind of barrier so he couldn't be humiliated publicly"[197]. Robert C. Harrison, another of his classmates, would recall that, "everybody found him boring because he spent most of his time claiming that he was a poor Jewish boy from Brooklyn." To his Jewish classmates, he would explain that they could not understand him simply because he was "poor Jewish". As an adult, Mailer would declare that: "It never occurred to us that we were in an incredibly subtle ghetto"[198], although his obsession with his identity seems proof of the contrary. The rift between his sheltered childhood and his student life obliged him to question his self-hood: "In college, it came over me like a poor man's rich fever that I had less connection with the past than anyone I knew."[199] At Harvard, he was seeking an identity: "Certainly in my years at Harvard the question of my identity was paramount. The most interesting question to many of us in those days was, what do you really think of me?"[200]

Mailer was truly tormented. If, on the one hand, he never actively struggled for the Jewish cause, on the other, he could not help but assume his Jewishness, even separating his friends into two groups: the Jews and the non-Jews. It was impossible, he explained to George W. Goethals, for a goy to comprehend a Jew. And to Jack Maher, he confessed the difficulties he had experienced trying to function in a non-Jewish world. At Harvard, furthermore, he confided in Adele, he had suffered, and had felt "like a fish out of water"[201]. It is not surprising that Mailer would seek his revenge, and when he was later to have some power as a recruiter for *The Advocate*, he treated the Brahmin novelist John P. Marquand's son with calculated condescension.

In his fascination with the establishment, he also came to affect a Harvard accent and adopted "the quiet grays, the understated shirts, and the challis ties that Mt. Auburn Street Club men wore."[202] Some of his classmates even maintained that Mailer ended up appropriating "the ethos of the seductive new environment, that he wanted to *be* Harvard."[203] On hindsight, he affirmed that he had forged his identity at Harvard, and that his university years had been among the most important experiences in his life.

Paradoxically, Mailer's inability to define himself was aggravated when *The Naked and The Dead* became a bestseller. He had lost the guidelines of his origins: "Success had been a lobotomy to my past, there seemed no power from the past which could help me in the present, and I had no choice but to step into the war of the enormous present, to accept the private heat and fatigue of setting out by myself to cut a track through a new world."[204]

Identity is a recurrent theme in his writings, especially in *Marilyn*, a novel-biography, or *Harlot's Ghost* and "A Harlot High and Low", his novel and his article on the CIA. While Marilyn was married to Arthur Miller and they were almost neighbors in Connecticut, Mailer had often tried to meet her. But the much-desired meeting was thwarted by her husband's jealousy. As an orphan, speculated Mailer, Marilyn Monroe was haunted by her lack of identity. Through her acting career, she sought "the close fit of a role"[205] while she had found in Arthur Miller "a character on whom [she] can rest [her] identity"[206]. *Death of a Salesman* appealed to her because it argued that "every moment of existence went into sustaining one's identity, and the moment one weakened, it was over"[207]. An argument that Mailer reiterated in *Harlot's Ghost*, in which the hero, Harry Hubbard also realized that, "One matures within an identity. One regresses without it"[208]. Indeed, if the CIA captivated Mailer, it is in part because he saw it as "a mammoth of shuffled identities"[209], a universe where "the facts are wiped out by artifacts, proof enters the logic of counter-proof; and we are in the dream, matter breathes next to anti-matter."[210]

Saul Bellow shared the same preoccupations as Mailer. This search of self appears in *Henderson the Rain King*, in the passage where Henderson explains, "I am a becomer"[211], or in *The Adventures of Augie March*, when Augie confesses to Mr. Mintouchian, "I tell you I have always tried to become what I am. But it's a frightening thing. Because what if what I am by nature isn't good enough?"[212]

Mailer was to transpose in fiction the vulnerability of his personal identity. Many of his heroes have dual racial backgrounds: Sam Slovoda is a quarter Jewish, as is Tim Madden in *Tough Guys Don't Dance*, Rojack is half Jewish, and Harry Hubbard, a later hero indicative of the author's own evolution, only an eighth Jewish. As Leslie Fiedler observed, alienated intellectuals such as Bellow and Mailer who began their writing careers creating mythical Jewish characters in the forties and fifties, later "moved on to imagine themselves as mythical Gentiles: paleface Protestant noble savages, great muscular conquerors of women and jungles, aging athletes, who, to parents of these writers, would still have represented the absolute Other."[213]

While a number of Jewish critics believed that Mailer had been disloyal to his heritage, these feelings of betrayal often distorted their objective interpretation of the man and his works. Fiedler, himself a Jew, illustrates this in his reading of *Ancient Evenings*, which he analyses as "one more goyish transgression", where "the return to Egypt becomes for Mailer a deliberate inversion of the myth of the Exodus—in which he is able to project once more his lifelong fantasy of becoming the golden goy..." in his surrogate Menenhetet.[214]

Mailer's obsession with Waspdom is further resumed in his collection of poems, *Death for the Ladies (and Other Disasters)*, where he even questions whether or not he is capable of becoming the Golden Goy:

> If
>
> Harry Golden
> is the Gentile's Jew
> can I be-
> come the Golden Goy?[215]

This poem, remarks Kate Millet, is a reflection of his "romance with Aryan manliness, one of the most puzzling and ubiquitous of his paradoxical qualities"[216]. Sergius O'Shaughnessy is one of his best examples of the golden goy. As described by Fiedler, he is a "superstud, superjock, and, of course, a mythic Goy." Mailer even planned to write another novel in which the mythical hero Sergius—"a kind of urbanized Hemingway"[217]—and his adventures are conceived during the dreams of Sam Slovoda, a small frustrated Jew and would-be minor artist. "One of [Mailer's] basic problems, remarks Fiedler, has been a temptation to believe that, after all, he himself is the Goy O'Shaughnessy rather than the small Jew Slovoda, who, in defeat and distress, has dreamed O'Shaughnessy."[218] Decades later, at the time of his death, the novel was still never written.

Like his author, Sergius is a composite between a Hemingway macho and "the Cossack rapist out of the erotic Jewish nightmares of the great-grandmothers of living American Jews."[219] Although the Cossacks—as opposed to the Jews—were implacably barbaric, they had the strength, the animal vitality of the Irish and they incarnated the force which Mailer sought. "He had a thing about the Irish," wrote Adele in her biography, "He loved them. Although he never denied his Jewish background, he wasn't happy about it. If there were such a thing as Jews Anonymous, Norman would have been a charter member. I sometimes thought he really wanted to be Irish; and if not Irish, WASP and rich. He did get rich."[220] Did Mailer never stop fleeing the *schlemiel*?

Toughness is a trait which he extolled in the WASPs and Irish both. During a conversation with Cy Rembar several years ago, he claimed it was the quality that he respected most about them. In *Cannibals and Christians*, he portrays the WASPs as an "iron people", with "iron power"[221], and names Harry Hubbard's half-brothers Rough and Tough, praising their integrity. Uprightness for Mailer is a capital virtue: In *The Armies of the Night*, the poet Robert Lowell expresses his opposition to the Vietnam war by refusing President Johnson's flattering invitation to a garden party organized for artists and intellectuals. He also admires WASP perseverance. Although consistently hostile to technical progress, in *Of a Fire on the Moon*, Mailer lauds the first trip to the moon as a symbol of success and power.

However, there are also elements of hatred in his fascination. Mailer does little to temper his criticism of the WASPs. He despises their sense of conformity, describing them as plastic, soulless robots, and blaming them for the country's demise: America, through its government, has become a totalitarian nation. In *The Presidential Papers*, he explains that totalitarianism manifests itself through attempts "at reducing complexity, minimizing expression or eliminating differences in personality and culture. For the essence of totalitarianism is that it beheads. It beheads individuality, variety, dissent, extreme possibility, romantic faith, it blinds vision, deadens instinct, it obliterates the past."[222] Mailer believed in the celebration of differences and, as he recounted in *Genius and Lust*, saw America as "a nation of transplants and weeds; the best was always next to the worse."[223]

He loathed Protestant avarice, WASP hypocrisy and greed, WASP blindness, which has led to their inevitable decline. They are "a race which was born to dominate and might never learn to share", who had exploited "the hardworking hard-used flesh of five generations of immigrants and although they were Christian did not want to hear about the rights of others." He went on to observe that "the sons of immigrants were so often king, [and] yes the WASPs did not understand what was going on."[224] In *Miami and the Siege of Chicago*, the author explained that "the muted tragedy" of WASPs was that "they were not on earth to enjoy or even perhaps to love so very much, they were here to serve… and so much of America did not wish them to serve any longer."[225]

He further elaborates: "I have the impression that the upper classes of England are superior to the upper classes of America. For one thing, if they're hypocrites, they're hypocrites with a certain style; if they're humbugs, they're humbugs with particularly interesting voices. Just as people there's something godawful about the upper classes of America; they really are horrible people."[226]

However, despite whatever animosity he felt, Mailer simultaneously aped the upper classes and wanted to belong to this elite, which had initially refused him a right of entry. Adele, once more, would remark in her biography: "One thing I noticed about Norman almost from the beginning was how impressed he was by other celebrities, especially if they were rich and Waspy. There was something deferential in his behavior toward them, and it was even more pronounced when drunk."²²⁷ When married to Adele, his social life, and the innumerable parties he gave, focused mainly on the American literati, stars like himself. When, in 1962, he married Jeanne Campbell, the granddaughter of Lord Beaverbrook**, the financier, his social universe expanded to include not only America's blue-bloods, but also international social and financial giants. Norris Church, Mailer's last wife—his sixth—whom he met in 1975, shared his appetite for power, thereby exacerbating his social aspirations. For many years, they dined out three evenings a week, frequenting socialites such as Kennedy's sister, Pat Lawford, hostess Jan Amory, city planner Marietta Tree, real estate barons Jerry Lipkin and Alice Mason, business tycoon Bill Paley, dress designer Oscar de La Renta, or socialite Slim Keith. They could be seen at fashionable charity events and fashion shows, organizing parties at home of up to two hundred guests, where Mailer's mother was inevitably present. The couple left an indelible mark on New York's glamorous social scene. Mailer, noted Norman Podhoretz, "had wound up practically living in a tuxedo. So attired, he would appear at least once a week in the society page photographs, and when I would occasionally bump into him at some party or other, it would invariably be a black-tie event."²²⁸ These dinners, explained Mailer to a *New York Magazine* interviewer in 1983 had become "sort of the last of my very small gifts to be developed. It's sort of like finding a new sport, the kind of sport you could never play when you were young."²²⁹ Jan Amory added that she felt Mailer was "dabbling in our world... he's on the outside looking into this zoo of animals."²³⁰

Mailer, for the wealthy upper class, was an *enfant terrible*, a Marcel Proust of the New World who brought them a moment of respite from their conventional and monotonous insularity. And Mailer, still hostage to his earlier insecurities, cultivated his eccentricities for fear that "they will become bored with me, and then boom I'm out."²³¹

His socializing was not limited to New York and, decked out in his Brooks Brothers uniform, he would go summering in Northeast

---

** Lord Beaverbrook was a newspaper magnate and former member of Churchill's war cabinet.

Harbour, the quintessential upper class WASP enclave, where his CIA novel, *Harlot's Ghost*, is partly set. Rosen, the novel's token Jew, determines that these New Englanders are viscerally anti-Semitic, and states that he "would never be allowed to go to those woods."[232] With his Harvard friends David Place and Lou Cabot, Mailer would go sailing, a favorite WASP activity, and play chess with the other men. Forty years later, he had become an honorary member of one of Harvard's final clubs to which they now deemed he merited late admission. Expecting unlimited orgies and depravation, the community at large was pleasantly surprised to find Mailer "so normal"[233]... or so they thought.

His increasing need to erase the early anti-Semitism he had been subjected to at Harvard, and in the army, propelled him to create a consummate WASP protagonist who was partially Jewish, with whom he could identify. Harry Hubbard allowed Mailer to re-create himself, and embark on the fantasy life he desired. In the author's vicarious existence, it was his ancestors who had arrived seven days after the landing of the *Mayflower*; it was his great-great grandfather, Doane Hadock Hubbard who had built the family house, appropriately called "The Keep", in Mount Desert in Northeast Harbour, where the author still vacationed. Through Hubbard, Mailer also gave himself the right credentials, Buckley School, the Knickerbocker Grays, St. Matthews, admission to the final clubs, at Yale this time, for diversity... He now also became a member of the CIA, which, he confessed, he had always wanted to join, had he come from the right background.

Although unmistakably mesmerized by grand Waspdom, its elegance and refinement, its class and idiosyncrasies, which had been little explored by his middleclass literary peers, he was unable to endorse its unlimited decadence. Aristocrats had invented the rules and, until recently, were the only ones who could afford to violate them. The poet Robert Lowell incarnated the gentility Mailer so admired. In *The Armies of the Night*, not only does he acknowledge Lowell's talent, which he inevitably compares to his own, but depicts him as a *grand maître* who had effortlessly, unlike Mailer, seduced his audience through his ease and self-confidence. Much to his chagrin and despite his pin-striped suit, Mailer perceived himself as the poet's antithesis, as "a clown of an aristocratic baron [who] would rather be an eagle or a count or rarest of all, some natural aristocrat from those damn democratic states."[234]

Meanwhile, in *Tough Guys Don't Dance*, Meeks Wardley Hilsby III is a true eccentric, a specimen unique even to his class and such a carry over of his English counterpart that, even in prison, he is referred to as the Duke of Windsor. While at Exeter he gangled "along in his chinois, his patent-leather pumps and his old dinner jacket that he wore every day to class (to the consternation of half of the faculty) his satin lapels faded and scuffed, his purple socks and heliotrope bow tie standing out like neon signs in Vegas."[235] Mailer was naturally attracted to Meeks's extravagance, so different to the blandness he repudiated in his Brooklyn background.

Otherwise, Mailer's disdain of WASPs lay in their decadence, exhibited either through homosexuality—yet again—or even insanity. He does not beat about the bush. Homosexuality, he writes in *The Prisoner of Sex*, is the "game reserve" or the playground of the upper classes; for the middle classes, it was a perversion, and for the lower classes, "a species of poor man's copulation". "Buggery, he abruptly concludes, is as fundamental to prison as money to social life."[236] Although he regretted his public school education, he exposed the shortcomings of his cherished Protestant prep schools, where their degenerate chaplains sodomized young boys such as Hubbard. He also demonstrates how the CIA, a sort of post-graduate Harvard, Princeton or Yale, was beleaguered by the same weakness. Spawned by those prestigious schools and universities, like Harlot the protagonists of the novel exhaust themselves battling their effeminacy, when not succumbing to it. Speaking of his mentor Hugh Tremont Montague, Hubbard declares that, "This impulse was the ongoing daily torment of his years at Harvard, then later at St. Matthew's where he ground his teeth in sleep. Indeed, he had not entered the ministry for fear that he would, one good day, dive deep into his impulses and betray the church. The sexual energies, in consequence, were in-held. As he shook my hand on introduction and stared into my eyes, he was a force and I was a receptacle. He was clean as steel and I was a punk."[237]

Homosexuality, however, was not limited to the upper class WASP boarding schools, or to the CIA: it haunts even the best homes of the rich and/or famous, as exemplified by Wardley—the hero of *Tough Guys Don't Dance*—who at fourteen gains access to his father's pornographic albums in exchange for sex with the butler. A barter he justifies with aristocratic nonchalance: "I gained entry to my father's private library by way of the butler—who was also the photographer, remember? All for no more than the promise that I would unbutton his fly—old-fashioned buttons for the butler, not zippers!—and go gooey-gooey down there. Which I did. I always pay my debts. Paris is well worth a Mass!"[238]

Unlike the Jews, upper class WASPs were often a product of fragmented families, emotionally repressed by their religious ethics and fraught with alcoholism. Harry Hubbard, who has little contact with his egocentric divorced parents epitomizes this fractured background. For Florence King in *WASP, Where is Thy Sting?*, "the children of the upper-class WASP father often [seemed] more like expensive pets than children"[239]. Predictably, the alienation emblematic of these families could and did lean to severe mental illness. "Is there a nice rich Episcopalian family or fine Presbyterian clan in our American world which does not have its important secret member raving mad? [...] WASPs live on the thin juiceless crust of the horror beneath, the screaming incest, the buried diabolisms of the grand and the would-be grand."[240]

Mailer's personal, social and professional insecurities, fanned by his constant exposure to Waspdom, were the driving force behind his ambition and creativity. He believed that he would write the masterpiece that would require "the seat of a Zola and the mind of a Joyce to do it properly." He continued that "Dostoyevsky and Marx; Joyce and Freud; Stendhal, Tolstoy, Proust and Spengler; Faulkner and even... Hemingway might come to read, for it would carry what they had to tell another part of the way."[241] Mailer was convinced that the only way to achieve his goal was by ruthlessly eliminating his rivals. He thus wrote two devastating essays, "Evaluations: Quick and Expensive Comments on the Talent in the Room", published in 1959 and "The Children of the Goddess", published four years later, in which he did his utmost to destroy the fiction writers of his generation. His scant praises were reserved for those, unlike James Jones, Gore Vidal or William Styron, who threatened him the least. His first essay resulted in the end of his friendships with Jones and Styron, and intensified his already ambivalent one with Baldwin. Mailer once again came off as the Harvard jock who had become a bad sport.

Styron, whom he feared would become literature's Mohamed Ali, was the brunt of his most vehement attacks. Mailer claimed that Styron lacked any substantial recognition, which inevitably infuriated him. Styron concurred with his wife Rose's opinion that Mailer's acrimony could be imputed to his "pent-up homosexuality"[242], for he was exceedingly jealous of the friendship between Jones and Styron. Later Mailer would admit that he had been driven to denigrate his contemporaries, Styron in particular, because he deemed they had devaluated him by creating "too small a window to look out on the world we have known."[243]

Despite his uninterrupted success, his behavior toward his fellow writers continued to reek "with the odor of an acute literary illness"[244]. In 1968, when Norman Podhoretz published Mailer's "The Battle of the Pentagon" in his magazine *Commentary*, Mailer led him to believe that he would write a favorable review to redress the wrong that had been done to Podhoretz's book, *Making It*. To Podhoretz's stupefaction, Mailer did just the opposite. In his review, "Up the Family Tree", he attacked the very premise of *Making It*—that success had replaced sex as the individual's focal point of desire—then proceeded to attack the literary Establishment, the "family" itself.

On the subject of his contemporaries, Mailer was later to confess: "I hated their talents. I despised and loathed everything about them that was the least bit good. It killed me every time they did something that I couldn't."[245] He even renounced writing the Jewish novel about his own family, because he felt that "Singer could do it better"[246]. Once again, haunted by the *schlemiel's* specter, he did not want to lose...

Decidedly, Mailer was the ultimate Jewish prince. Stifled by his doting mother, he fantasized about enlarging his fiefdom. At sixteen, when he was given his passport to Harvard, he was bewildered to discover how limited a passport it was for non-WASPs, especially Jews. He was no longer Norman Malech, Norman King, but a ghettoized Jewish immigrant in the WASP's Promised Land where he was taught that the White Anglo-Saxon Protestant was "the landlord of our culture, and his values were with rare exception those that defined it." And that Americans "ate, slept, worked and dreamed WASP".[247] Profoundly threatened in his identity, Mailer sought to re-create himself, always allegiant to his mother, but aware that integration into the WASP world, notwithstanding its decline, remained an essential passage in fulfilling his promised destiny of literary messiah.

CHAPTER III

Mailer and the Weaker Sex

Fan in particular, and women in general, have been a constant source of obsession in the author's life and work. A product of an overbearing mother and of a patriarchal Jewish heritage, for decades the Women's Liberationists—whom Mailer compared to German tanks—would chastise him for the misogynistic attitude he adopted toward the 'weaker sex' as a result of his fixation. In this "battle of the sexes", he would constantly attempt to justify himself.

Eva Figes claims that the Jewish woman was, "far from being a mother of all races of men, the national order was reversed, and woman [was] born out of man, no more than a single rib." If "the male seed [was] recorded in great detail [...] the woman was no more than a bearer of male children."[248] Sterility was the worse of all possible curses; fertility, the greatest of rewards. The role of the woman in traditional Judaism has been synthesized by Charlotte Baum, Paula Hyman and Sonia Michel in *The Jewish Woman in America*: "A female child was destined to be merely a good wife, and she was a financial burden as well since she would need a dowry, but a male child would not only ultimately assume all the responsibilities of Judaism— including reciting the memorial prayer for his parents—he might even bring renown to his family as a scholar [...]. And of course, only a male child could be the Messiah."[249]

If Jewish culture attached great importance to learning, a girl's schooling was at best limited. Her family considered the daughter's energies best spent caring for the younger children, while her brothers devoted themselves to Talmudic studies. The status of scholar was their passport to respect within the Jewish community. However, until 1972, women were even excluded from the rabbinate.

In *Promised Land*, Mary Antin describes the attention bestowed on her brother for his academic achievements: "No wonder he said in his ritually prescribed prayer, 'I thank Thee, Lord, for not having created me a female.' It was not so much to be a girl… Girls could not be scholars and rabbonim."[250]

While young Jewish males growing up like Mailer in immigrant America, "faced the problem of how to define their lives with relation to Jewish origins and American environment […] Jewish girls faced the problem of whether they were allowed to define their lives at all."[251] As a result of this patriarchal education, and the guilt they felt toward their mothers, writers such as Mailer Bellow, Roth and, to a certain extent, Malamud, tended to project a very negative image of women in their work. This is well expressed by Morris in Philip Roth's *My Life as a Man*, when he chastises his brother Peter Tarnopol: "What is it with you Jewish writers? Madeleine Herzog, Deborah Rojack, the cutie-pie castrator in *After the Fall*, and isn't it the desirable *shiksa* in *A New Life* a kvetch and titless in the bargain? And now, for the delight of the rabbis and the reading public, Lydia Zuckerman, that Gentile tomato. Chicken soup in every pot, and a Grushenka in every garage. With all the Dark Ladies to choose from, you luftmenschen can really pick'em. Peppy, why are you still wasting your talent on that Dead End Kid? Leave her to heaven, okay?"[252] Carol Zonis Yee pertinently remarked that the modern Jewish woman is active, creative and outspoken. Yet, "if she looks in modern letters for her counterpart, she finds herself portrayed as threatening, destructive, and the keeper of the home with its attendant misery (while impressing on her men that the outside is worse)."[253]

Given his desire to distance himself from his background, Mailer created few Jewish heroines, and those he did create—Jessica, Denise or Eleanor—were quickly denigrated. Like many Jewish authors, Mailer re-oriented anti-Semitism away from himself, to project it onto his female characters. In his work, women are furthermore allotted an auxiliary role, and their existence depends on the function they serve in a man's life, as the woman's existence depends on her role as wife and mother. Whether it be Eleanor,

Denise, Deborah, Ruta or Cherry, they belong in the category of Mailer's two-dimensional characters who have no true autonomy outside of the protagonist's sphere.

Leslie Fiedler's assessment of American writers in general seems to apply most particularly to Jewish authors: He claims "they rather shy away from permitting in their fictions the presence of any full-fledged mature woman, giving us instead monsters of virtue or bitchery, symbolic of the rejection and fear of sexuality."[254] According to Joanna Russ, in *Images of Women in Fiction*, twentieth century literature divides women into two categories: the devourer bitch and the maiden victim.[255]

Mailer shares this Manichaean approach to women: in his world they are either victimizers or victims. He has created a certain number of "bitch goddesses" such as Hallie, Lulu, Deborah or Marilyn, who use their powers to destroy men. Interestingly, with the exception of Deborah, the "bitches" are all blond. And despite their destructive tendencies, their victories are always ephemeral: Mailer makes certain that men ultimately destroy his heroines. Hallie and Lulu are trapped in unhappy marriages; Deborah is killed by her husband, and Marilyn, according to Mailer, did not commit suicide, she was murdered…

His literary treatment, however, is not an oversimplified parody. It is contradictory, paradoxical, and this ambivalence is in itself a part of his heritage. The ambiguous stature of women, particularly blatant in Hasidism, is equally apparent in traditional Judaism. If the Old Testament presents her above all as a child-bearer (Genesis 3:16), she is also depicted as an important public personage (Proverbs 31). The Talmud is also inconsistent in its presentation: While Shabbat 152a states, "though a woman be a pitcher full of filth… yet all speed after her"; Shabbat 1562a claims, "The rejoicing of one's heart is a wife", and she is portrayed with veneration, "Let a man be careful to honor his wife, for he owes her all the blessings of his house" (Baba Mezia, 51a).

In much the same way, Mailer's heroines are forever torn between the extremes of vice and virtue. Deborah, as she tells Rojack, is "more good and more evil than anyone alive"[256], while Marilyn is, on the one hand, "the sweet angel of sex", and on the other, "a formidable monster of publicity"[257]. Hers is a truly split personality, "a devil in the guise of an angel"[258], "one hard and calculating computer of a cold and ambiguous cunt... and the other tender animal, an angel, a doe at large in blond and lovely form."[259] In a similar manner, Cherry is also "an angel within a whore"[260]. Otherwise, in *Of a Fire on the Moon*, the author confesses that he is unable to fathom the complexity of women, and that he "spent his formative years and manhood in search of [their] true nature"[261]. In an interview with Buzz Farber for *Viva*, in 1973, he admits that, "the greatest vanity we have is to assume we know what is going on with women"[262]

When Mailer did create realistic portraits of women, they tended not to be fictional. In one of his articles, Gordon Graham concludes that these portraits are precise descriptions, and not products of the author's imagination and he backs up his argument with a series of examples ranging from a description of Jackie Kennedy's artificial presentation of herself in a tour of the White House in *The Presidential Papers*, to Pat Nixon's perfunctory projection of herself at the 1972 Republican Convention, in *St. George and the Godfather*, or Pat Collins's standardized interview on the moon landing in *Of a Fire on the Moon*.

Notwithstanding this quest for objectivity, Mailer's hostility to women was flagrant from the outset in *The Naked and the Dead*. Most of the novel's male characters are outrageously misogynistic, reveling in their sexual conquests and infidelities. Unanimously, they agree that, "there ain't a fuggin' woman is good"[263], although as objects of sexual gratification, they cannot do without them. Cummings sees woman as a sparring partner. Sexually sadistic, his power-obsessed libido overflows onto his opinions concerning domination and war. When he makes love to his wife Margaret, 'it is fantastic for a time, he must subdue her, absorb her, rip her apart and consume her". "I'll take you apart", he says to her, "I'll eat you, oh, I'll make you mine, you bitch."[264]

Twenty years later, during an interview with Paul Carroll for *Playboy*, Mailer expressed just the same attitude to lovemaking: "Sex is not only a divine and beautiful thing; it is a murderous activity. People kill each other in bed."[265]

In Mailer's work, young Jewish women do not fair any better than their Gentile counterparts. As early as *The Naked and the Dead*, he writes: "Shy, sensitive girls may end up as poetesses or they may turn and drink alone in bars, but nice, shy sensitive Jewish girls usually marry and have children, gain two pounds and worry more about refurbishing hats and trying a new casserole than about the meaning of life."[266]

Although he unquestionably admires women, as he admired his own mother, Mailer fears their power over men—above all, over him: "He had seen too many women down too many men, some with a campaign of applied force masterful as Grant on the Appomattox, some by the simple frustration of what was best in her mate at the best of times."[267], he writes in *The Prisoner of Sex*. As Frederic Jameson resumes, in Mailer's work, "sex [...] always stands for power relationships."[268]

Like his heroes, the author is undoubtedly attracted to strong women because they represent a greater challenge: a man's dominance over a resilient woman is the ultimate confirmation of his masculinity. To subjugate women "was not tyranny to him, but equality, for dominance was the indispensable elevator which would rise his phallus to the height from which it might seek transcendence... And sexual transcendence, some ecstasy where he could lose his ego for a moment, and his sense of self and his will, was life to him."[269] Such an attitude implies a constant struggle for power between the sexes, and the male and female protagonists which crowd Mailer's literary universe endlessly repeat this pattern of conflict. Kate Millet notes: "Mailer's sexual journalism reads like the sporting news grafted onto a series of war dispatches. As the formula of 'fucking as conquest' holds true, the conquest is not only over the female, but over the male's own fears for his masculinity, his courage, his dominance and the test of his erection."[270] In *The Naked and the Dead*, Cummings finds himself alone "to fight out battles with himself"[271] upon Margaret's body. Meanwhile, Rojack wonders whether he would not be better off retreating from a marriage which he views as a lost battle: "I worked to withdraw, count my dead and look for love in another land, but she was a great bitch, Deborah..."[272].

Rojack fairly well sums up his author's sexual politics: "all women are killers", "women must murder unless we possess them altogether"[273]. To curtail her power over him, he is compelled to kill Deborah. Later, he explains his success within the police and with the Mafia by the power politics he had been forced to deploy in his relationships with the women he had known: Deborah, Ruta or Cherry. Denise, Sergius's mistress, is equally a killer. When their affair is over, Sergius notices, "The look in her eyes, that unmistakable point for the kill that you find in the eyes of a very few bull-fighters... And like a real killer, she did not look back."[274] As Kate Millet concludes, Mailer sees "masculinity as a precarious spiritual capital in endless need of replenishment and threatened on every side." Even in his non-fiction, women remain killers: Valerie Solanis in, *The Prisoner of Sex*, is described as having "fired a gun on Andy Warhol and almost succeeded in killing him"[275]; Kate Millet is seen as "the perfect gun"[276]; while Marilyn is held responsible for the deaths of Johnny Hyde, Clark Gable, Jack Kennedy and Bobby Kennedy's girlfriend...

The *rapport de force* between the sexes are extended into a form of psychic cannibalism in which, once again, Mailer maintains his masculine troops in command. Sexual intercourse is converted into an act of absorption by the male of the female numa, a victorious "[digestion of] the new spirit which entered the flesh."[277] When Sergius, in "The Time of Her Time", makes love to Denise, they are like "two club-fighters"[278]. He slaps her across the face, "brings a cry from her and breaks the piston of her hard speed into something softer, wetter, more sly, more warm, [and he] felt as if her belly were opening finally to receive [him]."[279] He insults her, sodomizes her, until she finally submits to his will and experiences her first orgasm. Ruta is also very aggressive to begin with, but when Rojack treats her with violence, causes her physical pain and sodomizes her, she too submits to him, and "wants no more than to be a part of [his] will."[280] There is "nothing more promising, so warm... as the melting of a battle-ax"[281], also writes Mailer, apropos of Bella Abzug.

If, in Mailer's work, most women—hence most bitch goddesses—are either unwilling or unable to grant men the subservience they desire or deem they deserve, certain women, like Elena, are created just for that purpose. She is the quintessential submissive woman, a rarity both in Mailer's life and in his fiction. She belongs to that category of women described by Nona Balakian, whom men turn to as they might "to vitamins, expecting to be soothed or renewed and to bolster their waning sense of self"[282]. In *The Deer Park*, she soothes Eitel's self-doubt through her idolatry. After they first make love, she calls him a king. With Sergius, she is governed. He is "like a circus master tapping his whip; she [is] a trained animal and he [can] wipe his fingers in her hair"[283]. Eitel alludes to his "fragile manhood"[284]—a Maileresque obsession—and thus chooses a woman who offers him unlimited veneration. Yet, despite Elena's vulnerability and lack of social sophistication, she sees through Eitel's motivations and tells him so: "You stay with me 'cause I'm somebody you can feel superior to, that's how you get your opinion of yourself…"[285] She is equally aware that unfaithful women are often more attractive to men. So, like many of Mailer's heroines, she describes with unsparing detail her other affairs, sparking off her lover's typically male masochism and kindling his sexual ardor.

Ultimately, to Mailer as to his heroes, the desirability of a woman is in close correlation with the number of lovers she has known and the quantity of her admirers. She is like a barometer of the permanent competition between men. As Cummings claims in *The Naked and the Dead*, "the average man always sees himself in relation to other men as inferior or superior. Women play no part in it. They're an index, a yardstick among other gauges, by which to measure superiority."[286] Mailer's wives and mistresses all had a gallery of suitors; his heroines, not fortuitously, are pursued by a host of admirers, to whom, more often than not, they succumb. Deborah is courted by a legion of men—politicians, racing-car drivers, tycoons, playboys, not to mention her first husband, a count. Rojack meets her during a double date with her lover of the moment, another hero, Jack Kennedy. In the serialized version of *An American Dream*, Rojack wins Deborah away from Jack Kennedy. During their tempestuous marriage, she scores five adulteries. At the time of her death, she is juggling between a lover in the American government, a diplomat in the Russian embassy, and a civil servant in the British embassy. Cherry also has a cohort of lovers, from Barney Kelley to Shago Martin, not to mention the Mafioso Tony Ganucci. When Rojack kisses her for the first time, he almost swoons because, he explains, "she was too much for me [...] There was something in it of the iron motor in the hearts of a good many men she must have kissed"[287] Similarly, in *The Deer Park*, Lulu taunts and spurs Sergius on with her conquests: "To the pride of having him so beautiful a girl, was added the bigger pride of knowing that I took her with the cheers of millions behind me. [...] I knew I was good when I carried a million men on my shoulders."[288] She also tells Sergius that he is not as good a lover as Eitel, her first husband, whom she had previously described as a sorry bed partner. Then, like many other Mailer heroines, she leaves no stone unturned and reveals the most intimate details of her past and present sex life.

Social status also ranks among Mailer's main concerns and he has always been attentive to the role women could play in his social advancement. In this, as in many other aspects of his author's nature, Rojack appears as an emblematic hero, the one who most faithfully reflects Mailer's own fantasies. Alfred Kazin even considers *An American Dream* a "novel of ambition, a snob document"[289]. Rojack, socially inferior to his wife Deborah, sees himself as "her footman"[290]. "Marriage to her, he confesses, was the armature of my ego; remove the armature of my ego and I might topple like clay."[291] By rejecting him, Deborah endangers Rojack's fragile identity and precipitates her murder: "With such a nice finality that I thought again of the moon and the promise of extinction which had descended on me. I opened a void—I was now without a center... I did not belong to myself any longer. Deborah had occupied my center."[292]

Deborah, with her upper class Anglo-Catholic ancestry, rejects hybrids such as Rojack: "her detestation of Jewish-Protestants and Gentile-Jews was complete".[293] She maligns his modest Jewish origins: "You really look like some peddler from the Lower East-Side", and never allows him to forget that he is a "marginal socialite", with "weed's roots; Jewish father, immigrant stock; Protestant mother,

New England banking family, second drawer."[294] Nonetheless, Rojack feels empowered by his wife's glamour and social superiority. When their sexual relationship is satisfying, he describes it as "a procession through a palace, each stroke a step upon a purple walk".[295] He is flattered and reassured by "the smell of *foie gras* in Deborah's world and Deborah's friends."[296] She has been "his entry to the big league… [He] loved her the way a drum majorette loved the power of the band for the swell it gave to each little strut."[297] By contrast, he denigrates Ruta for her simple origins and crass ambitions, determining that only "something as corrupt as a banquet plate of caviar laid on hundred-dollar bills could enrich her odor (evocative of poor European alleys and lean rats)."[298]

Over-sensitive to social status, Mailer criticizes those of his heroines who, like Ruta, lack class. Initially, although Eitel hopes that, despite her vulgarity, he can "make something"[299] of Elena, he soon realizes that his victim is incapable of the least social refinement: she shall never escape the modesty of her background. He watches her as she stares out of the window in resignation, "like a peasant, much as her parents must have stared out of the window of their candy store"[300]. Elena realizes that Eitel's entourage will never accept her and concludes: "Maybe I like high society and the way it thinks I'm dirt"[301]. Her lack of worldly grace is ultimately the cause of their estrangement.

Yet, while Mailer portrays Elena with compassion, he ridicules Denise—also not to the manner born—for her pretentiousness and intellectual aspirations. Denise is condemned by Sergius as "one of those harsh alloys of self-made bohemian from a middle-class home"[302]. Her manner of speech—"an ugly New York accent with a cultured overlay"[303]—greatly irritates him. But Mailer's heroine has the very accent that Harvard had ridiculed in Mailer. So Mailer identifies closely with Denise and endures "the sweat of the cost of acquired culture when you started low and you wanted to go high."[304]. She adores T.S. Eliot and Sergius "was tempted to tell her how little Eliot would adore the mannerless yeast of the Brooklyn from which she came…"[305]. Sergius is conscious that "she would not make that other world so fast—nice society was not cutting her crumpets thus quickly because she was gone on Thomas Stearns Eeee."[306]

Denise's ambition is reflected in her sexuality, when she makes love with "a rage to achieve"[307]. Ultimately, she is not only a symbol of Jewish self-hatred, or of Mailer's own self-deprecation, but she also reflects, like most of the author's male and female characters, his "monomaniacal determination to get along in the world"[308].

Beyond these portraits which populate his work, Mailer's attitude to women is neatly summarized in his anti-feminist bible, *The Prisoner of Sex*, first published in *Harper's Magazine* in 1970, followed by a hard-cover edition the following year. In America, confronted with social, political and professional iniquities, the growing discontent of women culminated in the 1960s. Their movement was led by Betty Friedan, author of the groundbreaking work, *The Feminine Mystique*, published in 1963. Mailer, as the archetypal male chauvinist pig, rapidly became one of the movement's prime targets. In *The Prisoner of Sex*, he presents himself as a self-appointed Jewish patriarch, reasserts his conservatism, his Hebraic beliefs, and claims that "the prime responsibility of a woman is to be on earth long enough to find the best male possible for herself and to conceive children who will improve the species."[309] Besides allotting women the traditional roles of wife and mother—the very ones he sought to free himself of—he reiterates a series of comments so disparaging about women that they can only have been intended as provocations. He repeats a statement already made during a television program with Orson Wells—"Women should be kept in cages"[310]—and recopies sentences he had previously written in *The Presidential Papers*—"most men who understand women at all feel hostility toward them. At their worst, women are low, sloppy beasts."[311] He continues to compare the Women Liberationists to "a squadron of enraged Amazons, an honor guard of revolutionary (if we could only see them) vaginas."[312], and fears that they might usurp the power, kill all men with the exception of a few, reared as slaves to provide semen banks for the future. He viewed the Women's Movement as unfair, unforgiving, totalitarian in its disrespect of sexual differentiation and its endorsements of technological society through their advocating extra-uterine reproduction.

Beyond this extravagant indictment, Mailer used *The Prisoner of Sex* as a means of replying to Kate Millet's *Sexual Politics*, where she accuses him of reducing sex to issues of violence and power. He was also responding to assaults from Germaine Greer in *The Female Eunuch*, to Ti-Grace Atkinson's essays, to Valerie Solanis's manifesto, SCUM (Society For Cutting Up Men), or Mary Ellmann's *Thinking About Women*…

While adamantly opposed to Women's Liberation, he began to measure the movement's strength and perceive it as a threat. Pragmatically, he was forced to admit that women are indeed abused: "Yes, the argument is that women are a social and economic class exploited by a ruling class of men."[313] After spending a part of the summer in Maine taking care of his family, Mailer learned to empathize with the housewife. He confesses: "Yes, he could be a housewife for six weeks, even for seven years if it came to it, even work without help if it came to it, but he did not question what he would have to give up forever. So he could not know whether he would have found it endurable to be born a woman or if it would have driven him out onto the dreary avenues of the insane."[314]

Later, Mailer would congratulate Betty Friedan, founder of NOW (National Organization For Women) and support its bill of rights, demanding a constitutional amendment giving equal rights to women; a law forbidding sex discrimination in employment; a revision of tax laws to permit the reduction of home and care expenses for working parents; the establishment of day-care centers on the same basis as parks, libraries and schools; the right for women to be educated to their full potential, equal to men at all levels of education, the revision of welfare; abortion on demand; laws to provide women with more dignity, privacy and self-respect, the right of women to go back to work after childbirth without loss of seniority and to be paid maternity leave as a form of social security; the possibility to control their own reproductive lives through access to contraceptive information and devices…

Mailer was more tolerant of abortion than contraception. Although, as he told Joseph Ruddy in 1969, he considered a woman who aborts to be, "a murderess"[315], he condoned it as a personal choice. A few years later, in *St. George and the Godfather*, although he condemns abortion as the killing of human potential and the technological violation of mystery, he argues that the control over one's body is a basic human right. He sees the decision of bearing a child as "an act of self-recognition", revealing a woman's loyalty either to "the recollection of magic"[316], or her own practicality. If a woman is not ready to "devote herself to such a creation, then why not assume that she [is] in the right to deny life?"[317] With time, Mailer's position has become increasingly liberal. At the Republican Convention in Houston, in 1992, he sided with "the Amazons" against the implacable conservative pro-life concept, which equates abortion with murder.

On the other hand, Mailer's views on contraception have always been intransigent and remained so. They are best resumed in *The Presidential Papers*: "I hate contraception... it's an abomination. I'd rather have those fucking Communists over there."[318] He particularly loathed the pill, claiming that it "reduces the fuck to a species of upper masturbation"[319]. By contrast, the diaphragm at least offered "a chance each night... to remove the plug and have a child."[320] Thus, in *An American Dream*, Cherry and Rojack experience apocalyptic sex once "that corporate rubbery obstruction [he] detested so much" is removed from Cherry's vagina. "[Their] wills now met"[321] and Cherry was to become pregnant.

In her autobiography, Adele describes how Mailer, her husband, brutally reached into her to pull out her diaphragm, throwing it across the room in a violent rage and screaming: "I hate those fucking things. They'll give me cancer."[322] Suddenly a devout Jew, he proceeded to rant in endless monologues on the waste of his semen. For the "prisoner", contraception, excluding the possibility of childbirth, was associated not only with technology but also with homosexuality. In *Fear of Flying*, Erica Jong resumes all that Mailer despises in the use of contraception: "The diaphragm has become a kind of fetish for me. A holy object, a barrier between my womb and men. Somehow, the idea of baring his baby angers me. Let him bear *his* own baby! If I have a baby, I want it to be all *mine*!"

Mailer's opinion on the subject of contraception remains unchanged. In 1994, during an interview with Madonna, he declared that "Safe sex is part of the insanity of this country"[323], and vehemently criticized the use of condoms, despite the threat of AIDS.

His earlier reservations about abortion, his abhorrence of contraception are a result of a need to reassure himself. Procreation becomes a gauge of his virility. In *The Presidential Papers*, Mailer even confesses this vulnerability: "As you get older, you begin to grow more and more obsessed with procreation. You begin to feel used up. Another part of one's self is fast diminishing. There isn't that much of oneself left."[324] If he sometimes parodies male vanity—as in the fourteen "lays" of Minetta in *The Naked and the Dead*, or D.J.'s allusion to the "grab for your dick competition shit" in *Why Are We in Vietnam?*—he was certainly a prey to the same weakness.

These attitudes toward abortion and contraception, although rooted in his male chauvinism and personal insecurities, are also an integral part of the religious education imposed upon him. In traditional Judaism, "the spilling of the seed" is viewed as a serious transgression. Sterilization was prohibited, although rabbinical law could more willingly tolerate female birth control. A man was obliged to be fruitful and multiply: Deuteronomy 23:2 forbids vasectomies and any other form of male sterilization. Yet, Judaism is more firmly opposed to abortion than to contraception, since it is not only the waste of a man's seed, but the annihilation of potential life. Abortion is only permitted when the mother's life is endangered. The *mitzvah*, the sacred act of procreation as stated in Isaiah—"He did not create [the world] a waste, but formed it for habitation" (45:18)—is fundamental to Judaism. Consequently, the sages ruled that if a man had lived with his wife for ten years without producing children, it was his duty to repudiate her and wed another in her place. The Jewish view of procreation as a religious duty is diametrically opposed to the Catholic sanctification of celibacy and abstinence. With his eight children, Mailer is in keeping with his Jewish roots.

In March 1971, following the publication of *The Prisoner of Sex* in *Harper's*, the Theatre of Ideas proposed a debate between Mailer and a panel of feminists. Leading feminists like Kate Millet, Ti-Grace Atkinson, Gloria Steinem and Robin Morgan rejected the idea of a verbal match with this epitome of the "male chauvinist". They not only refused to participate, but they also declined to be present at the event. The meeting was finally organized not as a debate but as a series of presentations modulated by the "Prisoner of Sex" in person. Jackie Ceballos, the president of NOW, Jill Johnston, the *Village Voice* writer, dance critic and militant lesbian, Diana Trilling, the literary critic, and most importantly, Germaine Greer, the Australian feminist whose bestseller, *The Female Eunuch*, was on the point of publication, were to attend the conference. To reporters, Greer announced that she would seduce Mailer, and "carry him like a wounded child across the wasted land"[325]. Many celebrities attended: Stephen Spender, Arthur Schlesinger Jr., Betty Friedan, Cynthia Ozick, Jules Feiffer, Elizabeth Hardwick, John Hollander, Jack Newfield, Anatole Boyard... Weeks before the event, tickets had sold out at double the price of the most popular musicals. On the day, the conference rapidly degenerated into a "happening": Jill Johnston and two of her lesbian friends, dressed in well-patched jeans and boys' shirts, locked into an embrace and rolled together on the floor. Horrified, shocked to the core of his Hebraic machismo, Mailer begged Johnston to "be a lady"[326]. However, deeming the spectacle worthy of posterity, in 1972, he had Donn Pennebaker turn it into a film, entitled *Town Bloody Hall*.

That same year, Mailer appeared at the Stony Brook campus at the State University of New York, where he made other denigrating comments on Women's Liberation. By the end of his speech, half of his audience had already expressed their disapproval, deserting the hall, slamming the doors as they left. In 1972, again, he published *St. George and the Godfather*, another address to the feminists. He compared their movement with the black issue. While sympathetic to the black American's plight, he expressed his intolerance of Women's Liberation, arguing that the American woman's struggle was merely the result of her ennui confronted with "the pointlessness of middleclass life". In an interview given to David Kenby for the New Yorker, he admitted that with the Women's Liberation, he ultimately felt "like the British when they lost India", fearing that men might lose "their co-starring role in conceiving a child, their purchase on the womb." At seventy-five, he was divided: "One part of him grudgingly [accepted] Women's Liberation; the other part [was] a critic who wouldn't let go", judging that the success of the movement depended on its symbiosis with the corporation. Women's Liberationists, he said, had become "the gilt-edged peons of corporation"[327]. In fact, Mailer remains deeply entrenched in his role of Hebraic patriarch. Many years later, in *The Time of Our Time*, he was no more favorable to feminism: "Women's Liberation, contributing to no cause but its own, has become tiring. Their agenda was sexist: women were good and men were no damn good."

Many Jewish women supported the movement, no doubt because they were more educated than their "sisters" from other religious backgrounds. They were thus better equipped to assert themselves outside their homes, in professional life. As they were both female and Jewish, they were also doubly stigmatized, and thus were more motivated to secure their position in American society. Betty Friedan claimed that her passion for equal rights for women stemmed from "a passion against injustice, which originated from [her] feelings for the injustice of anti-Semitism."[328]

Bella Abzug, another important figure of Women's Liberation, was the second Jewish woman elected to Congress, where she served three terms for Manhattan's West-Side, from 1971 to 1977. She was also one of Mailer's most virulent critics within the movement. Renown for her "powerful vocal chords and not-so-conventional manner", she did not stand on ceremony and told Mailer outright: "Your views on women do not impress us. In fact, we think you stink. We think your views of women are full of shit."[329]

In the final analysis, "the Prisoner's" only ally within the movement was Gloria Steinem—also Jewish—the journalist who was also co-founder and editor of *Ms.*, a magazine oriented toward women, dealing with their problems not only as mothers and wives, but also directed toward the public issues concerning them. Since 1972, Steinem has given many lectures, organized countless actions and written a great deal on behalf of feminism. She is equally the co-founder of the Women's Action Alliance and the National Women's Political Caucus. In a way, like Mailer, she has focused on aiding the "underdog", and has been instrumental in encouraging poor, black working-class women into the movement. Although she chose not to participate in the feminist panel sponsored by the Theatre of Ideas, she was nonetheless supportive of "the Prisoner's" political beliefs and actively participated in his mayoral campaign. When Mailer found himself adrift on his fortieth birthday, he celebrated it with her in a *tête-à-tête* dinner. Insensitive neither to her charm nor to her support, he attempted, unsuccessfully, to seduce his fan, who was probably the only "supportive Amazon" in the movement.

Parallel to the Women's Movement was a Jewish feminist movement led by Letty Cottin, acclaimed for an article she had written in *Ms.* on anti-Semitism in the general feminist and lesbian-feminist movements. The Jewish feminists fought to improve their status within Judaism, and many Jewish women with a strong religious identity became part of this movement because they felt that the general movement failed to correlate their religious and feminist concerns. Jewish feminism did not focus so much on self-realization, but more on educational and religious equality. Whether as part of a general movement or within Jewish feminism, Jewish women have proven to be more liberal and more active in defending minority rights. They have been a major force in social change and the major nemesis in "the Prisoner's" patriarchal program: ultimately, they have taken Denise Gondolman's revenge.

Mailer does not, however, limit his misogyny to feminists, but extends it even to women writers. As Gloria Steinem explains, he deems that women, like blacks, have a more animalistic sense of life, which he envies. Yet, men are more intellectually gifted, possess a better notion of strategy and political power, as well as a greater capacity for action. In his review of Mary McCarthy's, *The Group*, Mailer condescendingly refers to it as "a lady book"[330], implying that a woman writer is necessarily inferior, if at all existent. Mary Ellmann explains that his critical and political prose is based on a system of values so ridiculously male chauvinistic that it constitutes a new aesthetics, which she defines as "phallic criticism"[331]. In *The Deer Park*, he describes intelligence as "masculinity of mind"; in *Cannibals and Christians*, he condemns the "dead-stick prose" of mediocre writers, praising the accomplished ones for setting a "virile example", resuming that since "style is root" (penis), the best writing requires "huge loins". If his article, "Evaluations: Quick and Expensive Comments on the Talent in the Room", is aimed at denigrating his literary peers, he claims outright that he is unable to read women authors, and that no really exciting female work could exist until one was written by a whore. He speaks pejoratively of their work as "always fey, old-hat, Quaintsy Goysy, too dykily psychotic, crippled, creepish, fashionable, frigid, outer-Baroque, *maquillé* in mannequin's whimsy, or else bright and stillborn." In a second article, "The Children of the Goddess", he only deigned to devote a footnote to female writers, gracing them with faint praise.

Mailer's disdain took an institutional turn when he became president of PEN (Poets, Editors, Essayists and Novelists) in 1984. The American PEN is the largest of the association's one hundred and thirty centers around the world. In 1986, Mailer organized the club's forty-eighth International Congress, the first to be held in America since 1966. The under-representation of women was flagrant. Betty Friedan openly asked Mailer why so few women had been invited, to which he answered, "Oh, who's counting?"[332] Betty Friedan and the rare women who took part in the congress demanded that PEN apologize in a manner that was "not perfunctory", and asked that this omission be immediately rectified. Mailer argued that many women he had invited—Mavis Gallant, Nathalie Sarraute, Iris Murdoch, Mary McCarthy, Eudora Welty and Marguerite Yourcenar—had refused to attend. While addressing this issue of under-representation, he managed in a typical Maileresque fashion to further infuriate women writers by insisting that men writers were more qualified to attend: "Since the formulation of the panels is reasonably intellectual, there are not many women, like Susan Sontag, who are intellectuals first, poets and novelists second. More men are intellectuals first, so there was a certain tendency to pick more men than women." At the end of the congress, he added insult to injury by presenting an ultimate backhanded apology, stating that: "We did not want a congress that would establish a political point at the cost of considerable mediocrity"[333].

Were Mailer's heroines inspired by the women he knew? In an interview with Laura Adams for *Partisan Review* in 1975, he claims they were not, explaining that he found it unadvisable to fictionalize women, "especially wives"[334]. Yet Denise Gondolman is a counterpart to Beatrice Silverman, his first wife, who was Jewish, young, intellectual and domineering. Eleanor and Elena also share many traits with his second wife. Both, like Adele, are bohemian, and Elena is a female victim. Deborah's murder in *An American Dream* and Sam's fantasizing about killing Eleanor were generated by Mailer's stabbing of Adele. His third wife, Lady Jeanne Campbell, member of a prominent English family and brought up in England, undeniably resembles Deborah. Cherry is a synthesis of his fourth and fifth wives, Beverly Bentley and Carol Stevens. Beverly is a Southern blond, like Cherry. Carol was a singer in a Harlem nightclub, also like Cherry. Norris, his last wife, has no double. They were married until his death, and maybe he did not feel the need to immortalize her through fiction.

In truth, the link between his inspiration and his life is essentially reflected in his marriages. They allowed him the wealth of concrete, daily experiences with women. As he writes in *The Prisoner of Sex*, he had been "four times beaten at wedlock"[335]. Marriage occupies all his novels, often revealing his views and failures. When it is not a battlefield, an arena of pure hostility and antagonism, it is total ennui. "The act of marriage," he writes of the McLeods' union in *Barbary Shore*, "having divorced them from all passion and all friendship so that they live in guilt and hate and very occasionally in love."[336] In *The Naked and the Dead*, Goldstein's tedious marriage laps around him like "a warm bath"[337]; while Sam and Eleanor's marriage in "The Man Who Studied Yoga", was at best "a pomade of affection, resentment, boredom and occasional compassion", the couple eventually turning to pornographic movies to escape the dullness of their existence. *The Death of the Ladies* abounds with pejorative allusions to the home and mother, as well as dreary Sunday afternoons spent with the wife.

Mailer believed that he could socially escape his Jewishness by becoming integrated in a non-Jewish milieu. Since his college days, according to Bea Silverman, he had always wanted to "lay *shiksas*", and of his six wives, only two—Bea and Carol—are Jewish. His first marriage was to Bea. His second choice was Adele, a goy, in the hope that he might free himself from the problems inherent to endogamy. In Roth's *Portnoy's Complaint*, Alexander questions his psychiatrist on the subject of goy women: "But what was I supposed to be but her savior? A brainy, baldy, breaking Jew… who neither drinks nor gambles nor keeps show girls on the side… a regular Messiah!"[338] Mailer felt marginal, badly assimilated into society; marrying a goy reassured him. To other Americans, the Jewish and the Asian men seemed fragile but intelligent, an image radically opposed to that of American virility, which grossly lauded the brutal strong male: the real jock. Many Jews, as well as men belonging to other minorities, integrated these negative stereotypes and vented their rage and frustration on their wives as a means of sublimating the rejection they experienced due to prejudice. Thus, Mailer incorporated this tortured vision fundamental to his religion into his own sexuality. He was persuaded, as he explained in *The Prisoner of Sex*, that circumcision is "the fastest way to relocate the libido from the genitals to the brain and mouth"[339].

In *Of a Fire on the Moon*, he states that he cannot understand people who marry their mirror images: "he has always gotten married in a hurry to women who were remarkably different, except for his final inability to get along with them."[340] For Mailer, each marriage was a passport to another culture, as he confesses in *The Armies of the Night*: Of Bea Silverman, he claims he had learned something "of Jewish genius and of revolutionaries and large indiscriminate love for the oppressed". Adele Morales taught him a "love of painting and sensuality and drama and Latin desperation". With Jeanne Campbell, he experienced "a love-affair with England". Beverly, an actress, initiated him to the Southern mystique[341] and he expressed with a tender nostalgia his regrets over the failure of their marriage: "The sense of love as a balm for the vacuums of the day was departed from them—they were sealed from one another; a run of seven years was done and his heart throbbed like a bruise in the thigh"[342]. Although Mailer was conscious of the disastrous effects divorce had on his offspring—he spoke of "the vortex of all post-marital pain"[343]—he was ultimately responsible for each of his separations. His married life was fraught with conflict, which arose from his mother's constant intervention, his alcoholism, his infidelities, and his insistence that love and marriage were a perpetual struggle for power. In short, "love [was] a dialectic, man, back and forth, hate and sweet"[344].

These *rapport de force* were often the consequence of a Jewish son's upbringing, described by the feminist, Aviva Cantor, as "apron-string bonding"[345]. The mother initially creates this interdependency during adolescence, in order that her son remain as emotionally dependent on her as an infant. He is taught that by doing something she disapproves of, or by not fulfilling her desires, he becomes the cause of her grief. The mother uses guilt and nagging as a means of submitting the son to her will. Inversely, the son retaliates by withholding his emotions and withdrawing into himself. "Apron-string bonding" results in egocentricity. Mailer's interdependence with others—especially with women—is ultimately subject to his power over them. Furthermore, Mailer is the archetypal Jewish prince, spoiled by his mother, who expects the same treatment from other women.

Simultaneously, he is attracted to challenging women; although certainly not to women within his profession, who present a threat to him. In 1981, he brought up the subject during a discussion with Jeffrey Michelson and Sarah Stone: "I've usually been drawn to women who are not necessarily that interested in my work. My present wife [Norris] had read one book of mine before we met. She hardly knew anything about me. It's probably analogous to the poor, young, rich girl who wants to be loved for her literary fame because you know more about it than anyone else and you know literary fame has little to do with your daily habits. I mean, finally you're an animal who lives in a den and goes around, and finally you know, has to be liked or disliked as an animal first"[346]. In relationship to his wives, ever the fighter in white armor, Mailer resumed that he also liked "to marry women I can beat once in a while and who fight back"[347]. With the exception of Carol Stevens, his fifth wife, and Norris, his last wife, Mailer's personal life had always been subjected to the *rapport de force* inculcated during his childhood.

He met Bea Silverman, his first wife, in his junior year at Harvard. She was a talented music major at Boston University. They eloped in 1944, so that Fan could not prevent "her little genius"[348] from getting married. The couple later had one daughter, Susan. Like many Jewish men who married another Jew, Mailer chose a woman from a more modest social background: Bea was the daughter of a local butcher. This first union soon became a struggle for power. Of all his wives, Bea was the one who most resembled Fan: she was Jewish, domineering, and strong. Not surprisingly, she was also the daughter-in-law that Fan disliked the most. She criticized her for her competitiveness and her unfaltering desire to be "top banana"[349]. Fan's relationship with Bea exemplified the classic Jewish mother-in-law, daughter-in-law discord, which is much like "two captains trying to gain control of a ship's bridge"[350].

The rivalry between Bea and Mailer had doubtless the most destructive influence on their marriage. Mailer considered Bea as "a pre-mature Women's Liberationist"[351]. She was enlisted in the WAVES (Women's Emergency Services) as a lieutenant, which irritated him. Mailer was determined to enlist as a private, because he felt that if he were made an officer, he would find himself working behind a desk, rather than involved in the combat. Predictably, he did not enjoy the idea of his wife holding a position of authority superior to his: would he be expected to salute her before "putting it in"[352]? Moreover, he was hostile to the presence of women in the army: war, of course, was a man's activity. Most importantly, Bea suffered from a sense of inferiority with regard to her husband's charisma, his personality, and his fame. Even before *The Naked and the Dead* was published, while

Mailer was in the process of writing it, Bea began a novel of her own about women in the Navy. The more Mailer came into the literary limelight, the more Bea waned and wilted to the point of severe depression.

In 1954, after Bea, Mailer married Adele Morales, a Spanish-Peruvian abstract painter who became his mentor to bohemia and Greenwich Village. It was a period of professional dissatisfaction in the author's life, and he sought refuge in drugs, promiscuity and alcohol. Although they had two daughters together, Dandy and Betsy, the tumult of their marriage would lead to Mailer's stabbing of Adele after a party at their house, in 1960. Adele, however, was devoted to her husband and refused to press charges. She did all she could to minimize the incident: "He's not a violent person. I think, basically, he's a very good person. In some ways, he's immature, but he's also very boyish"[353]. Yet despite Adele's indulgence, Fan could only respond myopically and protectively to "the trouble". Nothing, of course, was her son's fault: "If Norman would stop marrying these women who make him do these terrible things…"[354]. Mailer, true to his natural egotism, was more concerned with his reputation, fearing that he had "destroyed forever the possibility of being the Jeremiah of our time"[355]. Adele lived in Mailer's shadow and yet he played Pygmalion, building her into the strong woman he needed, that paradoxical feminine entity which challenged and defied his authority, while threatening his masculinity. She continued to be entranced by Mailer, constantly bating his jealousy in order to sustain his interest, "contented to have found a lover whose need for drama equaled [her] own."[356] By touching his Achilles' heel, she remained his sparring partner during an eight-year marriage.

His marriage to Jeanne Campbell in 1962 would only last one year. They divorced after the birth of their daughter, Kate. When they met, Jeanne was a journalist and correspondent in America for *The Evening Standard*, her father, the Duke of Argyll's, newspaper. Her grandfather, Lord Beaverbrook, was vehemently opposed to the match and disinherited her. Meanwhile, Mailer complained: "She'll give up ten million dollars for me, but she won't make me breakfast"[357].

Fan too disapproved of the marriage. She had little patience with Jeanne and her aristocratic family, while Jeanne, who believed she was marrying a powerful, dynamic literary man, found herself bound to a spoiled mother's boy. Independent socially and financially, well established in her career as a journalist, she was a stimulating, intelligent, strong-willed partner for Mailer. Jeanne, according to Bill Ward, a long-time resident of Provincetown, "wouldn't take shit from anybody"[358]. As Bea described her, she was the "ultimate *shiksa*"[359]. Like Daisy for Gatsby, or Deborah for Rojack, she was Mailer's passport to power, to "the big league". "Suddenly, because he was married to Lady Jeanne,, he was nobility"[360]. And like Alexander Portnoy, Mailer didn't seem "to stick his dick up these girls as much as [he stuck] it up their backgrounds"[361].

His marriage to Beverly, a Southern actress, was another story altogether. It lasted seven years, from 1963 to 1970. Initially, Fan was well disposed toward her, finding her open and generous. Unfortunately, the couple, who had two boys, would rapidly fall apart, as would the relationship between mother-in-law and daughter-in-law.

Beverly's insistence on having both a career and a family life was an important element of conflict in their marriage. In order to appease these tensions, Mailer set up a coffeehouse theatre, Act IV, so that she could continue acting. Yet, in a typical Maileresque fashion, when he directed the play, *The Deer Park*, instead of giving the lead role of Elena to Beverly, he gave it to his ex-wife, Adele. "My acting was something I had that he didn't have", concluded Beverly[362]. It was not so much that Mailer wanted to be an actor himself, but he was jealous of anything that his wife might have in her own right. It infuriated Mailer that, at the beginning of his career, before she met him, while she was working on The Godfrey Show, she had changed her name. Beverly soon realized the cause of his anger: "Because I changed my own name, that meant to him I was not entirely his own creation— and worse, to his mind, maybe that of another man. I was my own creation, [and] that really got to him."[363]

Beverly came from a family of nine children. Strong-willed, she was the only one to stand up to her father, an Army Air Corpsman.

Although she considered herself "tougher than the other ones"³⁶⁴, she was no match for Mailer. Soon overwhelmed by him, conscious that "all his ladies do for a while, then he tramples them"³⁶⁵, she began to drink heavily. Beverly was soon to be humiliated, not only as an actress, but also as a woman. Mailer was flagrantly unfaithful. When she returned home from the maternity ward with their first son, Michael, he was out all night, womanizing. She threw her wedding ring out of the window. When their second son, Stephen, was born, her husband was having an affair with an airline stewardess. By the time their marriage came to an end, he was involved with both Susan Nye and Carol Stevens, his future wife, who was pregnant with his child. Sadistically, Mailer went so far as to impose other women on Beverly, in their home. This promiscuity was yet another means for him of establishing his power in the struggle he immediately forced onto the women closest to him. It comforted his virility. Adding violence to adultery, Mailer would often beat Beverly, who would find herself with a black eye and a swollen face. He once even threatened to throw her out of the window, as Rojack had done to his wife, Deborah.

Mailer had in fact met Carol Stevens, the blues singer, shortly after he had left Adele, in 1961. Theirs was an episodic affair, which lasted from the summer of 1970 until 1975, when he left her for his last wife, Norris Church. Mailer only married Carol in 1980, in order to legitimize their daughter, Maggie Alexandra, and to honor the years they had spent together. Once again, the author made the headlines. *People* quoted: "IN A MERRY MARRIAGE-GO-ROUND, MAILER PLANS A DOUBLE WEDDING TO WIVES FIVE AND SIX"³⁶⁶. Norris was understandably disconcerted, but for Mailer, it was a means of legitimizing "every one of the little buggers".³⁶⁷

Carol Stevens, in love with Mailer through his marriages with Jeanne and Beverly, had been convinced that theirs was "an historic love-affair", and that "they [would] end up together"³⁶⁸. She was the first of his wives not to fight back. In fact, she did not even respond. Such a show of indifference from a strong woman could only intrigue Mailer. Again, according to some of his friends, he began to play Pygmalion.

Mailer met his last wife, Norris in 1975 with whom he would later have a son, John Buffalo. He furthermore adopted her son, Matthew, by an earlier marriage. Norris was a model and artist. She was apparently the only one capable of braving the storm. She was the most compatible with Mailer because, although strong, she seemed the most adept at catering to his whims, while sharing his ambitiousness, his need to "[be] a winner"[369].

Unlike Carol and his other wives, Norris became extremely close to Fan and remained so. When she arrived in New York, in 1975, Fan found an apartment for her in her building. Norris accompanied Fan to temple, dined with her several times a week, saw her every morning and spoke with her every evening. In short, Norris, despite the fact that she is a *shiksa*, became Fan's best and only friend. Fan found her "easy to be with, and like Norman, she has a very honest personality. She's unique, very different from Norman's other wives. She has character. She knows when to overlook things and she doesn't fight and scream", concluding that, "she was what Norman needed, though, in looks and knowledge and character—a true person."[370]

Emma Gwaltney, who introduced Norris—her close friend—to Mailer, analyzed the success of their marriage: "It seems to me [Norris] is wiser about how to get along with Norman than some of the other ones… For some time, Fig and I noticed a feeling of competition that women had with Norman. [Norris] doesn't do that at all. Adele wanted to be a painter, Beverly wanted to be an actress, and Bea was just very, very smart. It seemed to me that sometimes their ambition gave rise to a little bit of challenge. But [Norris] is very supportive."[371] Mickey Knox, one of Mailer's oldest friends, thought that Norris incarnated all the elements that the author had been seeking in his previous wives, and that she is "the one woman who had everything: beauty, grace, intelligent, talent and a very strong will."[372]

With Norris as with Carol, Mailer was involved with a woman who did not fight back. He could neither provoke her nor destabilize her. Yet, despite the happiness he found with her, he could not remain faithful. According to "the Prisoner": "Infidelity, once it becomes the confirmed habit of one's youth and middle-age, does not go gently into the long dark night of finding oneself a senior citizen."[373] In 1983, he began a nine-year long relationship with Carole Mallory, a model and actress. She wrote a fictionalized account of their affair, *Flash*, which was published in 1988. Very much in love with Mailer, she alluded to her displeasure at being "a fuck-and-run. His sexual gymnasium"[374]. She claims that, "he wouldn't let me control him. He controlled me."[375]

After the publication of *Flash*, she embarked on a successful career in journalism, specializing in confrontations between two prominent figures. In 1990, she organized an interview between Gore Vidal and Mailer, which appeared in *Esquire* the following year. It was probably this interview that marked the end of their relationship. Mailer, jealous as always, felt that Carole had flirted with Gore Vidal. When he saw the draft of the magazine's cover, a photograph of her kissing his arch rival, his anger knew no bounds. He broke up soon after, on the pretext that Norris had just discovered their liaison, which of course was untrue: she had known about Carole from the start.

Carole Mallory, however, was convinced that Mailer had left her because he feared he could no longer control her. In 1995, 'Page Six', the gossip column of *The New York Post* announced a second book by Carole: *On Mailer*. She explained that she would not have it put to press before John Buffalo became an adult, although Mailer, surprisingly, granted her permission to publish it. She does, however, describe him as "her mentor, Henry Higgins Pygmalion"[376]

Mailer, Jewish patriarch and Jewish prince, adept of a "virility cult"[377], could only be ambivalent and male chauvinistic toward the "weaker sex". His rage against women was mainly due to the fact that he depended on them for his nurturing and his identity. Although he admitted that men in America had not fulfilled their role, he feared that as a result of society's process of feminization, women were becoming "more selfish, more greedy, less romantic, less warm, more lusty and filled with hate"[378] Mailer came to apprehend the power of women, a dread which began with his mother and was later incarnated by the Women's Liberationists. In his relationships with women, he used the *rapport de force* he had initially learned in his childhood in order to protect himself, convinced that "no matter what brutalities men have exercised upon women, they've obviously lived in sufficient awe of [them]. They didn't destroy women. But if you ever reversed it, if women had all the power, there would be very little to keep men safely on earth, I can tell you that."[379]

CHAPTER IV

Mailer: The Jeremiah

Mailer believed that one of the writer's primary goals was to clarify a nation's vision of itself. Despite his integration into Waspdom, he assumed the messianic role of the Hebrew prophet, chastising the American people for allowing their country to fall into a state of decadence, "authority and nihilism stalking one another in the orgiastic hollow of this century"[380]. Mailer saw it as his mission to save his country, proclaiming in *The Armies of the Night*: "Let the bugle blow. The death of America rides in on the smog. America—the land where a new kind of man was born from the idea that God was present in every man not only as compassion but as power... Deliver us from our curse. For we must end on the road to that mystery where courage, death and the dream of love give promise to sleep."[381]

To him, the writer is "the marrow of the nation"[382] who must "settle for nothing less than making a revolution in the consciousness of time"[383]. Although he greatly admired the early Gentile authors such as Hemingway and Faulkner, he reproached them for their social and political detachment: "Their vision was partial, determinedly so, they saw that the first condition for trying to be great—that one must try to save. Not souls and not the nation. The desire for majesty was the bitch that licked at the literary loins of Hemingway and Faulkner: the country could be damned. Let it take care of itself."[384]

Like many of his contemporaries and their forerunners of the 1930s, Mailer gave traditional Judaism little credit, and transposed his religious aspirations onto politics. In 1947, soon after embracing his leftist doctrines in *Barbary Shore*, he described himself as a "Jew radical"[385]. By the mid-fifties, with the evolution of Communism, and his much-improved status in American society, Mailer no longer sought the nation's salvation through politics but through the individual notably the hipster. From political radicalism, he transferred his religious faith onto spiritual radicalism; his religious awareness was awakened to Jewish mysticism and the belief in reincarnation, which would remain a fundamental aspect of his vision.

As late as 1998, in *The New York Times*, Mailer was quoted as saying, "What people don't understand is that religion has been a major theme of all my work… For the last fifty years, my preoccupation has been religion. What might God be? I am searching for a notion of God that is alive in me."[386] He had earlier defined himself as a secular Jew for whom the customs of conventional Judaism are of little importance. He had created multi-faceted heroes such as Rojack, projections of himself and his unrealized fantasies. Rojack is a Harvard graduate *summa cum laude*, a war hero, the only intellectual in American history to win a Distinguished Service Cross, an ex-congressman, a television personality, a professor of existentialist psychology, an author, a boxer and a consummate stud… Yet as a cultural hybrid straddling the world of his Jewish origins and the gentile extremes of Waspdom, he is also a marginal man. Speaking of himself in *Christians and Cannibals* Mailer says that he is, "alienated from the self by a double sense of identity and so at the mercy of self which demands action and more action to define the most rudimentary borders of identity."[387] Thorstein Veblen, in his delineation of the prototype Jew, claims that the assimilation of both cultures is a necessary prerequisite for the gifted Jew to become, "a creative leader in the world's enterprise".[388] The emancipated Jew is therefore, "a specialist in alienation", as defined by Isaac Rosenfeld.[389]

Like Mailer, the emancipated Jew was the cosmopolitan capable of adapting anywhere and belonging nowhere. With Spinoza, Heine, Rosa Luxembourg, Trotsky and Freud, Mailer found rabbinical Judaism too archaic and constricting. He felt the need to create a more direct and personal relationship to God, much in the same way as he sought to create his own identity.

This sentiment of isolation was shared by many of his contemporaries notably Salinger, Rosenfeld and Ginsberg, to name only a few. Their desire for a more utopian society led them to express their dissatisfaction through dissent. In 1952, in an article written for the *Partisan Review*, Mailer defended this position: "Is there nothing to remind us that the writer does not need to be integrated into his society, and often works best in opposition to it... It is worth something to remind ourselves that the great artists... certainly the moderns... are almost always in opposition to their society and that integration, acceptance, non-alienation, etc., etc., have been more conducive to propaganda than to art."[390] Thus, Mailer "vowed to serve as a radical sentry and sound the alarm about the dangers the nation faced from totalitarianism, repression, conformity"[391]. Although many traditionalists who sought affirmative Judaism were offended by Mailer's apparent negativism, Leslie Fiedler remarked that the "negativist is no nihilist": Mailer and many of his contemporaries affirmed the existence of tradition, if only to contest it.[392]

For Mailer and his peers, the onus of the blame lay on capitalist values. America, they argued, was "built on property and such inhuman abstractions of human energy as money, credit and surplus value"[393]. The paradox is that "life in America becomes more economically prosperous and more psychically impoverished each year."[394] Like other Jewish authors, Mailer wanted to write 'the big one', the novel that would awaken social, political and spiritual consciousness and create great changes in America.

To Mailer, the novel, which he deemed a sacred vessel, was the best means of bringing about this transformation: "there's nothing more beautiful than a marvelous novel; to me a novel is better than a reality... I mean there's something beautiful about one mind being able to come up with a vision that's not Godlike but close enough to be Godlike to give us a vision of how marvelous the Lord's mind might be"[395].

Mailer is also a modern Moses whose dream of justice is shared by the Old Testament prophets. Hugo Valentin judges that Moses was "the first to proclaim the rights of man", arguing that: "The recollection of Egyptian bondage with the concomitant emphasis upon liberty are among the most important facts of Jewish history. In ancient Jewish life, these resulted in egalitarian and libertarian emphasis in Jewish religious thought and marked a sympathy for the oppressed and the enslaved."[396]

For much of the Jewish intelligentsia, as for Mailer, social and political injustices could be righted through political reforms. The author has always had "an umbilical attachment to the left"[397] and viewed Marxism as a guide to change. Since its conception, Marxism has greatly attracted Jews, Marx, himself having been a converted Jew. Although the Marxist interpretation of history and humanity is implacably materialistic, and diametrically opposed to Jewish and Christian beliefs in the creation of man in God's image, Marxism and Judaism share many of the same goals. Both express a desire to perfect the world and establish an ideal society. For those Jews no longer attached to the Torah and the Talmud, and who felt no allegiance to capitalism, Marxism became a secular offshoot of Judaism, which was adapted to their need for a messianic vision.

In 1998, in an interview with Jean-Louis Turlin for the French newspaper, *Le Figaro*, Mailer equated religion and politics: "the spiritual quest and political involvement is the same combat"[398]. As early as the mid-1950s, Mailer had become increasingly interested in spiritual radicalism. In 1955, he bought a share in *The Village Voice*, run by his friends, Dan Wolf and Ed Fancher, in order to express his radicalism and his adherence to counterculture. Discouraged by the comparative failure of *Barbary Shore* and *The Deer Park*, he saw himself as a literary outlaw, and this further estranged him from the social and literary WASP establishment. This was the period during which he drowned his anger and frustration in drugs and alcohol, identifying with the hipster, that social outcast he so romanticized. The hipster thus became not only an outlet for Mailer's religious aspirations, but also a means of self-justification.

His presence at *The Village Voice* was, however, short-lived. After only a year, Mailer found the newspaper too conservative, and thus an inappropriate conveyor of his radicalism. Kevin McAuliffe sums up Mailer's conflict at the *Voice*: "As his moods got blacker, he became more and more impossible. Cover this. Cover Sex. Murder. Dope. Revolution."[399]

A year later, in 1957, Mailer published his seminal article, "The White Negro", in *Dissent*, which was to appear in 1959 in *Advertisements for Myself*. Here Mailer, like Joseph, is "the Jewish Dream Peddler", and these dreams are reflected in his endorsement of hipster and counterculture, presaging the hippie and black movements of the 1960s. As he explained in the article, his transition from political to spiritual radicalism was the evolution of a conscious interest in politics, to an unconscious preoccupation with murder, suicide, orgy and psychosis.

To critics such as Diana Trilling, this transition from political to spiritual awareness, away from Marxism, was a development "[allowing] Mailer to probe modern society on a deeper level than that of political and economic determinism."[400] In "The White Negro", the hipster usurps the role allotted to Marx's proletariat. He is a new-sprung trinity incarnating the bohemian, the juvenile delinquent and the Negro. He bears an uncanny resemblance to the psychopath, as defined by Mailer's friend, the psychiatrist Robert Linder, in *Rebel Without a Cause*: "A rebel without a cause, an agitator without a slogan, a revolutionary without a program: in other words, his rebelliousness is aimed to achieve goals satisfactory to himself alone; he is incapable of exertions for the sake of others. All his efforts, hidden under no matter what disguise, represent investments designed to satisfy his immediate wishes and desires."[401]

Linder's psychopath and Mailer's hipster may depend on the same "instinct of rebellion"[402]; the sedition of Mailer's hipster is primarily a means of freeing American society from the yoke of repression. A new American existentialist, the hipster had emerged from the shadow of the Holocaust and the atomic bomb. This "discontented nephew of the proletariat"[403] came to terms with the tyranny of death and destruction by withdrawing from society and depending on himself alone in his quest for sense: "If the fate of twentieth century man is to live with death from adolescence to premature senescence, why then the only life-giving answer is to accept the terms of death, to live with death as immediate danger, to divorce oneself from society with the rebellious imperatives of the self. In short, whether the life is criminal or not, the decision is to encourage the psychopath in oneself, to explore that domain of experience where security is boredom and therefore sickness, and one exists in the present, in that enormous present which is without a past or a future, memory or planned intention, the life where a man must go beat until he is beat, where he must gamble with his energies through all those small or large crises of courage and unforeseen situations which beset his day, when he must be doomed with it or doomed not to swing."[404]

In *The New Novel in America: The Kafkan Mode in Contemporary Fiction*, Helen Weinberg points out that the Jewish writer, whether it be Bellow, Salinger, Gold or Roth, is almost systematically dedicated to "the imperatives of self"[405]. Mailer, however, is alone in emphasizing the acceptance of death, darkness and the unconscious, and the necessity of endangering oneself in that acceptance. The quest of self-hood to Mailer includes evil; Marion in *The Deer Park* and Rojack embrace evil in order to overcome it and find their identity. The notion of the Evil Impulse, the division of the universe into two opposing principles is also at the root of Cabalistic thought.[406] This medieval mystical school would subsequently influence the development of Hasidic mysticism, but the Hasidim would replace the radical dualism of the Cabala with the theory of the *Yetzer ha'va* or evil urge, and the *Yetzer tov* the urge to do good. Both coexist within the individual. The theologian, Martin Buber, considered these inclinations toward good and evil as similar in nature, not antagonistic. Evil should not be excluded as it was in Mosaic Law, but incorporated for the benefit of the individual. Mailer clearly shares this belief, as is illustrated by his selection of the Hasidic tale "With the Evil Urge", which he included in *Commentary*, in his discussion of the Hasidic tales.

In *Good and Evil*, Buber explains that: "... the 'evil urge' as passion, that is, the power peculiar to man without which he can neither beget nor bring forth, but which, left to itself, remains without direction, and leads astray, and the 'good urge' as pure direction, in other words, as an unconditional direction that leads towards God. To unite the two urges implies: to equip the absolute potency of passion with one direction that renders it capable of great love and of great service. Thus and not otherwise can man become whole"[407].

Creativity was another path leading to self-realization and salvation. To Mailer, the 'real world' is mechanistic and Machiavellian and should be placed in opposition to an imaginative world created by the artist, a writer like himself, whose reality is constructed on truth. Eitel describes such a reality in *The Deer Park*: "... when all else is lost, when love is lost and adventure, pride of self and pity, there still remains that world we create, more real to us, more real to others, than the mummery of what happens, passes and is gone... Try for that other world, where orphans burn orphans and nothing is more difficult to discover than a simple fact. And with the pride of the artist, you must blow against the walls of every power that exists, the small trumpet of your defiance."[408]

The hip movement presented itself in opposition to the 'real world'; it had no specific leader and escaped precise definition. A form of neo-primitivism, it resulted from the individual's sense of godlessness and over-civilization. Reacting against the conformity and repression inherent to American Puritanism, hipsters denounced the country's uncritical belief in technology and the dehumanization it bred, as illustrated in its architecture. Mailer's country had become: "...an empty promiscuous panorama where no one can distinguish between hospitals and housing projects, factories and colleges, concert halls, civic centers and airport terminals. The mind recoils from the thought of an America rebuilt completely in the shape of those blank skyscrapers forty stories high, their walls dead as an empty television screen, their form as interesting as a box of cleansing tissue propped on end. They are buildings which reveal nothing so much as the deterioration in real value of the dollar bill."[409]

In his vision of the future, he saw that, "New cities with great towers must rise in the plain, cities higher than mountains, cities with room for four hundred million to live, or that part of four hundred million who wish to live high in a landscape of peaks and spires, cliffs and precipices".[410] As described by Donald Kaufmann, America's architecture revealed "man's passing into an animal graveyard of the senses."[411]

In order to avoid "extinguishing the animal in us", hip thus advocated the return to a simpler, more natural existence based on intuition and instinct. Because intuition is hostile to external control, the individual needed "to create a new nervous system for [him]self through the senses."[412] Rojack, for example, learns to make an effort to "trust the [authority] of his senses."[413] To Mailer, intuition led to a subjective grasp of realty, "to an absolute relativity where there are no truths other than isolated truths of what each individual feels at each instance"[414]. On the same lines, hip morality encouraged the individual to do as he felt at all times. Mailer thus stresses the importance of the unconscious, which he esteems is endowed with an immense teleological sense. Rojack, after his murder of Deborah, meditates on hidden motives, "the messages of one's experience are continually saying, 'Things are getting better', or 'things are getting worse. For me. For that one. For my future, for my past, mmm?' It is with this thing that they move, that they grope forward this navigator at the seat of their being"[415]. This "messenger" kept communing with the "harbor of his calm", and Rojack's situation improved or worsened depending on whether he listened to his instinct or his Jewish intellect, which Mailer so disdained.

In their own way, hipsterism and Mailer upheld one of the fundamental ethics of rabbinical Judaic: the actions of an individual are laden with significance. A man's acts become *mitzvots*, acts of holiness, and through them, his existence is sanctified. The six hundred and thirteen commandments of the Old Testament were a guideline by which the individual could attain such sanctity. First to have set a rationale for the *mitzvot*, the Hinnuk proclaimed that through good actions an individual becomes good: "Were he to rouse his spirit and endeavor to occupy himself diligently with the Torah and the commandments, even if not for the sake of Heaven, he would immediately incline toward the good and by the power of his deeds he would destroy his evil nature because men's hearts are drawn after their actions."[416]

Similarly, the modern theologian Joshua Heschel, author of *God in Search of Man*, upheld that the individual's action was not secular.

Heschel maintained that every act the individual performed was proof of the fact that the world was meaningful. He stipulated, like Mailer, that action must be coupled with belief: "Jewish observance... consists of acts performed by the body in a clearly defined and tangible manner... of the right intentions and of putting the right intention into action. Both body and soul must participate in carrying out a ritual law, an imperative, a mitzvah."[417]

Despite the fact that Mailer, and his *alter ego*, the hipster, expounded the death of God, Mailer made a clear distinction between American and French existentialism. For the author, the French existentialists had created a theory of atheism, which upheld, in opposition to Hipsterism, that life is rational, and death, emptiness.

Hip was also based on the mysticism of the flesh. Its source was the Negro whose cultural mentor was the Negro jazzman. The White Negro, the hipster, like the Negro, lived on the fringe of society and was also a member of America's underground. He too depended primarily on his instincts, his sexuality in particular, for self-realization and survival. To Mailer, White America was alienated from its instinctual life, for which he blamed, in part, Freudian analysis. Notwithstanding his recognition of the psychoanalyst's "genius", he deemed his theories "were doctrine-like, death-like, and philosophically most dreary"[418]. In 1956, Mailer became a fervent supporter of William Reich, author of *The Sexual Revolution*.

Mailer would soon adhere to Reich's analysis of the correlation between sexual and political repression, and his belief in the therapeutic value of the orgasm. A genuine disciple, Mailer would have a Reichian "orgone box" built for himself in the country and in the city, designed to absorb psychic energy and release it to the person using the box. In Connecticut he had a huge wooden egg resembling an Easter Egg in which he would shut himself from time to time, while in his New York apartment, he constructed a carpet-lined box large enough for him to stand in, where he would scream, anticipating the concept of primal screaming. Reich was actually imprisoned for disregarding an injunction not to manufacture the "orgone box", which only added to his aura of a cult figure for Mailer.

Not only did Reich influence the author's lifestyle, but he was also the pivotal influence on "The White Negro", the orgasm being the hipster's ultimate act in self-realization through his fusion with God: "... that God which every hipster believes is located in the senses of his body, that trapped, mutilated and nonetheless megalomaniacal God who is It, who is energy, life, sex, force, the Yoga's *prana*, the Reichian's orgone, Lawrence's "blood", Hemingway's "good", the Shavian life-force; "It"; God; not the God of the churches but the unachievable whisper of mystery within the sex, the paradise of the limitless energy and perception just beyond the next wave of the next orgasm."[419]

In Judaism, sex and God were inextricably linked, on the condition that the relationship was heterosexual and remained within the framework of marriage. Although Mailer disregarded the conventional aspect of marriage, he alluded to sex as mystical, a conviction underlined in Job, in the Old Testament: "And I shall behold God out of my flesh". (Job 19:26) Jewish mystics also recognized this union, which Mailer further referred to in *The Prisoner of Sex*, when he claimed that "sex is the mirror of how we approach God"[420]. The transcendence experienced by Rojack and Cherry when their orgasm is accompanied by the fluttering of "angelic wings in the room"[421] is yet another example of this spiritual trinity. In *Pontifications*, Mailer upholds that "the first time that someone has a profound sexual act, when it's all over, it proves to them God's existence"[422].

Violence however was a prerequisite to the hipster's self-realization, which is contrary to all Jewish values. Mailer postulated that rage is noisome to creativity when directed toward the self: the externalization of anger through violence was therapeutic and cathartic. Without this expurgation, one could neither grow nor love. He told Mike Wallace that violence and creativity seemed to have "some sort of twin-like relation"[423]. Living in the specter of the Holocaust, Mailer upheld that individual acts of violence are preferable to the collective violence of the state. The author finally melded his concept of sexuality and violence with Hemingway's emphasis on courage. The hipster, he proclaimed, must "find his courage at the moment of violence, or equally make it in the act of love"[424].

Although Mailer received much critical acclaim for "The White Negro", his theory of violence has been seriously contested throughout his life. In 1960, three years after the article was published, he stabbed Adele. In 1981, he was responsible for the release of prisoner Jack Abbott who soon after stabbed and killed an East Village waiter. Charles Brossard, author of *Who Walks in Darkness*, a novel published in 1952 in which he combined the concepts of existentialism and hip, which greatly influenced Mailer's own hip philosophy, defended Norman's position: violence and pain, he asserted, were in essence "a form of engagement for Mailer of reality"[425]. Overall, despite its brilliance, critics viewed "The White Negro" as a dangerous apology of violence. Irving Howe, head of *Dissent*, went so far as to recommend the censorship of the controversial passage in which, in the name of courage, Mailer endorses the gratuitous murder of a fifty-year old store owner by two eighteen year-old juvenile delinquents: "The psychopath murders—if he has the courage—out of necessity to purge his violence, for if he cannot empty his hatred then he cannot love, his being is frozen with implacable self-hatred for his cowardice. (It can of course be suggested that it takes little courage for two strong eighteen-year old hoodlums, let us say, to beat in the brains of a candy-store keeper, and indeed the act—even by the logic of the psychopath—is not likely to prove very therapeutic, for the victim is not an immediate equal. Still, courage of a sort is necessary, for one murders not only a weak fifty-year old man, but an institution as well, one violates private property, one enters into a new relation with the police, and introduces a dangerous element into one's life. The hoodlum is therefore daring the unknown, and so no matter how brutal the act, it is not altogether cowardly.)"[426]

At a precarious moment in Mailer's career, he needed to share in the attention the beatniks were getting from the American literati. So, although Mailer distinguished between the hipster and the beatnik—the former was chic, the latter, slovenly; the former was physical and Faustian, the latter cerebral and sentimental—although he disagreed with Beat atheism, he courted the movement. Their leaders however, whether Allen Ginsberg or Jack Kerouac, disapproved of the violence incarnated in Mailer's hipster, especially as they had made serious forays into the world of violence in the 1940s. At the time, Ginsberg, Kerouac, Burroughs and Herbert Huncke frequented the criminals of Times Square. By the mid-forties, Burroughs was playing with thieves and in 1948, Ginsberg was busted for being a member of a large gang of thieves. In 1950, Burroughs had slaughtered his wife. Ginsberg may have admired Mailer's courage in publishing "The White Negro", yet he and Kerouac finally shied away from the hipster's cool detachment, so contrary to the gentleness, warm-heartedness and "Dostoevskian Alyosha-Myshkin-Dimitri compassion"[427] they embraced.

Yet, despite their differences, when *Life Magazine* published a disparaging article about the Beats in 1959, Mailer reacted with sympathy and strategy by organizing a party, an act of revenge against the literary establishment also designed to attract publicity. The object of these festivities that took place in the Village was to celebrate "The End of the Beats", which he dubbed "The Funeral of Hip" or "The Burial of Hip". Other literary stars such as Susan Sontag, James Baldwin and the poet, Tuli Kupferberg, were invited, but Mailer, as the proud father of his White Negro, not surprisingly stayed in the forefront of this counter-cultural event.

Soon after 1961, restless and disillusioned, conscious that there were fewer "White Negroes" than the multitudes he had fantasized, the general concluded he had "gained strength [but] lost troops"[428] and decided to move the remaining troops onto other battlefields. By 1968, the year of his prize-winning victory over the Establishment, he looked back on this earlier period and confessed that, "He had lived for a dozen empty hopeless years after the Second World War with the bitterness, rage and potential militancy of a real revolutionary"[429], and was now content to write movie scripts and novels, and spend time with his family.

At the same time Mailer, like many religiously or socially radical Jewish intellectuals who were against the Establishment, became an enthusiast of Martin Buber and Hasidism. In this post-war period when the Jews and their culture were rapidly gaining recognition, the Hasidim, the Yiddish storytellers, Maimonides, medieval Hebrew poetry, and the Rabbis of the Talmud had become fashionable. While the Jew in particular was seeking his identity in evocations of Eastern European Jewry, as symbolized by the novels of Singer, the literary establishment as a whole shared in this interest. In fact, Buber's two-volume collection, *Tales of the Hasidim* had the greatest impact on non-Jewish writers of any other Jewish work of the period, whether they were religiously inclined or not.

Mailer saw himself as a "non Jewish Jew, an alienated American"[430]. While "riding the electric rail of long nights on marijuana"[431], he read *Tales of the Hasidim, The Early Masters* and *The Late Masters*, and discovered that they were the first piece of devotional prose, which had not been deadening to him. The tales also helped him in defining himself as a Jew by giving him "a rudimentary sense of clan across the centuries"[432], although he was otherwise ignorant of Jewish culture and lacking even the desire for it. On reading the tales, he depicted himself "like an orphan discovering that in fact he has a beautiful mother"[433].

In 1962, Mailer's curiosity peaked and he actually asked Norman Podhoretz to take him to an Hasidic Synagogue. As Mailer promised to dress and behave properly, Podhoretz agreed to accompany him to a Lubavitcher Hasidic synagogue on the eve of Yom Kippur, not far from where Mailer had grown up. The author was immediately fascinated by the Hasidic Jews, regarding them as "a bunch of crazy motherfuckers, hard core and mean and tough"[434]. They spoke loudly, stamped out their cigarette butts on the floor while waiting for the rabbi in their minimalist synagogue. Mailer had finally found in a group of Jews the virility he so admired in the Irish and the WASPs.

Soon after, Mailer asked Podhoretz if he could write a column about Buber's *Tales of Hasidim* in *Commentary*, the prestigious journal of the American-Jewish Committee run by his 'friend'. True to himself, Mailer's approach was far from traditional in discussing Buber's tales from an existentialist point of view. He did however attract the attention of the Jewish literati, relieved that for the first time their *enfant terrible* was publicly addressing the question of his own Judaism. Even though Mailer had agreed with Podhoretz to do a bimonthly column in which he was to reprint selected stories from Buber and write commentaries on them, he had a limited attention span and his enthusiasm rapidly waned: after six installments, the column ceased.

However short-lived, the author was incited to write this column in great part because it was a means for him of addressing the fundamental issue of good and evil, of expressing his preoccupation with God and the Devil. In an interview for *Partisan Review*, when Mailer was asked whether a secret or hidden pattern was at work in his novels, he answered: "But I will say only one thing, which is that I have some obsession with how God exists. Is He an essential god or an existential god: is He all-powerful or is He, too, an embattled existential creature who may succeed or fail in His vision? I think this theme may become more apparent as the novels go on."[435]

As he states in *Of a Fire on the Moon*, all his other beliefs sprang from his vision of God as "embattled": "Every other one of his notions had followed from that, for if God were a vision of existence at war with other visions in the universe, and we were the instruments of His endeavor just so much as the conflicting cells of our body were the imperfect instruments of our will, then what now was the condition of God?"[436]

As mentioned earlier, this duality is a fundamental tenet in Jewish mysticism. The Hasidic movement was founded by the Ba'al Shem Tov (Master of Good Name) in Poland in the 1730s and 40s. It came as a response to the despair and the evil that had been engendered by the massacres a century earlier, which had left the country economically devastated and a large part of the population homeless and impoverished. Many Jews no longer able to study turned away from rabbinical Judaism, adopting Hasidism and its de-emphasis on the study of the Talmud. Instead, they insisted that God should be worshipped spontaneously, with fervor and exaltation. Hasidism came to be described as "the rebellion of the half-illiterate rural Jew against the supremacy of the learned urban Jew"[437]. In his first column for *Commentary*, Mailer expressed that he had finally found an unconventional and unorthodox Jew with whom he could identify. Although he would never have been a member of the Jewish Establishment—not even two centuries before—he could however see himself as "some bright trouble-making Reb with a wild beard, an odium for ceremony, a nose for the psychic *épée*, and a determined taste for the dramatic in words, in writings, in the life of dialogue— that was not altogether impossible"[438].

In Hasidic mysticism, the rabbi, the scholar was replaced by the *rebbe*, *tzaddik* (holy man in Hebrew), the *ba'al shem*. For the first time in Judaism, he was the leader who acted as man's intermediary with God. He was also a combination of guru and miracle-worker, endowed with magical and healing powers. It was his capacity as a magician that particularly appealed to Mailer, whose work increasingly reflected his serious interest in the occult. In his commentaries on Buber's *The Tales of Hasidim*, Mailer explained that esotericism was in direct contradiction to the decadent, mechanized American society he so deplored. "Our taste for miracles has left us," he wrote. "Man in the Middle Ages lived with dread as a natural accompaniment to his day. His senses insulated by the daily use of daily drugs [...] his mind not guarded by a society which was anti-supernatural, medieval man was therefore able to live with gods, devils, angels, and demons, with witches, warlocks and spirits."[439]

He reproached such writers as Joseph Heller, Mary McCarthy and James Jones their inability to address the mystical dimension of life, as well as the issues of anxiety and dread. Mailer now believed that modern society's major affliction was the conflict between being and nothingness, and concluded that even Heidegger and Sartre had inadequately dealt with: "the new continent which shows on our psychic maps as intimations of eternity…"[440]. Furthermore, scientists who had once acknowledged the mystery of the universe by depending on intuition and metaphor had now become the slaves of technology. Rojack however remains the spokesman of the author's esotericism when he proclaims that men are fearful of murder, "not from a terror of justice so much as the knowledge that a killer attracted the attention of the gods; then your mind was not your own, your anxiety ceased to be neurotic, your dread was real. Omens were tangible as bread."[441]

Mailer especially approved of the focus the Hasidim placed on dialectics: they believe that the clash between opposing forces is fundamental to the human condition, and that the right form of struggle is necessarily constructive. The author, as he told Oriancia Fallaci in an interview in 1969, considered himself a Marxist because he reasoned dialectically, not because he believed in dialectical materialism[442]. In the first column he wrote for *Commentary*, he applauded the Jews for their "irreducible greatness" which he found "in the devil of their dialectic which places madness next to practicality, illumination side by side with duty and arrogance in bed with humility"[443]. This emphasis on dialectic was not unique to Hasidism but was also fundamental to rabbinical Judaism as expressed by Joshua Heschel in *God in Search of Man*: "Jewish thinking and living can only be adequately understood in terms of a dialectical pattern, containing opposite or contrasted properties. As in a magnet, the ends of which have opposite magnetic qualities, these terms are opposite to one another and exemplify a *polarity* of ideas and events, of *mitzvah* and sin, of *kavanah* and deed, of regularity and spontaneity, of uniformity and individuality, of *halacha* and *agada*, of law and inwardness, of love and fear, of understanding and obedience, of joy and discipline, of the good and the evil drive, of time and eternity."[444]

This dialectic—"the boiling cauldron of opposites"[445]—described by Mailer in *The Prisoner of Sex*, is equally evoked by Irving Malin in *Jews and Americans*. One of the focal points of Jewish-American literature, argues Malin, is precisely this dualism, which expresses itself as a tension between the Promised Land and Galuth (Exile), father and sons, past and present, and above all, between head and heart[446]. Yet, despite these dichotomies, the Jewish-American author never reached the nadir of defeatism typical of Gentile writers like Melville or Faulkner. Instead, the Jew managed to reach a level of reconcilement and transcendence. Joseph, the "dangling man" assented to regimentation, David "called it sleep", Herzog fell asleep, Moonbloom was reborn, Leventhal became involved in life, Fiedelman loved men and women, and Rojack was "something like sane again"[447]. On the subject of his novels, Mailer claimed that they were parables about the movement of individuals through history and that, "Man instead is corrupted and confused but even in the corruption and sickness there are yearnings for a better world."[448]

Unique to Judaism, particularly to Hasidism, is the belief that man is God's moral equal, since both are bound by a covenant of mutual protection. This was greatly appealing to Mailer's unconventionality and liberalism. According to Elie Wiesel, "We are to protect His Torah, and He, in turn assumes responsibility for Israel's presence in the world. Thus, when our spirituality—the Torah—was in danger, we used force in protecting it; but when our physical existence was threatened we simply reminded God of His duties and promises deriving from the Covenant."[449] Wiesel's *The Gates of the Forest* is a tale of four rabbis who are together in a Nazi concentration camp and hold a special tribunal to place God on trial: "I intend to convict God of murder, for he is destroying his people and the law he gave them from Mount Sinai. I have irrefutable proof in my hands... The trial proceeded in due legal form, with witnesses for both sides... The unanimous verdict: 'guilty'."[450].

The reciprocity between man and God was implied in Mailer's commentaries on *The Hasidic Tales*: unlike any Christian, when the Jew was in the desert, he had the option "to speak directly to God, [bargain] with Him, [rise] to scold Him, [stare] into God's eyes like a proud, furious, stony-eyed child"[451]. In the same way, Goldstein in *The Naked and the Dead*, reproached God for his acceptance of anti-Semitism. Golstein "smacked his fist against his palm in exasperation. How can You permit the anti-Semites to live, God? he asked. He was not religious, and yet he believed in a God, a personal God with whom you could quarrel, and whom he could certainly upbraid. 'Why don't You stop things like that?' he asked bitterly."[452]

According to Mailer, having betrayed God both in the desert and with Christ, Jews have been questioning over the centuries if, mystically, they belong to a "God of righteousness" or a "devil of treachery"[453]. Unable to sustain this query, they have escaped into the mechanistic jargon of philosophy, psychoanalysis, social action, productive process and the arts in contemporary society. Mailer himself viewed the Holocaust as the devil's "signature"[454], and believed that given "no Messiah was brought forth from the concentration camps"[455], in despair the Jews have transferred their religiousness to mundane preoccupations such as housing, social planning, interfaith councils and improvement of the PTA in the suburbs. Also in the guise of compensation, Mailer maintained that "half of the American Jews have fallen in love with a super delicatessen called Miami, and much of the other half have developed a subtly overbearing and all but totalitarian passion for the particular sallow doctor who is their analyst"[456]. This, he concluded, was the reason why organized Judaism had waned and why the synagogues had come to resemble recreational centers attended only by those who wished to please their mothers.

Mailer believed that God was embattled, not omnipotent, because for him it was the only justification for evil: "The idea of an omnipotent God leaves me apathetic, at best, and cold with anger, at worst," he said, "because if God is all-powerful, then there is a rather ugly show going on. I would rather think God is doing his or her best against adversity"[457]. Hence, like Rabbi Abraham Joshua Heschel, Mailer posits that "God is in search of man", and that without man, God's plans for the universe could not be realized; man's life is thus bound with God's purpose. Man is God's symbol and agent in the cosmic scheme, "the instrument of his endeavor"[458] giving God strength against the devil. In the same way, Heschel states that "man's life [...] can upset the balance and order of the universe."[459] This is expressed by Cherry in *An American Dream*, when she declares, "I always end up with something like the idea that God is weaker because I don't turn out well... I believe God is just doing his best to learn from what happens to some of us"[460]. Rojack illustrates how, while man is helping God through virtuous acts, he also brings about his own salvation.

Like the Sabbatian mystics, Mailer believes even today that God is an "embattled existential creature", at war with the devil. The author's spiritual quest still continues, yet as recently as 1997, in Jesus' autobiography, *The Gospel According to the Son*, Mailer, in a manner similar to Jesus, concludes that, "God and Mammon still grapple for the hearts of all men and women. And yet, since the contest remains so equal, neither the Lord nor Satan can triumph."[461], a view diametrically opposed to the one exposed in the New Testament, where God is perfect.

In her articles "Sex, Creativity and God" and "An American Dream: Mailer's Walpurgisnacht", the critic Jessica Gerson argues that Mailer's attitude about women is rooted in Jewish mysticism[462], and not only as a result of the male chauvinism and latent homosexuality the Women's Liberation accused him of. The Cabala is a masculine doctrine that tends to emphasize the negative, if not the demonic, aspects of women. The Cabala's 'bible', the *Zohar* (Book of Splendor) stipulates the existence of two worlds: the first, *Ein Sof* (infinite in Hebrew), is unintelligible to all but God; the second, that of the *Sephiroth* (emanations from God), is intelligible to man. The *Sephiroth* resembles a tree, with the feminine and negative principles on the left, and the positive, masculine ones on the right. Only when the two poles are united, creating harmony and beauty, can grace flow between heaven and earth. The feminine side is equated with intelligence, rationality and craft; the masculine, with intuition and inspiration.

In *An American Dream*, Deborah is the "devil's daughter", a "Great Bitch who delivers extermination" and "transmits messages to some distant force. Rojack had thus come to envision himself as her puppet and had come to believe in grace and the lack of it, in the long finger of God and the swish of the devil, [he] had come to give [his] scientific apprehension to the reality of witches."[463] Similarly, Marilyn's potential to kill is presented as supernatural, and Mailer suggests that her mere presence at Kennedy's inauguration during a stopover at Dallas airport could have been in part responsible for Kennedy's later assassination. Mailer also hypothesized that the Kennedys were involved in her death and that her ghost might have "given a witch's turn to the wheel at Chapaquiddick"[464].

Apart from the negative aspect of the *Sephiroth*, the mystics maintain that there exists a benign dimension to femininity, illustrated in Mailer's work by Elena in *The Deer Park* and Cherry in *An American*

Dream, through redemptive love and creativity; or in *Marilyn*, by Monroe's career as an actress. When Rojack seeks salvation and asks God for a sign, he meets Cherry—allegorically an angel, and the antithesis of Deborah, the witch. In *Jewish Magic and Superstition: A Study in Folk Religion*, Joshua Trachtenberg points out that Jewish mysticism holds the belief in the presence of angels as man's helpers on earth, and his mediators in the heavenly court.

Ancient and medieval Jewish sources portray women with the same ambivalence: they are on the one hand the daughters of Lilith, the female demon of Jewish folklore said to have been the first rebellious wife of Adam, renown as a child killer and seducer of pious men; on the other hand, they are *Shekhinah*, the gentle loving presence of God, the daughter, queen, bride and lover celebrated in prayer and Sabbath liturgy.[465]

In Mailer's work, these two aspects of femininity are associated with the two sexual orifices, the vagina and the anus. The vagina he identifies with creation, "the province of the Lord", while the anus is "the kitchen of the devil". With his maid Ruta, who is a symbol of negative femininity and German to boot, Rojack alternates between anal and vaginal sex: "a minute for one, a minute for the other, a raid on the devil and a trip back to the Lord."[466] In "The White Negro", Mailer had claimed that "good orgasm opens his possibilities and bad orgasm imprisons him"[467]. In much the same way, as elucidated in Louis M. Epstein's *Sex Laws and Customs in Judaism*, Judaism considers that the sexual act should not exclude the possibility of procreation. Mystics also believe "that sexual connection for carnal pleasure alone opens the world to evil influences and dethrones God"[468].

Apart from Mailer's condemnation of contraception. His attitude to masturbation is equally as negative. Masturbation is an example of "bad orgasm", or "carnal pleasure alone", which the author and the Jewish mystics viewed as "a waste of nature", anti-life. In the *Zohar*, it is deemed the worst sin recorded in the Scriptures[469]. Masturbation, according to the author, leads to insanity, a form of self-violence, a symbolical suicide. Violence turned outward, such as rape, is preferable. Mailer equally condemns masturbation because it does not allow for growth, for the testing of the self involved in dialectics: "If one masturbates, all that happens is, everything that's good and beautiful in one, goes up the hand and into the air and is lost. Now what the hell is there to absorb? One hasn't tested himself. You see, in a way the heterosexual act lays questions to rest, and makes one able to build up new answers."[470]

Mailer agrees with the mystics' belief that conception was God's reward for "good orgasm", apocalyptic sex, that mystical union between man and woman in which He partakes. While Cherry becomes pregnant, Deborah's marriage is childless. She "lost the baby, it came brokenly in birth, in terror, I always thought, of the womb which was shaping it... tearing by this miscarriage the hope of any other child for Deborah." Her miscarriage and ensuing infertility are symbolic of God's disapproval of Rojack's marriage, in which he had "torn free some promise of his soul and paid over in ransom."[471]

The occult plays an important part in Mailer's work, and he even came to consider the artist or writer as a magician of sorts. In *Pontifications*, he states, "It's as if art seeks to restore men and women by reproducing in them that sense of lost spell, as if the artist is some sort of magician or midwife between the lost life of the primitive and the modern world of technology."[472] In *Pieces*, he also alludes to the mysterious force propelling the work of art by claiming that "writing has its own occult force. At its best we never know where our writing comes from nor who gives it to us"[473]. In an interview with Christopher Ricks, on the subject of *Ancient Evenings*, he even claimed that the novelist was telepathic: "I couldn't understand why it sat so comfortably. Then I realized. Novelists have been using it for years. That God-like posture. The author is looking into everyone's head."[474]

Apart from the psychic powers Mailer bestows on his female characters, his work in general is seeped in esotericism. Rojack is obsessed by magic. After killing Deborah, he is convinced his shirt has magical powers and after meeting Cherry, he feels endowed with gifts that allow him to perform certain psychic tricks: "The prizefighter said 'Oil it' to Cherry and I fired a battery of guns at him. His laughter stopped in the middle; he scowled as if four bad eggs had been crushed on his head... in a magic spite, feeling as wicked as a titled child, I shot an arrow into her big toe... and saw it twitch on the beat."[475] Cherry also remarks that he looked as if "he'd been painted by a touch of magic"[476]. Meanwhile, as he watches Cherry sing, Rojack sends mental darts throughout the nightclub. His powers mirror the Jewish mystical belief that certain individuals are endowed with special esoteric aptitudes. The mystic Nachum proclaims that "A Jew with a wave over there, and if he moves his hand this way, he moves the world that way"[477]. Cherry also rewards Rojack for his courage by giving him Shago's umbrella, which in mystical terms could be considered a magic rod or talisman. This umbrella is a conveyor for God's messages, counseling Rojack in his next confrontation with Kelly who represents evil. When Kelly takes it away from Rojack, stunned with fear, he lacks the necessary courage to walk the parapet a second time. Cherry's death will be his punishment.

In *The Deer Park*, Marion Faye spends part of his evenings immersed in his tarot cards. Later, in *The Executioner's Song*, Gary Gilmore's lawyer, Dennis Boaz not only believes in the tarot but also in numerology, while Gilmore's grandmother, Baby Fay, was a medium who gave weekly séance sessions from her bed. Tim Madden, the hero in *Tough Guys Don't Dance*, participates in séances where he sees his wife, Patty's, decapitation. As magic-ridden as Rojack, Gary Gilmore believes he is protected by a guardian angel, has premonitory dreams about his execution and upholds the concept of reincarnation. As superstitious as many of his characters, Mailer believes that Provincetown in Massachusetts is ghost-ridden by both the Pilgrims and the whaling captains. In *Executioner's Song*, Gary's mother Bessie feels that her son is a victim of the haunted house he had grown up in, while Kittredge Hubbard in *Harlot's Ghost* thinks that the Donne is haunted, and frequently communicates with her dead relatives.

Coincidences also play an important part in Mailer's esotericism. In *An American Dream*, Jack Kennedy's name is mentioned in the first sentence. Nine lines further, a man named Kelly is alluded to. Later on in the chapter, one learns that the man's middle name is Oswald. This chapter appeared in *Esquire* a month after Kennedy's assassination; yet it had been written three months earlier. In the same way, *Barbary Shore* is a novel about an important Soviet agent, William McLeod, who lives on the top floor of an inexpensive rooming house. A year after the novel's publication, Mailer rented a room in a similar boarding house on Fulton Street, where, coincidentally, Colonel Rudolph Abel, considered the most important spy in America, was also living at the time.

Finally, omens punctuate Mailer's works as the essence of magic which resides in a state of consciousness where the past and the future seem interchangeable. Indeed, classical Hebrew has two tenses, the present and a second tense where the past and the future are barely distinguishable. In fact, Cabalists believe that omens provoke events and that the future exists only because it has already been described. Thus, in conceiving the universe, God had already constructed it. In *An American Mystery*, a few days before the president's assassination and her husband Oswald's slaying, Marina believes that a broken mirror presages an imminent death. The non-progressive Judaic notion of history actually maintains that events co-exist. Heschel defines this Jewish vision, "less as a vertical movement through time than as a horizontal simultaneity"[478].

In 1953, James Jones first introduced the concept of karma to Mailer, who later synthesized his beliefs in reincarnation on *Pontifications*: "I have this belief in karmic balance—that we come to life with a soul that carried an impost of guilt and reward from the past. And at the end of each life we may be reborn, which I think is a reward in itself. Which not everyone gets. Some people's souls die, literally die, just as the body dies; some people's souls die in a given life. As you know, I believe in two kinds of death. Final death as some species of oblivion, and transcendental death, where you're reborn in some form of existence that gives fair measure for your previous lives."[479]

Mailer finds that a world with reincarnation is more logical than a world without it, in which man's existence would be merely a waste. For him, God is a kind of cosmic artist involved in reincarnation, for when disappointed, He returns to certain of His projects in order to improve them. Ugliness and beauty are also seen as a form of karma: those individuals drawn to beauty have a healthy karma while attraction to ugliness reflects unpaid karmic debts.

Karma would play an especially important role in *Ancient Evenings*, through Mailer's hero Menenhetet and his four successive incarnations, or in *Executioner's Song*, where Gary Gilmore is obsessed by his past and future lives. The belief in life after death is one of the main reasons why Mailer chose to set *Ancient Evenings* in Egypt. Cabalists believe that, much like angels, the souls of the dead can intercede in paradise, favorably or unfavorably, for the living. And the Egyptians upheld that, on dying, the Ka, one of the seven souls or spirits of the deceased, continued into a next life. The Ka was man's double or genius and resembled the individual both in body and character. The Ka could exist eternally or it could perish, but when an individual died a second time, the second death was permanent.

Gary Gilmore in *Executioner's Song* sustains that not only will he be executed during his present lifetime, but that he had also suffered the same fate in eighteenth century England. Just as Mailer attributed Marilyn's death to a karmic debt, Gary asserts that his execution is the result of his sins in a former life. Gary also tries to persuade Nicole to commit suicide, justifying her death with the conviction that they will be reunited in their next life. The notion of rebirth acts as a palliative for Gary, allowing him to fantasize about another kind of life to which he would be better suited.

Although a self-appointed Messiah, Mailer has not often been identified as such because his Jewishness, at least on the surface, is less apparent, given the sparseness of his Jewish settings and characters. Mailer's sister even remarked: "I'm always amazed coming from the same family, by the whole strain of Norman's writing. He's really writing from a different area of consciousness than anything from his life or background."[480]

Apart from his hybrids, ranging from the classical *schlemiel* such as Sam Slovoda to his venerated hero Rojack, his purely Jewish characters were more often than not treated with distance, or even disdain, a point remarked on by the critic Sam B. Girgus, who notes that, "His handling of Jewish characters or themes often has been ambivalent at best or negative at worst"[481].

When Mailer was younger, and less removed from his origins, Jewish characters were more present in his work. This is illustrated by Goldstein, his Orthodox Jew, or Roth, his agnostic Jew in *The Naked and the Dead*. Notwithstanding Goldstein's endurance and courage, or Roth's intelligence and sensitivity, the author has already relegated them as *schlemiels*: Goldstein emphasizes suffering—"I think a Jew is a Jew because he suffers. Olla Juden suffer"[482]—and Roth is epitomized by his self-pity.

Similarly, Mailer was criticized in his non-fiction for shunning his Jewish heritage. The Jew was absent in his strategy for a revolution of minorities in "The White Negro". Donald L. Kaufmann observed that it was in Mailer's "muted biography" that "Jewish Experience" made "its most conspicuous exit"[483]: in the biographical section of *Advertisements for Myself*, the author does not once evoke his Jewishness. Similarly, in "Responses and Reactions I", although he presents a résumé of his background, he denies the least ethnic involvement. In *The Presidential Papers*, ever the "non-Jewish Jew", Mailer criticizes the Jews for assimilating at the price of their ethnic roots, in the same way that he admonishes the Jewish author for sacrificing to America's commonplaceness in *Cannibals and Christians*.

By his late work, the author is better reconciled to his Jewish background. Having gained social recognition, he has in great part transcended the fetters of what he deemed to be the vulgarity and limitations of his lower-middleclass upbringing. He is less in conflict with his origins. In *Harlot's Ghost*, although he still ridicules Arnie Rosen, "as a bagel-baby from the middleclass purlieus of the Bronx"[484], a Jewish homosexual who dresses in three-piece suits and marries "a nice gray Episcopalian lady"[485], in order to help his advancement in the CIA, the author nonetheless portrays him as the counterpoint to Hymen Bosqueverde, the devout Orthodox Jew. In Montevideo, Bosqueverde gives his students Hebrew lessons in order to prepare them for the Bar Mitzvah, and Mailer describes their "mutual recital of Hebrew as if all the words were magical"[486], viewing their teacher with admiration and envy, aspiring, in his own way, to reach an analogous religiosity.

Mailer, as described by James Toback, is finally a "latter-day hell-fire Puritan as motivated by dread and concerned with the after-life as Jonathan Edwards".[487] Alfred Kazin also observes with insight that Mailer is "a great Jew" and that "instead of writing about the goddamn righteous Jew pushing carts on the Lower East-Side to send [his] kids to college", Mailer went into the mainstream of American life.[488] The author equally lamented the fact that "the Jewish intellect had not emancipated itself from its own tradition" personified by "the old Cabalists"[489]. Mailer thus liberated himself from the restrictions of his traditional Jewish origins and moved himself and his troops on a spiritual quest rooted in mysticism, the occult and reincarnation. As both a responsible general and writer, he aspired to enlighten both his troops and his country, leading them towards a Promised Land no longer bound to the tyranny of convention and totalitarian thought, where each could find his individual and collective spiritual truth.

CHAPTER V

Mailer: Politics and Anti-Semitism

Both politics and anti-Semitism have been a major concern throughout Mailer's work. By the beginning of the 1950s, vehement radicalism had become characteristic of the Jewish intelligentsia. Although the author's early career was marked by such radicalism, Mailer was twice born, "once as Bolshevik and once as human".[490] Although unable to renounce his liberal Jewish roots, from this period to the present day, Mailer's political thought had grown increasingly conservative. Otherwise liberal Jews have, almost systematically, equated "the right" with fascism and anti-Semitism. Since his first exposure to prejudice at Harvard, then in the army and later, throughout his adult life, anti-Semitism has preoccupied the author, and the specter of the Holocaust has remained constantly present in his opus.

Like the majority of the American Jewish population in the United States, Mailer's "home" is still more to the left, despite the moderation of his radicalism. Although as early as *The Naked and the Dead*, the author was incredulous as to the effectiveness of liberalism, he did however embrace many of its principles, so deeply ingrained in Judaism. Unlike the liberals in the novel who believe in man's perfectibility, General Cummings, the consummate fascist, maintains that the only motivations of an individual are wealth and power. Mailer believes that the will to dominate culminates in Nazism, fascism and American imperialism, all of which are manifested by the strengthening of the military. He further asserted that "this [was] going to be the reactionary's century", and may well represent the beginning of "their thousand-year reign"[491]. Cummings' antithesis, Lieutenant Hearn, the archetypal liberal, finds himself defenseless against his fascist superior who tries to convince him that his liberalism is simplistic and thus incompatible with reality: "Somewhere you picked it up so hard that you can't shake the idea 'liberal' means good and 'reactionary' means evil. That's your frame of reference. Two words. That's why you don't know a damned thing."[492]

In Mailer's 1954 *Dissent* essay, "David Riesman Reconsidered", he again admonishes the liberals for their inability to comprehend that the roots and nature of power in America were masked, explaining that the "forms of power are taken for the content, and there is no attempt to distinguish between those who lead and those who are led."[493] Mailer argues that, if this dissimulation justified the patriotic reasons for America's involvement in the Second World War, or shed light on the inhumanity of bureaucracies, it nonetheless grossly underestimated the ruthlessness of power politics. Riesman incarnated the liberal's facile rationalization and optimism, which so aggravated Mailer: "One feels Riesman's desire to find something justifiable, something *functional*, in all aspects of society. Ultimately, his credo seems to be that what-is must necessarily contain something good... At last all things are equal, are justifiable—one is drawn to quietism and acceptance."[494] However, Mailer was critical of liberalism as a father would be of a naive but favored son; his frustration stems more from disappointment than from detestation.

The Jews' struggle to transform society through social justice, civil rights and liberties has been greatly endorsed by the rabbis, especially those who embraced Reform Judaism. However, many Conservative or Orthodox rabbis have stressed the inherent relationship between Judaism and liberal objectives, emphasizing the Jews' responsibility toward the socially deprived. In "Reponses and Reactions", Mailer even considers himself a Jew "out of loyalty to the underdog".[495] The Jews, particularly women, have been more politically active than any other religious group in America. With the exception of certain high-status Protestants, they have also achieved the most professional and economic success. However, they have always remained allegiant to the American left, even to the detriment of their economic interests.

Jews have in fact been more loyal to their liberalism than to their Judaism, as numerous American presidential campaigns bear witness.

Franklin D. Roosevelt was the Jews' major presidential hero. Although he supported the Jewish cause by entering the Second World War on the side of the Allies, albeit he appointed many Jews to government posts, a majority of Jews chose to occult the fact that he had refused shiploads of Jews fleeing Nazi Germany entry into America and had never bombed the railway lines leading to the concentration camps. Meanwhile, if Dwight D. Eisenhower was a capital force against Nazism, in 1952 and 1956, a majority of Jews voted for the Democratic candidate, Adlai Stevenson, who had remained quite passive to their cause. Aware of John F. Kennedy's father's alleged anti-Semitic inclinations, the Jews, nevertheless, overwhelmingly underwrote his candidacy in 1960. Mailer even attributed Kennedy's victory to his own active support of the Democratic campaign. Ironically, the first appointment he made as president was Dean Rusk's as Secretary of State. Rusk, a renown anti-Zionist, had persuaded Truman to send American troops to Palestine in an attempt to impose a plan of trusteeship against the will of the Jewish forces. In the 1964 election, even though Barry Goldwater was half Jewish and proud of it, the Jews voted for the liberal Lyndon B. Johnson. Finally, despite Jesse Jackson's overt anti-Semitism, the Jews maintained their liberal affiliations and, reacting with Pavlovian predictability, voted for the left in 1984 and 1988.

Until this day, despite his growing conservatism, Mailer proved incapable of voting for a Republican candidate. In 1964, convinced that the country needed to be purged, he toyed with the idea of voting for Barry Goldwater against the Democrat, Johnson, fearing Johnson would lead the country "down a liberal straight-highway into the deepest swamp of them all."[496] Yet, he remained faithful to the liberal camp, a vote of confidence he justified by stating that Goldwater had "made his career by crying Communist, that was too easy; half the pigs, cowards and bullies of the twentieth century had made their fortune on that fear."[497] In the 1968 presidential election between the Republican, Richard Nixon, and the Democrat, Hubert Humphrey, the author felt that Nixon was probably the lesser of two evils: "Sometimes you have neither a man nor an idea, that's President

Nixon. Of course I preferred him to Humphrey for a simple reason, which is Humphrey was a weak man with a dead idea."[498] This time, unable to endorse the liberal vote, Mailer opted for abstention. Years later, in the 1996 elections, Mailer had a certain affection for the Republican candidate, Robert Dole, and yet, although he disliked two-thirds of Clinton's political program, he voted for him nonetheless, for the simple reason that Clinton had improved relations between blacks and whites in the Democratic Party.

Jews have embraced liberalism because it has always fostered pluralism, a necessary prerequisite for the integration of minorities into American society. More importantly still, Jewish left-wing liberals associate "the right" and conservatism with anti-Semitism. The historian, Lucy Dawidowicz, claims: "The Jewish experience in Russian and Austro-Hungarian empires established even more emphatically what Jews had learned in Western Europe: that the political right was at best conservative, avowedly Christian and committed to the preservation of ancient privileges; it could, often did become reactionary and even anti-Semitic."[499]

Similarly, Ernest Van Den Haag attests that, "To the Jewish mind, the Gestalt of the rightist usually requires anti-Semitism. Hence, Jews regard rightists as anti-Semites—no matter whether they are: they ought to be."[500] Mailer also equated "the right" with anti-Semitism: in *Cannibals and Christians*, he claims, "all of that Right Wing which runs from staunch Republicanism to the extreme Right Wing, and then half around the world through ghosts of the Nazis, all of the persecuted Right Wing which sees itself as a martyr..."[501] Mailer's obsession with Nazism and fascist rule was so profound that, in 1954, he seriously contemplated writing a novel set in a concentration camp. In his writings, the Holocaust is constantly alluded to and his German characters are systematically associated with some form of sexual perversion. In *An American Dream*, he portrays a German soldier as a homosexual mother's boy, and Ruta, as accepting heterosexual sodomy with Rojack. In much the same way, Mailer projected the European war scene onto his heroines by chopping their hair off—a post-war punishment inflicted on European women who had had sexual relationships with Germans. At the moment of their defeat, Denise Gondolman, Eleanor Slovada and Elena were submitted to such a fate. Nazi brutalities were described in *The Barbary Shore* and in *Oswald's Tale: An American Mystery*.

Like Mailer, the Jewish author lived in the shadow of the Holocaust, and the memories of fascism's horrors. Erica Jong's reaction on arriving in Germany, described in *Fear of Flying*, is a salient example of the prevalence of those recollections: "Suddenly, people on buses were going home to houses where they treasured clever little collections of gold teeth and wedding rings... The lampshades in the Hotel Europa were suspiciously finely grained... The soap in the restroom of the Silberner Hirsch smelled funny... The immaculate railroad trains were really claustrophobic and foul-smelling cattle cars... The conductor, with his pink marzipan pig face was not going to let me off... The station commander, with his high-peaked Nazi hat, was going to inspect my papers on some pretext and hustle me over to one of those green-coated policemen in black leather boots with a matching whip..."[502]

In America, the Jews' fervent participation in law and politics has been their means of self-defense against potential anti-Semitism, for in America too, Jews have equated the right with anti-Semitism. This was best exemplified by Henry Ford, the Detroit automobile magnate who published a weekly newspaper, *The Dearborn Independent* in which he incorporated a series of ninety-one articles under the title, "The Protocols of the Learned Elders of Zion". These forged documents, which Ford claimed were authentic, revealed a Jewish plan for world domination. Finally, in 1927, confronted with several million dollars of lawsuits for slander, he ceased to publish his anti-Semitic propaganda. The Jews also considered that it was the right who had imposed many of the quotas on the immigration laws, Ivy League colleges and professional schools; that they had restricted Jews' access to prestigious professions and careers, and refused to hire Jews or admit them to private clubs, resorts and certain residential areas.

In *The Authoritarian Personality*, Theodore Adorno explains the relationship between capitalism and anti-Semitism. He claims that capitalism has been responsible for the emergence of the authoritarian personality, the major catalyst of prejudice in America, fostering conventionalist thinking, autocratic traits, and simultaneously, submission and authoritarian aggressiveness.[503] All these characteristics can be associated with conservative America and the right, if not the far right.

Above all, the Jews' commitment to law is a result of their adherence to their own law, the five books of the Torah being comprised mainly of laws, and the Talmud, of explanations as to how they should be interpreted. For Jews, even the most mundane details of daily life are subject to their law. Jewish scholarship has been based principally on law and during the Middle Ages, knowledge of the law was the prerequisite for leadership in the Jewish community. Throughout history, the legal system has been of intense interest to the Jewish community because it has implemented social justice and social change. In Europe, during the eighteenth and nineteenth centuries, lawyers, advocates and barristers played a significant role in reforming society, not only to protect others, but also to protect themselves. As emphasized by Van Den Haag, for the Jews gentile law has always been the major source of protection against local aggressions and superstitions. Since the sovereign princes often depended on the Jews' skills, they protected them, up to a certain point, through the law.[504]

In general, American anti-Semitism has differed from its European correlate. In European governments, it was often part of a state policy and served as a means of diverting attention away from internal problems: hereditary monarchies justified it as a defense of Christianity; Hitler, to achieve cultural purity; the Soviet Union, in the name of the proletariat. In America, however; anti-Semitism has never had a legal status, but has been expressed through social and economic discriminations, particularly from the 1920s to the 1940s. Furthermore, it was most prevalent among the socially and economically disfavored because it was a means for them of venting their emotional frustrations, reflecting their lack of education and their limited social experience. This group adopted the classic prototypes of the Jew as dishonest, pushy, unethical in business and clannish.

These prejudices date back to the Middle Ages when Jews, excluded from Christian society and its professions, were forced to become moneylenders, thus forming closely-knit groups. These images, however, were often integrated by Jews, resulting in what Kurt Lewin named "negative chauvinism", whereby certain individuals belonging to an underprivileged group, ashamed of their membership, remove themselves as much as possible from anything that reminds them of their group.[505] Mailer's ambivalence to his Jewish roots, his glamorization of Waspdom and his consequent self-hatred are projected onto some of his characters: Denise Gondolman in "The Time of Her Time" can only reach orgasm after being sodomized and called a "dirty little Jew"[506] is just one manifestation of the internalization of the anti-Semitism to which the Jew was submitted.

Politically, it is true that the Jews have been emancipated from their ghettoes by the eighteenth and nineteenth century revolutions of the left. Following the French Revolution, the left, as opposed to the right, declared that nationality, not religious affiliation, determined citizenship. In their systematic fear of the right, Jews, however, have tended to occult the existence of leftwing anti-Semitism. Charles Fourier, the father of French socialism, warned the masses that, "in dealing with the Jews; one is bound to expect lies and nothing but lies"[507], while Marx, despite his Jewish ancestry, asked, "what is the worldly basis of Judaism, if not practical need, egotism? What is the worldly cult of the Jew? Hustering. What is his worldly god? Money."[508] More recently, the foreign policies of the liberal Social Democratic parties in nations as diverse as Sweden, Denmark and Austria have been furthermore far more conciliatory toward the Soviet Union than towards Israel.

The Jewish *angst* of the right and of anti-Semitism is linked to their wariness of bureaucracies which they associate with repression and persecution. During the Depression, notes Nathan Glazer, when the United States was faced with rampant poverty, numerous Jews avoided government jobs.[509] Later, Mailer would show the same reticence towards the army, in *The Naked and the Dead*, and soon after towards the FBI and the CIA, both closely connected to the American right wing. The secret service became a focus in Mailer's work as early as 1952, with the publication of *Barbary Shore*, and his criticisms are clear in his treatment of Leroy Hollingsworth, the archetypal secret service bureaucrat and spokesman for monopoly capitalism to which he was vehemently opposed. Later, in an open letter to President Kennedy, Mailer also warned against the CIA strategies in Cuba. In his film, *Maidstone*, the author imagined a secret service based on the CIA, which threatened the hero, an autobiographical portrayal of Mailer, whose role he also played. In *St. George and the Godfather*, Mailer resumes his conspiracy theories when he confesses that it would have been his life's ambition to come up with evidence that the CIA was tripping on American elections.

Finally, in Mailer's later work *Oswald's Tale: An American Mystery*, the author did not exclude the possibility that Lee Harvey Oswald, Kennedy's alleged murderer, was also employed by the United States' secret services, specifically COINTELPRO, as also suggested by David Wise in *The American State Policy*. Between 1954 and 1971, the FBI concluded a COINTELPRO operation that was a secret arm of the United States government where taxpayers' funds were used for a wide diversity of covert techniques and crimes. Of the seven programs, two were in the scope of Oswald's activities, the Socialist Workers Party and the Communist Party. In 1963, he wrote to both New York groups stating that he would like to contact Party members when he moved to the Baltimore-Washington area.

According to Diana Trilling, Mailer was "absolutely paranoid on the subject of the FBI."[510] Viewed from Mailer's standpoint the FBI, the police, the DEA and the justice system were all corrupt. Mailer even thought the FBI was tapping his phone. He also claimed in *The Presidential Papers* that the FBI was "a high church for the true mediocre"[511] and in *Pieces* compared its efficiency to the concentration camps at Buchenwald.

Yet, his most significant act of protest against the FBI and the CIA was his creation of the Fifth Estate, which became the focal point of his fiftieth birthday, held at the Four Seasons Restaurant in New York. Mailer invited 5,000 people asking $50 a couple. Among his honored guests were Shirley MacLaine, Jack Lemmon, Senator Javits, as well as the press, including the editors of leading newspapers and national magazines. All of his children, three of his wives, including Lady Jeanne, Adele, and Carol, and of course his mother were also present. The Fifth Estate was to comprise a group of citizens to monitor the FBI and the CIA and appraise the American public in which ways these organizations were manipulating public opinion and to what extent they had been possibly instrumental in the assassinations of John F. Kennedy, Martin Luther King Jr. and other public figures. The Fifth Estate was actually to become the fundraising division of a group called CARIC (Committee for Action/Research on the Intelligence Community). CARIC had grown out of the anti-war movement and was headed by Tim Butz and Winslow Peck who had backgrounds in military intelligence. The Fifth Estate also published a magazine called *Counter Spy* that listed in each of its issues the names of CIA agents around the world. The CIA, soon infuriated, accused Mailer and CARIC of endangering national security. After the death of CIA agent Richard Welch, for which Mailer deemed CARIC indirectly responsible, as well as a personal and political distancing from his radical past, he once again moved his troops to a more conservative territory.

In fact, by the mid-1970s with his growing entrenchment in WASP society and his waxing political conservatism, the author instead decided that the CIA was a "noble institution."[512] The early 1990s marked the completion and publication of *Harlot's Ghost*, a testimonial of his continued fascination with WASP society and power as manifested by the CIA. Six months after the publication of *Harlot's Ghost* in 1991, Mailer went to CIA headquarters in Langley, Virginia where he addressed five hundred agents and received several standing ovations. The former radical and father of the Fifth Estate now claimed his support of "wet jobs" (the KGB term for covert assassinations) and his approval should Iraqi dictator Saddam Hussein be granted such a fate.

Finally, the relationship between liberalism and charity has been one of the most essential ones for Mailer as well as for the Jews in general. As early as the Old Testament, *zedakeh,* charity, which also included the notion of social justice, played an important role in the Jewish community. As described in Exodus, the landowner was expected to share his produce with the poor: "For six years you shall sow your land and gather in its yield; but the seventh year you shall let it rest and lie fallow, that the poor of your people may eat" (Exodus 23:10-11). Furthermore, at the end of every three years, the landowner was also obliged, and as outlined in Deuteronomy, to take a tenth of his produce and make a charitable donation to those in need, whether the Levite, the stranger, the fatherless or the widow. Maimonides also emphasized the legal obligation to give charity in his code of Jewish law, the *Mishneh Torah,* in the section entitled "The Laws of Giving to the Poor". Additionally, in the Middle Ages, the Jews were not only forced by law to contribute to the poor but were jointly answerable for taxes or fines levied on members of the community. Finally, charity in ghetto society was also more or less equivalent to justice and giving to the poor, the orphans, and the helpless was a religious duty. The charity box or *pushke* was a characteristic of the Jewish home in the Eastern European Communities. Small sums of money, in order to aid both local and Palestinian causes, were dropped into these boxes at least weekly and was collected at least once a year. Thus, through time, the maintenance of the poor by the wealthy became both a custom and an obligation.

Given their heritage, it is therefore not surprising that in the United States, the Jews have been by far the major donors to the philanthropic organizations; Mailer himself having given generous donations to his *alma mater,* Harvard. Otherwise, despite the fact that there existed many similarities between the Jews and the Puritans, they differed radically on this issue. While the Puritans and the Protestants in general maintained that each individual received what he deserved, the Jews focused instead on responding to the individual's needs, specifically his material ones.

Mailer, as most Jews, therefore endorsed welfare to a greater extent than members of other religious or ethnic groups. Though contrary to his own economic interests, the author, as many liberals, supported confiscatory taxes, massive welfare programs and other efforts to redistribute wealth. Although on one hand, Mailer, as he expressed in *St. George and the Godfather*, believed that the individual should work for a living, he simultaneously questioned whether the unemployed did not have as much right to require payment as those businessmen who have become wealthy through exploitation and useless work. Ultimately, he favored the militant welfare rights groups who demanded their "share of the waste,"[513] concluding that among the rich, there were those who were deserving and those who were not. As long as some individuals had become rich through exploitation or inutile work, Mailer then believed that it was acceptable to be paid for not working at all. The author was conscious, concurrently, that those who abused the system were violating the fights of those who were industrious. Yet, he was willing to countenance this as the requisite price for alleviating poverty.

In addition to economic aid for the poor, Mailer also found it essential that the poor were given responsibility, maintaining that they should be encouraged to plan and administer their own poverty programs, since they were the most aware of their own needs. The author also asserted that less money should be spent by the government in investigative operations, leery, like many Jews, of all forms of censorship, and asserted that these funds would be much better spent in job-training programs for the unemployed.

Mailer's altruism for the poor and his empathy toward the underdog also extended to the criminal as exemplified by *The Executioner's Song* or his active endorsement of prisoner, Jack Abbott. For the author, criminality also required far more imagination and courage and no more prevarication than law abiding. Though in some ways the criminal undoubtedly offered a threat, in Mailer's view, he also brought vitality. Mailer, in fact, even mistrusted laws, finding that it was the legal system that often perpetuated injustice. As the author demonstrated in his movies, *Beyond the Law* and *Wild 90,* and especially in *Miami and the Siege of Chicago,* Mailer came to perceive the world of the police and the criminal as one in the same: "The criminal attempts to reduce the tension within himself by expressing in the direct language of action whatever is most violent and outraged in his depths; to the extent that he is not a powerful man, his violence is merely anti-social like self-exposure, embezzlement, passing bad checks. The cop tries to solve his violence by blanketing it with a uniform. This ...explains why cops will put up with poor salary, public dislike and a general sense of bad conscience; they know they are lucky. They know they are getting away with a successful solution to the criminality they can taste in their blood."[514] While Mailer also felt that the police were so irresponsible that they had to be monitored by civilian view boards, he was in a way more optimistic about the criminal whom he esteemed could be rehabilitated through society's intervention, as he noted in *Running Against the Machine*: "We also advocate a program that would transform our goals from mere inhuman detention centers to environments conducive to genuine social rehabilitation. Inmates should be provided with opportunities for academic, artistic, and vocational education. In addition, apartments or halfway houses shall be set up in family situations on social visits."[515]

He was also convinced that an open admissions policy had to be created at City College in New York in order that ghetto youths would be encouraged to finish their studies, diminishing simultaneously their temptation to crime. Finally, given the author's systematic fear of bureaucracies and authoritarianism, which, again like many Jews, he had come to associate with Nazism, it is not completely unforeseen that he held serious reservations with regard to the police.

As early as 1949, Mailer was helping prisoners in Spain who had been the victims of Franco's fascism. With Bea and his friends the Linenthals, Mailer made a trip to Barcelona, hiding pesetas in condoms which he and his friends then inserted into toiletry tubes and jars and crossed the Spanish-French border, closed at that time, in order to give the money to contacts in Spain who would in turn aid the prisoners.

By the early 1960s, Mailer's empathy for outlaws was reinforced by his personal confrontations with the law. In the summer of 1960, he was arrested in Provincetown, Mass. for police interference. In November of the same year, he was again arrested for his refusal to pay a nightclub bill, also obtaining another acquittal. A few days later, the White Negro's skirmishes with the law culminated with the stabbing of his wife, a hearing in felony court and a sojourn in Bellevue's psychiatric ward.

At this time, Mailer had frequent correspondence with criminals, most of whom wanted assistance with their writing. In 1963, one of these prisoners named Raimondo was released and came to the author seeking work. Mailer supplied him with odd jobs such as window washing until, shortly after, Raimondo forged one of the author's checks. Although the prisoner disappeared not only with the money, but also with Mailer's maid, the author was more disappointed than angry. Yet, very philosophical, he had no regrets. Endowed with a strong sense of *zedakah,* he conceived that due to his success, it was his duty to aid the underprivileged.

Always remaining sympathetic to the criminal, despite the fact that in this case the criminal had murdered two men, Mailer undertook *The Executioner's Song,* the biographical novel of Gary Gilmore, the Utah state prisoner who was executed in 1977; Gilmore being the first prisoner executed in America in ten years. Mailer's portrayal of Gilmore was one of extreme empathy. Regarding Gilmore, the author also focused on the issue of capital punishment of which he basically disapproved, sharing the attitude of other liberals as well as his Jewish predecessors. Earlier in *The Presidential Papers,* Mailer exposed his declaration of capital punishment by stating that: "I would never like to see a law passed which would abolish capital punishment, except for those states that would insist on keeping it. Such states would then be allowed to kill criminals provided that the killing is not impersonal, but personal and public spectacle; to wit that the executioner be more or less the same size and weight as the criminal... and that they fight to death using no weapons or weapons not capable of killing at a distance... The benefit of the law is that it might return us to moral responsibility. The killer would carry the other man's death in his psyche. The audience in turn would experience a sense of tragedy, since the executioners, highly trained for this, would almost always win. In the flabby American spirit there is a buried sadist who finds the bullfight contemptible. What he really deserves is gladiators. Since nothing is worse for a country than repressed sadism, this method of execution would offer ventilation for the most cancerous emotions of the American public."[516] Despite the fact that Mosaic Law fixed capital punishment for various crimes, in practice since the Second Jewish Commonwealth, it was eliminated because it was opposed by the Jewish community at large; thus, the Jews found means of skirting it by imposing so many limitations that its enforcement, at least in the majority of cases, became unfeasible. Instead, fines and other penalties were prescribed on the criminal. In *The Executioner's Song*, Mailer claimed apropos of Gilmore that the question of the execution of any individual was nothing but a legally sanctioned murder, "blood atonement." Yet, in an article Mailer wrote later in 1981 on capital punishment, he did admit his confusion, his ambivalence on the matter, given that he also realized that capital punishment might be justifiable as it was a manner of controlling dangerous pathological behavior by placing a necessary restraint on the individual.

In the same way that Mailer was sensitized by Gilmore's correspondence, he was equally moved by Jack Abbott's letters. As well summarized by Michiko Kakutani in a *New York Times Book Review*, "the 'ordinary' criminal who espouses a radical code of thought, after all, has long exerted a certain hold on the literary imagination."[517] Mailer, sharing Jean-Paul Sartre's fascination for the criminal, allowed Abbott to "play him like a violin,"[518] asking the author, for instance, to shop for his clothes of which he was allegedly deprived in prison. Abbott was a state-raised convict who had been guilty of several assaults as well as the murder of a fellow convict while in prison. Errol McDonald, a young black editor at Random House, as well as Mailer and other writers, sent letters to Abbott's patrol board insisting upon his talent as a writer as well as his capacity to earn a living as an author; Mailer promising him a job as his editorial assistant upon his release. Besides writing the introduction to *The Belly of the Beast*, a brilliant work, which consisted of Abbott's prison correspondence, Mailer immediately met him at the airport and received him at his home upon Abbott's acquittal from prison in 1981. Very much to

Norris's discountenance, Mailer, notwithstanding Abbott's murder of a restaurant waiter six weeks later, wanted custody of Abbott as well as his permanent release. The author was greatly criticized for his role in Abbott's acquittal given his attitude of defensiveness that "Culture is worth a little risk."[519]

Otherwise, Mailer's early political life was marked by radicalism. Many Jewish immigrants and their descendants repudiated material success as both an ideal and as an indicator of individual worth and were drawn to socialism and other leftist movements, which were supportive of the underdog, with whom they could identify. As pointed out by Arthur Hertzberg, socialism and anarchism furthermore offered surrogates to the weak male models that many young Jews were to inherit, Mailer being a salient example.[520]

The author, himself, became especially politicized during his sojourn in France between 1947-1948 when he came under the influence of Jean Malaquais who was soon to become his political mentor. Malaquais was a Trotskyite who had also been the secretary of André Gide and who was also awarded the Prix Renaudot for his second novel. He was a socialist who was vehemently anti-fascist, a Jew himself. Initially, Malaquais found his protégé to be politically naive, describing him as "a boy scout, both intellectually and mentally; like somebody from a kibbutz."[521] He considered Mailer, unlike the Europeans of his generation, as apolitical, having no knowledge, for example, of the Russian Revolution, despite Mailer's Russian Jewish origins. However, by the time the author returned to America, he was not only a sophisticated politician, but like Malraux, Malaquais and other European intellectuals, Mailer believed now in the importance of political engagement.

The author thus became an ardent and active supporter of the former democratic vice-president, Henry Wallace, in the 1948 presidential campaign, much to the dismay of Malaquais, a fervent anti-Stalinist; Wallace being strongly aligned with the American communists. Yet, like many of the American-Jewish intelligentsia, Mailer was soon not only disenchanted with Wallace but more importantly with communism in general. Thus, always under

Malaquais's influence, Mailer spoke at the Waldorf Peace Conference in 1949 where he reproached both the United States and the Soviet Union as moving toward state capitalism. He further announced that "so long as there is capitalism, there is going to be war. Until you have a decent, equitable socialism, you can't have peace."[522] This subject Mailer further elaborated upon in his second novel, *Barbary Shore* published in 1951, and even dedicated to Malaquais. In *Barbary Shore,* he addressed the evils of American monopoly capitalism and Soviet state capitalism, both of which were, in the final analysis, directed toward war and its production. Mailer perceived that arms production was an essential part of the economic programs of both countries. As world markets had been saturated with goods and as developing nations had been increasingly subject to state capitalism or nationalization, it had been steadily more complicated for American monopoly capitalists to find outlets for their products. Consequently, the United States involved itself in military production: "for there was a new consumer and new commodities, and every shell could find as customer its enemy soldier."[523] Concurrently, the state capitalists of the Soviet Union had been unable to raise Russia's standard of living by furnishing goods and services, which were essential and thus became prisoners of the production of machinery and tools that would enable further production. They had therefore become engaged in "seizing new countries, stripping them of their wealth and converting their economy to war."[524] Thus, both superpowers were producing "wholly for death,"[525] this decadence terminating only when "we are faced with mankind in barbary."[526] As a result, Mailer, at this point like Malaquais, saw the only panacea in revolutionary socialism as described in *Barbary Shore* by William McLeod, the former Stalinist: "It conceives of a society where the multitudes own and control the means of production in opposition to what exists everywhere today. It holds the true conception of equality where each works according to his ability and each is supplied according to his needs. It views the end of exploitation and the beginning of justice."[527]

Otherwise, by 1952 he found an outlet for his radicalism when invited by Irving Howe to become a contributing editor of *Dissent,* a quarterly journal devoted to socialist thought. At this point, Mailer firmly believed that it was only by aiding the impoverished and the disadvantaged that America could combat its decadence. The author expressed his socialist views in *Dissent* by stating: "As socialists we want a socialist world not because we have the conceit that men would thereby be more happy—those claims are best left to dictators—but because we feel the moral imperative in life itself to rescue the human condition even if this should ultimately mean no more than that man's suffering has been lifted to a higher level, and human history has only progressed from melodrama, farce, and monstrosity, to tragedy."[528]

Simultaneously, although Mailer had become disenchanted by Communism as he had already proclaimed, his radicalism was still questioned by the American government, his father being investigated as a security risk by a Civil Service check in 1953 for his association with a "concealed communist"—his son. However by 1955, Mailer had become immersed in spiritual radicalism, leaving aside his political focus until the 1960s when he considered running for Mayor in 1960. Parallel also to his increased interest in religion during this period, the early 1960s through 1972 marked a period where politics were also a pivotal force in much of his writing beginning with an article he wrote for *Esquire* covering the Democratic convention in 1960 until the publication of *St. George and the Godfather* in 1972.

During the 1960 presidential campaign, Mailer renewed his activist role in politics with his career as a writer. Commissioned by *Esquire* to report on the Democratic convention, the author besought by Kennedy's charisma not only voted in a presidential election for the first time since 1948 but also actively endorsed Kennedy's candidature. Since the president had won only by a very narrow margin, the author was, with his habitual arrogance, convinced his article in *Esquire* had made a decisive difference: "My piece came at the right time for him—three weeks before the election. It added the one ingredient Kennedy had not been able to find for the stew—it made him seem exciting, it made the election appear important. Around New York there was a turn in sentiment; one could feel it; Kennedy now had glamour."[529] Mailer also identified with Kennedy projecting upon him his outlaw status, comparing him to other "outlaw" presidents whether Jefferson, Jackson, Lincoln or Roosevelt.

Thus, though unsolicited, Mailer composed a series of essays later collected in *The Presidential Papers* where, like a Jewish patriarch, he advised him on foreign affairs, juvenile delinquency, capital punishment and the requirements for existential leadership. Concurrently, notwithstanding that Mailer was bewitched by Kennedy, he still remained critical of what he esteemed to be his weaknesses; his lack of imagination, his political manipulations and his occasional lack of moral leadership. Yet, despite his shortcomings, Kennedy was still Irish and was also still part of the social WASP elite which Mailer aped and into which he aspired to become fully integrated.

At the same time, even though the author had a particular fascination and admiration for Castro, romanticizing his aggression toward Batista and his followers, viewing him as a cherished and charismatic outlaw figure who provided him with some sense that there were heroes left in the world, by 1961 Mailer's enthusiasm in general for the far left had begun to diminish. In an interview in England with Richard Wollheim, he described his socialist preference now *faute de mieux*, considering many socialists including his friends as prigs.[530] Mailer's growing conservatism was more apparent by the end of the decade in *The Armies of the Night* and particularly in *Miami and the Siege of Chicago*.

Yet Mailer, like many liberals, was very much in opposition to the war in Vietnam still perceiving that both communism and capitalism were each in their own way, as he expressed in *Cannibals and Christians*, malignancies. He also felt that America's position in Vietnam was ambiguous given that the United States was bombing Vietnam on the one hand, while offering it aid on the other.

Mailer also contested L.B. Johnson's support of the war deeming that the president, like D.J. in *Why Are We in Vietnam?*, was using the war as an outlet for his pent-up violence. He perceived, too, that America's intervention was, in the final analysis, another manifestation of the totalitarianism and oppressiveness besieging the country at large. Mailer therefore agreed in late 1967 to participate in the March on the Pentagon taking an active position against the war, the subject of his non-fictional novel *The Armies of the Night* published a year later. Although the author's final allegiance as he stated was with the villains who were hippies, those who in his estimation believed in life's mystery, during the march the author still began to question the extent of his allegiance to the New Left and their 'White Negroes', apprehensive now about their self-indulgence, hedonism and drug infatuation. Mailer now considering himself a 'Left Conservative'[531] came to view this segment of America's youth with only "gloomy hope".[532]

Mailer's reticence regarding the left increased considerably by the time of his coverage of the 1968 political conventions as exemplified by his observations in *Miami and the Siege of Chicago*. The author came at best to have very limited patience for the New Left: "The Left was not ready, the Left was years away from a vision sufficiently complex to give life to the land, the Left was still too full of kicks and pot and the freakings of sodium amytol and orgy, the howls of electronics and LSD. The Left could also find room to grow up. If the Left had to live through a species of political exile for four or eight or twelve good years, it might be forced to consider what was alive in the conservative dream"[533]. Furthermore, even though Mailer found that Nixon lacked either Kennedy's or Castro's charisma, he had come by now to respect him as a survivor who had triumphed over his earlier political defeats. However, during his coverage of the 1972 presidential campaigns, described in *St. George and the Godfather*, he was to become again very disapproving of Nixon, this time for prolonging the war: "4.5 million civilians and 1.5 million combatants being killed, wounded or made homeless on all sides in the three and a half years Nixon had continued the war..."[534], comparing the Republican position in South East Asia to Nazi Germany. Although he was much less sympathetic to the right and to the conservatives in *St. George and the Godfather*, much of his criticism was war-related; whether war be endorsed by a Democrat such as Johnson or a Republican such as Nixon, was inevitably associated, by Mailer, with the Holocaust. Yet, ultimately despite all his disapprobation of America and as he stated in *Miami and the Siege of Chicago,* the Jeremiah came also to the realistic conclusion that his country had treated him well, having permitted him to earn a living and status, one which his conservative side increasingly wanted to preserve.

During this phase of politicization, Mailer also decided to run for Mayor of New York City, an ambition he had already hoped to realize in 1960. He ran for Mayor in 1969, believing that if he became mayor he would never write again, but that "he would have his hand on the rump of History, and Norman was not without lust."[535] He ran on the same ticket as Jimmy Breslin, not surprisingly again an Irishman, and one whom he esteemed would be instrumental in galvanizing the support of the city's white working class and white ethnic community. The main focus of Mailer's program was statehood and neighborhood control. The candidate proposed that New York City petition to become the fifty-first state. Even though this supposed major economic conditions, for Mailer who remained loyal to his liberal idealism, the financial issues were still overridden by the spiritual ones. Operating on the premise that the city paid nearly five times the amount of tax money that it received in state or federal aid, the candidate estimated that if the city unfettered itself from the state, it could conserve billions of dollars, which could be utilized for its needs. More importantly, he considered that a city, like an individual, in order to perpetuate its spiritual growth, should be responsible for its own destiny and therefore resolve its own individual problems with its own resources. The candidate furthermore proposed that once the city achieved its statehood, it should thereafter grant autonomy to its neighborhoods. Each neighborhood receiving state funding would in turn manage its own municipal services and even its schools: "In the city-state, every opportunity would be offered to neighborhoods to become townships, villages, hamlets, sub-boroughs, tracts or small cities at which legal point they would be funded directly by the fifty-first state. Many of these neighborhoods would manage their own services, their police, sanitation, fire protection, education, parks or like very small towns if they wished, combine services with other neighborhoods. Each neighborhood would thus begin to outline the style of its local government by the choice of its services."[536] Mailer's advocacy of the decentralization of government and the redistribution of local power was a notion fundamental to conservatism. Mailer himself stated that "The conservatives are right that man must solve his problems through his own agency, but you can't ask the other half to do it until they have their own agency."[537] Simultaneously, he also remained faithful to the left by supporting the notion of *zedakah* as he expressed during his campaign: "I'm a man of the left in that I believe conservatives have exploited society. Government must see that the poor get the necessary resources to help themselves."[538]

He furthermore viewed much of his constituency, as he had in his thwarted campaign in 1960, as comprising "the underdog", the disenfranchised, the criminals, the prostitutes, the junkies and the hippies. The candidate hoped simultaneously to build a constituency between them and the artists and the intellectuals. Mailer's continued attraction to the marginalized individual was well synthesized by Joe Flaherty, his campaign manager: "If someone had been part of an experience foreign to his own (being Black, a convict, a prizefighter), Mailer found in him occult powers bestowed only on the children of the gutters.."[539] According to Flaherty, Mailer was having a "one-way love affair with street types".[540] Ultimately, as Mailer stated himself he proposed a "hip coalition of left and right"[541] which was uniquely Maileresque, in which he banned private automobiles, legalized gambling, provided free bicycles in the city's parks, and provided methadone to addicts. Among his proposals were his plans to build "Vegas East" at Coney Island, institute an annual Grand Prix in Central Park, have a central-city farmers' market which sold ethnic foods, build a zoo in every neighborhood, return national baseball teams to Brooklyn and Manhattan, grow ivy on housing projects, provide craftsmanship training in gardening, and use stained glass windows in public parks and gardens. Yet, probably his most innovative and most controversial proposition was one dubbed "Sweet Sunday"—where one Sunday a month all traffic including incoming ships and airlines were to be forbidden and all power except those in the hospitals were to be shut off.

Mailer's political career was however short-lived, he and Breslin being eliminated in the primaries, coming in next to last. Mailer's candidacy was distressing to many of his fellow liberals because the 41,000 votes he received were taken from Herman Badillo who would have probably otherwise won. Following his political defeat, Mailer meanwhile consoled himself by rationalizing that "Norman was lazy, and politics would make him work hard for sixteen hours a day for the rest of his life. He was so guilty a man that he thought he would be elected as a fit and proper punishment for his sins... He would never write again if he were Mayor (the job would doubtless stain his talent to extinction)..."[542]

Although Mailer had, since the late 60s and early 70s, maintained an interest in politics, as demonstrated by the years he devoted to his CIA novel, *Harlot's Ghost*, or his articles on Watergate, Jimmy Carter, George Bush, Clinton and Dole which he included in his 1998 collection of his writings *The Time of Our Time,* his political aspirations came to a quick halt after his 1969 defeat. Despite the fact that he remained a Democrat, his growing conservatism was incontestable, as demonstrated by his endorsement of the CIA and his continued disappointment with the left for its ineffectiveness as he expressed as late as 1991: "Intellectually speaking, liberal ideology had become about as stimulating as motel furniture. You could get through a night provided you didn't have to hang around in the morning. Liberalism was opposed to poverty, hunger, AIDS, drugs, corruption in high places, crowded prisons, budget cuts, sexism, racism, and opposition to liberation, but it had not had an idea in twenty-five years for solving those problems."[543]

For Mailer, like many Jews, his avid involvement in politics and political thought has been an offshoot of his Jewish roots, a transfer of religion to politics as well as a reflex of survival against anti-Semitism, which, as described by Jean-Paul Sartre, was "a poor man's snobbery"[544]. Mailer's early radicalism, again intrinsically linked to his Jewish background gave way to a growing conservatism which budded at the time of his renunciation of Wallace and his communist entourage and which continued until the end. Mailer, who was the radical general during the middle of the last decade, had long abandoned his radicalism, but remained loyal to the left as a lover to a past love. After his 1969 mayoral defeat, the general retired from his active political career and became a wise and more conservative political counselor and commentator, who enjoyed the benefits of fame and social status bestowed upon him by his growing alliance with the right, even questioning whether or not he had not become a "closet republican".[545]

CHAPTER VI

Mailer and the Negro

Mailer's preoccupation with the Negro was a major focus of his early and middle work. The apparition of "The White Negro" was his testimonial to the Negro's sexuality, perceived by his friend, James Baldwin and many other blacks as "White Negro bullshit."[546] However, the mid and late 1960s marked a change in Mailer's romanticizing of the Negro as he became increasingly aware that Black Power was the symbol of the Negro's anger and anti-Semitism. Gradually, although the black was to become a distant cousin rather than a venerated and protected younger brother, he was still a part of Mailer's spiritual family. Like Baldwin, Mailer recognized that, "... just as society must have a scapegoat, so hatred must have a symbol. Georgia has the Negro and Harlem has the Jew"[547].

At Harvard, Mailer was in a class where there were only four blacks out of a thousand students. Aware that, as a Jew, he was the object of prejudice, he must have already identified with other minorities, specifically the blacks, who were subjected to a similar fate. During his junior year, influenced by Richard Wright, he wrote "Right Shoe on Left Foot", a story about a black man in the rural South who comes to understand that passive resistance is the most efficient means of provoking the culpability in the white, sadistic Southerner.

Although in *The Naked and the Dead:* there are no black characters, probably an accurate portrayal of the Jim Crow Army of W.W. II, there are still many negative allusions made by the soldiers with regard to the Negro. As a target of white bigotry, the black first appears with Lieutenant Conn's reference to "the treachery and depravity of the Negro and the terrible fact that New York was in the hands of foreigners"[548]; Jews and blacks, being linked as they were both ostracized by the Gentile mainstream. While Conn's degradation of 'niggers' reoccurs several times in the early part of *The Naked and the Dead,* Mailer also insists upon the prejudice inflicted upon the blacks later in the novel when the Negro is depicted as wielding unmerited political influence: "I hear they got some niggers down in Washington that's a fact," as described by an anonymous soldier, probably Conn, who states, "I was readin' that in the newspapers they got a nigger down there tellin' the white men what to do"[549]. Part of the Negro's political influence was attributed to the fact that white politicians were having sexual relations with black women. As alluded to by one politician, "all the time he's pushing through those bills, to make the nigger a King Jesus, he's doin' it for good reason. That woman is runnin' the whole labor movement, the whole country including the President is being influenced every time she wiggles her slit"[550]. In *The Naked and the Dead,* it is the black woman in particular who is the incarnation of sexuality. Woodrow Wilson recollects a moment when "a colored girl, about eighteen [walked] past him, her bare feet swirling tiny clouds of dust before her. Under her sweater she [wore] no brassiere, and her pendulant breasts [looked] very full and soft." "One of these days," he says to himself, "Ah'm gonna try something like that"[551].

Although there are no black characters in either *Barbary Shore* or *The Deer Park,* by 1957 in "The White Negro", Mailer gave his incisive psychological analysis of the Negro. To him, the major difference between the black and the Jew was the fact that the Negro kept "the art of the primitive"[552] for his survival. While the Jew intellectualized, the Negro acted. As noted by Leslie Fiedler, it was surprising that the American-Jewish writers, in general, did not turn to the Negro as a model for their re-invented selves, given that the Negro was "the Jew's archetypal opposite, representative of the impulsive life even as the Jew [was] the symbol of the intellectual."[553] In Mailer's case, when he was not identifying with the WASP or the Irish, he was identifying with the Negro, whom he considered the anti-type to the Jew. The white Negro, the hipster, allowed the author the possibility to become black, to "absorb the existentialist synapses of the Negro, and for practical purposes [to] be considered a white Negro." Mailer later came to view himself as an "Honorary Black"[554], admitting that, "he was envious. They had the good fortune to be born black."[555] As observed by Leslie Fiedler, Mailer was not satisfied with a "pseudo-matrimony, or [with] being adopted by some colored foster-father", rather he desired to be "reborn as Negro, *becoming the other*"[556]. Mailer's white Negro bestowed upon the author another identity, allowing him to escape the intellectualization characterized by his Jewish roots, which he so detested.

Mailer's identification with an ethnic group other than his own, was a classic example of counter-ethnicity, a frequent tendency among both Negroes and Jews who desperately sought a sense of personal identity. As Lenora Berson pointed out, many found their selfhood by playing reverse roles and seizing upon their negative group image, which they adapted and elevated in their imagination[557]. While the entertainer Miles Davis, renown as a "super-spade" and a "lover of white beauties", converted to Judaism, Mailer the nice Jewish boy from Crown Heights took upon himself the persona of the black stud and became like his hipsters, a white Negro.

His seminal article, "The White Negro", was in great part inspired by his maid, a black woman who had actually been a whore. She had also given rent parties, in Harlem at her home, rather than in a bar, in order to raise money each month to pay her rent. Mailer became very close to her and regularly attended her parties. Through his maid and her black entourage, he drew many of his conclusions about the Negro.

In his essay, Mailer explained that the Negro was the ultimate hipster, the "White Negro", being only a pale replica. It was, he wrote, "no accident that the source of Hip [was] the Negro, for he [had] been living between totalitarianism and democracy for two centuries."[558] The Negro has had only two options, either to live a life of total subservience or one of perpetual danger: "Any Negro who wishes to live must live with danger from his first day, and no experience can ever be casual to him, no Negro can saunter down a street with any real certainty that violence will not visit him on his walk. The Negro has the simplest of alternatives: live a life of constant humility or ever-threatening danger. In such a pass where paranoia is as vital to survival as blood, the Negro has stayed alive and began to grow by following the need of his body where he could."[559]

Mailer, however, believed that despite the disadvantages and the prejudice to which the black had been forced to succumb, these very handicaps ultimately acted as his source of strength, forcing him to become especially sensitive to his surroundings. This heightened awareness was actually a trait the black shared with other minorities, all of whom needed to be acutely cognizant of the host group for their survival. Apropos of the Jews, with whom the Negro was often coupled, Isaiah Berlin perceptively remarks that: "…The Jews, like the strangers seeking to lose themselves, were compelled to devote all their energies and talents to the task of understanding and adaptation upon which their lives depend at every step. Hence the fantastic over-development of the faculties for detecting trends, and discriminating the shades and hues of changing individual and social situations, often before they have been noticed anywhere else."[560] James Baldwin in "The Black Boy Looks at the White Boy"—a portrait of himself as a Negro and Mailer as a Jew—adds: "And I think I know something about [Norman's] journey from my black boy's point of view because my own journey [was] not so really different, and also because I have spent most of my life, after all, watching white people and outwitting them so I might survive."[561] According to Mailer in "The Tenth Presidential Paper: Minorities," minority groups were "the artistic nerves of a republic," Negroes and Jews having had "a more intense awareness of their own value than the awareness of the white Anglo-Saxon Protestant for himself"[562]. Yet, despite this consciousness, minorities, whether Jewish or Negro, were unable to accept the marginality of their minority status and thus surrendered themselves to the conventionality of the white mainstream. To Mailer's chagrin, "the larger tendency among minorities [was] to manufacture a mediocre personality which [was] a dull replica of the manners of the white man in power. Nothing can be more conformist, more Square, more profoundly depressing than the Jew-in-the-suburbs or the Negro as a member of the Black Bourgeoisie."[563] The author bemoaned that "the average man in a minority group [was] no longer a member of that minority—he [was] instead a social paste which [had] been compounded out of the grinding stone of the society which [contained] him. He was not his own authentic expression. By this logic, the average Negro or Jew [was] not so much a black man or a Semite as a mediocre ersatz Protestant."[564] While the Jew had long acquiesced to the Protestant majority, the Negro now was "going through the bends."[565] Mailer concluded that, "It was therefore not an accident that many of the Negro leaders were as colorless as our leaders. The Negro knew he need merely ape the hypocrisies of the white bourgeois, and he will win."[566] Yet, Mailer was convinced that, contrary to what the Negro imagined, through his accommodation to white society the black did not "hasten his victory so much as he deadened the taste of it."[567] Unlike Sergius who maintains his minority status as an Irishman and a white Negro, to Mailer's regret, most minorities failed to retain their ethnic individuality and melted into the mould of conformist America. However, he recognized that it would be unrealistic for him to expect that the Negro should renounce the goals of security and stability, given the violence and hardship to which he had been subjected to in America: "The demand for courage may have been exorbitant. Now as the Negro was beginning to come into the white man's world: annuities, mental hygiene, sociological jargons, committee solutions for the ills of the breast. He was sick of a whore's logic and a pimp's logic."[568] Notwithstanding, Mailer believed, once again, that the extreme states of emotion and the ghetto life that the Negro had been subject to were essential to his spiritual habilitation. The author regretted that, "There is no one to tell [the Negro] it would be better to keep the psychology of the streets than cultivate the contradictory desire to be…a great, healthy, mature, autonomous, related, integrated individual."[569]

Mailer further elaborated on the limitations of the Negro's assimilation in the eleventh essay of *The Presidential Papers,* "Death–Ten Thousand Words a Minute", which focused on the Floyd Patterson–Sonny Liston heavyweight championship fight. Most blacks supported Patterson, which Mailer attributed to the Negro's desire for integration. While Patterson—polite, quiet, humble, industrious, Catholic and white—was the symbol of security, Liston, in total opposition, personified "the old torment"[570], the violent and dangerous aspect of black existence. Mailer thus romanticized and mythicized Liston, who incarnated the prototype black from whom he had earlier drawn his white Negro. Thus, the day following Liston's victory in the heavyweight championship, Mailer, heavily under the influence of alcohol, and with his habitual need to affirm himself and his masculinity in relationship to his black hero, verbally challenged Liston. Yet, with Mailer's unconscious white sense of superiority, he alludes to Liston's "chuckle of corny old darky laughter, cotton-field giggles"[571] or later to Ali's "sad plantation voice"[572]. One recognizes that despite his Jewish liberalism, he was still prisoner to white prejudice "having metaphorically reduced [the Negro] to his [ancestrally] original condition of servitude. From King of the Northern urban jungle where the white man is afraid to meet him on the street at night [the Negro] has been deported to a Southern cotton plantation where he knows his place and recognizes his master"[573]. Norman Podhoretz, commenting on "The White Negro", concludes: "I doubt if a more idyllic picture of Negro life has been painted since certain Southern ideologues tried to convince the world that things were just fine as fine could be for slaves on the old plantation."[574]

Apart from his psychological and sociological analysis of the black, Mailer also strongly emphasized the Negro's sexuality, an issue which became sorely controversial in both the black and white communities. Mailer was firmly convinced that since the black "had very few sophisticated pleasures of the modern world, he had to go into the basic pleasures, if you will, of existence, such as sex… there is no use getting around it that the Negro's culture has been a profoundly sexual one and it was built on a different premise than white culture."[575] In "The White Negro", he addresses the issue of desegregation in the schools of the South, of which he was in favor. He recognizes, however, that the white Southerner was mainly opposed to the reform because he feared it would lead to miscegenation: "The comedy is that the white loathes the idea of the Negro attaining equality in the classroom because the white feels that the Negro already enjoys sensual superiority. So the white unconsciously feels that the balance has been kept, that the old arrangement was fair. The Negro had his sexual supremacy and the white had his white supremacy, by this logic, the unconscious logic of the Southern white, it is fatal to give the Negro equality because that is the same as to give him victory."[576]

William Faulkner, very disapproving of Mailer's viewpoint, responded: "I have heard this idea expressed several times during the last twenty years, though not before by a man. The others were all ladies, northern or middle-western ladies, usually around forty or forty-five years of age. I don't know what his psychiatrist would find in this."[577]

Jean Malaquais furthermore claimed that Mailer had "romanticized the black man."[578] Ned Polsky argued in a similar vein that since "the white Negro [accepted] the real Negroes, not as a human being in his totality, but as the bringer of a highly specified and restricted 'cultural dowry', Mailer [created] an inverted form of keeping the nigger in his place."[579] Joseph Wenke ascertained that albeit Mailer intended to praise the Negro, he presented an image that could easily be misconstrued as condoning the classical negative stereotypes of the blacks as hedonistic primitives[580], while John Cooley concurred that Mailer created "a mass portrait of black sexuality. In so doing, he [denied] individuality by placing a single idea about sex and race in front of the facts of individual lives."[581]

Mailer's romanticizing of Negro sexuality was also ill received in the black community. James Baldwin was displeased that "an American Negro male is also to be a kind of walking phallic symbol; which means that one pays, in personality, for the sexual insecurity of others."[582] He reproached Mailer for the perpetuation of "the myth of the sexuality of Negroes, which Norman, like many others, refuses to give up."[583] Baldwin also questioned why Mailer "[maligns] the sorely menaced sexuality of Negroes in order to justify the white man's own sexual panic?"[584] Baldwin was furthermore infuriated that "so antique a vision of the blacks should, at this late hour, and in so many borrowed heirlooms, be stepping off the A train."[585] In the final analysis, Baldwin perceived that Norman "still sees us as goddamn romantic black symbols. We still haven't been granted ordinary human status, the right to go to the bathroom. Until Norman sees us with no more romanticism than he views Jewish storekeepers, he'll never understand or be on to what's happening, really happening."[586] Equivalently, Lorraine Hansberry, author of *A Raisin in the Sun*, a successful Broadway play about a black family's problems, judged Mailer as being one of the "New Paternalists."[587]

Paradoxically, Mailer's greatest black defender was Black Power leader, Eldridge Cleaver, author of *Soul on Ice*. Cleaver considered "The White Negro" as "prophetic and penetrating in its understanding of the psychology involved in the accelerating confrontation of black and white in America."[588] To him, the essay was "one of the few gravely important expressions of our time", one of "the first important chinks in the mountain of white supremacy."[589] In parallel, he was personally insulted by Balwin's "flippant, schoolmarmish view of "The White Negro", which he considered a "literary crime."[590] Cleaver's appreciation of Mailer might have been particularly comprehensible because both reduced human nature to over-simplified alternatives. In the same way that Mailer categorically divided individuals into one of two camps, "the Hip" or "the Square", Cleaver, in *Soul on Ice*, classified the white males as "Omnipotent Administrators" and black males as "Supermasculine Menials."[591] As he argues that, "the black man's penis was the monkey wrench in the white man's perfect machine"[592], it is understandable Cleaver should sympathize with Mailer's white Negro, declaring that after Mailer, "there's a shit-storm coming"[593].

Mailer's fascination and eulogy of the Negro continued. In 1965, it appears in his fiction through Shago, the black jazz musician in *An American Dream*. Although he is ultimately a stereotype of the black stud, possibly modeled after Miles Davis, Shago is undoubtedly Mailer's most developed black character. When described for the first time, Rojack says he resembles "some perfect recollection of a lord of Harlem standing at the street corner."[594] Shago, like Rojack, is another example of a character who hopes to achieve counter-ethnicity. The desire on the part of the Negro for such assimilation was often a means of self-validation. While Rojack seeks integration into the black world, Shago aspires to assimilate into the white one. When he first met Deborah, who judged him as "the most attractive man in America," he later explains to Rojack, "that I was at the big divide…They were ready to pick me up, make me a society singer"[595], adding that, "I wanted the society shit cause I was right for that, but I took one look at your wife and I gave it up."[596] Although he refuses to perform at Deborah's charity event, straddling two worlds, he had to find himself "a lily-white devil in a black ass…cut off from [his] own lines"[597]. He views himself as "a captive of white shit now"[598]. In fact, as incisively resumed by Rojack, Shago is "not white, [he was] just losing [his] black"[599]. John Cooley sees him as "a tragic figure, a black man who perceived too late that he was engaged in the white devil's work."[600] Yet, Shago ultimately chooses heroin, the street life of Harlem and his revenge against Rojack when he discovers he is having sexual relations with Cherry. On the other hand, following their violent dispute, Rojack is simultaneously empowered by his victory over Shago: "Some hard-lodged boulder of fear I had always felt with Negroes was in the bumping, elbow-busting and crash of sound as he went barreling down, my terror with him."[601] Their encounter permits Rojack, at least symbolically, to become black.

Two years later in *Why are We in Vietnam?* The Negro's importance is slightly diminished. If D.J., like Mailer, at times fantasizes that he is a Negro, no black characters actually appear in the novel. In a manner similar to the way that Mailer identifies with Cassius Clay in *The Armies of the Night,* D.J. compares himself to a black: "Maybe I'm a Spade and writing like a Shade. For every Spade is the Shade of the White Man, and when we die we enter their mind, we are part of the Shade. And when Spades die?—well that depends on how you dig Niggers you white ass chiggers says D.J. Come on now says D.J., what if I'm not the white George Hamilton rich dear son of Dallas, Texas, and Hallelujah ass but am instead black as your hole after you eat licorice and chew black cherries, what then, what if I'm some genius brain up in Harlem pretending to write a white man's rink fuck book in revenge..."[602] D.J.'s sexual prowess, which he claims is legendary, resembles Rojack's after he takes possession of Shago's umbrella—a phallic symbol, of course—and subsequently defeats him: "cause D.J., owning God's blessing, is well hung, in fact he has a dick like a nigger, but for hue, Renfrew."[603]

In this novel, Mailer also addresses, once again, the issue of prejudice, the association of Negroes and Jews in the bigot's mind. Rusty Jethroe, father of D.J., passes on to his son his negative notions about both minorities: "The Niggers are free, and the dues they got to be paid is no Texas virgin's delight; The Niggers and the women are fucking each other; The Yellow races is breaking loose;...The great white athlete is being superseded by the great black athlete; The Jews run the Eastern wing of the Democratic party; and Karate, a Jap sport, is now prerequisite to good street fighting."[604]

The evolution in Mailer's work between 1965 and 1967, and his unwillingness or his inability to create a black character during this period, might be a manifestation, not only of his growing conservatism, but also of his increasing ambivalence toward the black, one he shared to a lesser degree with the Jewish community at large.

Until this period, with the exception of certain earlier black nationalists such as Marcus Garvey, considered the "Black Hitler"[605] of the 1920's, Negro-Jew relationships, though equivocal, were generally empathetic. The Jews were probably the Negroes' greatest supporters. In the nineteenth century, they were already major contributors in the crusade against slavery. One of the most courageous of the Jewish abolitionists was Dr. David Einhorn, a Baltimore rabbi, who preached abolitionism in pro-slavery Baltimore. In the first half of the twentieth century, Jews such as Julius Rosenwald donated generously to improve the education of the Southern blacks and Joel Springarn provided the funds necessary for the organization of the NAACP (National Association for the Advancement of Colored People), the first national organization to advocate increased rights and opportunities for blacks... During the Roosevelt administration of the 1930s and 1940s, Jews with political influence endorsed federal programs to help the Negro communities. In the 1940s, Alexander

Pekelis of the American Jewish Congress created a Commission on Law and Social Action bringing in collaboration with the NAACP test cases on discrimination to trial; within a few years AIC and ADL became involved in a similar defense system for the Negro. When the Civil Rights Movement arose in the 1950s, many Jews, through their financial aid or their active participation and presence, were highly supportive. Mailer, like many Jewish liberals, endorsed the Civil Rights Movement but, as he stated in *Idol and the Octopus*, he was opposed to Martin Luther King's philosophy and strategy of passive resistance: "I'm against sit-down strikes. I'm against sitting down in Trafalgar Square, and cops having to carry them off. I think if you're not ready to fight the police, you mustn't sit down and let them carry you off. You must recognize that you're not ready to fight to the very end for your principles. I was carried off in a chair not so long ago, and I'm not proud of it..."[606]

When the Civil Rights Movement took a more aggressive turn, Mailer was initially favorable to this evolution. Since he had never given much credence to the goal of integration, he was reassured to find that the movement was becoming more self-assertive. In his view, expressed in *Existential Errands*, not only was assimilation generally degrading to a minority, but the Negro, if given adequate opportunities, could prove to have more potential than his white counterparts: "The Negro does not want equality any longer, he wants superiority, and wants it because he feels he is in fact superior. And there is some justice on his side for believing it. Sufficiently fortunate to be alienated from the benefits of American Civilization, the Negro seems better able to keep his health."[607] Thus, he felt that it was much more important for the blacks to build their own culture.

If the Jew was sympathetic to the Negro, the Negro was sympathetic to the Jew, especially over the suffering he had endured in Nazi Germany. As early as 1933, the black leader W.E.B. Dubois had stated: "It seems impossible that in the middle of the twentieth century a country like Germany could turn to race hate as a political expedient. Surely, the example of America is enough to warn the world. It all reminds the American Negro that all race prejudice has nothing to do with accomplishment, with genius or ability. It is an ugly, dirty thing. It feeds on envy and hate."[608] While minority victimization was their greatest bond, tensions began to emerge after the Second World War, when Jews, improving their economical status, were moving out of ghetto neighborhoods and Negroes, migrating from the rural South, were moving into these northern neighborhoods. The tenant-landlord and customer-storeowner relationship between black and Jew was to create much of the conflict between the two races, a tension well portrayed by James Baldwin in his essay, "The Harlem Ghetto": "Jews in Harlem are small tradesmen, rent collectors, real estate agents, and pawn brokers; they operate in accordance with the American business tradition of exploiting Negroes, and they are therefore identified with oppression and are hated for it. I remember meeting no Negro in the years of my growing up, in my family or out of it, who would really trust a Jew, and few who did not, indeed, exhibit for them the blackest contempt."[609] The complexity of these relationships is best described by Dick Gregory. In his work *Nigger*, written in the 1960s, he not only recounts the exploitation of the black by the Jewish merchant, selling him stale bread or spoiled fruit, but he also describes the Jewish store-owner's other facet, revealing his empathy and generosity towards his Negro customer. Like Mailer, he could be sympathetic to the underdog and allegiant to the Jew's tradition, which insisted upon the importance of *zedakah*: "When it came down to the nitty-gritty (however) you could always go to Mister Ben, before a Jewish holiday he'd take all the food that was going to spoil while the store was shut and bring it over to our house. Before Christmas, he'd send over some meat, even though he knew it was going on the table and he might never see the money. When push came to shove, and every hungry belly in the house was beginning to eat on itself, Momma could go to Mister Ben and always get enough for dinner."[610]

Mailer was also conscious of these relationships and addressed the issue of the tenant-landlord relationship with his habitual creativity. In response, he believed that it was imperative that the government take a small amount—one or two thousand dollars—of the money that was allotted to dispose and relocate slum tenants and demolish buildings, and offer it to each of the ghetto tenants to improve their homes. If the tenant spent the first one hundred dollars on drink, he would not receive any more funding. Although Mailer did not offer a solution for eliminating "the odious landlord", he had at least found one which could potentially increase the Negro's autonomy and self-respect.

Other conflicts were created where Negroes started vying with the Jews for certain professional positions. The Negro, considered as a member of an under-privileged minority, was often favored over the Jew and chosen for positions for which he was not qualified, a phenomena of "reverse discrimination"[611], which occurred particularly in the areas of teaching, school administration, social work and other branches of the civil service, where the blacks wished to enter.

The crisis between the two groups reached a peak in the late 1960s, with the 1967 Arab-Israeli war abroad and the 1968 Ocean-Hill Brownsville school district strike at home. In 1966, with the nomination of black militant Stokely Carmichael as chairman of the SNCC (Student Non-violent Committee), succeeded by A. Rap Brown, who continued his tactic of violence, advocating rioting and looting, the conflict between the Jews and the blacks began in earnest. Black and white students had initially organized the SNCC with the encouragement of Martin Luther King. Its goals, which were to be achieved through non-violence, were equal political and legal rights as well as integration. Instead Carmichael, and later Rap, insisted upon racial separation and affirmative action, where the blacks were to be compensated for their handicaps. The enemy changed from the "bureaucracy", or the "system", to the white liberal bourgeoisie. Carmichael and Rap identified their leadership with "Black Power". Even the Negro's identity was now shifted; he was no longer "a Negro", he was now "a black". Aligning with other militaristic black groups such as the Black Panthers, those Mailer judged as the "Achilles's heel"[612] of the New Left, the SNCC expelled its white members and adopted an ideology which was a blend of Separatism, Pan-Africanism, Marxism, and racial pride. Many of the Jewish members, fervent supporters of

Civil Rights, were insulted and hurt. In *The Armies of the Night,* Mailer seems to share this reaction, and reveals a certain animosity towards the blacks, which he described during the Pentagon March as, "Up to some collective expression of disdain, something to symbolize their detestation of the White Left—yes, Mailer was to brood on it much of the next day when he learned without great surprise that almost all of the Negroes had left to make their own demonstration in another part of Washington, their announcement to the press underlining their reluctance to use their bodies in a White War."[613]

Mailer was in fact very ambivalent on the subject of Black Power. As early as *Cannibals and Christians,* he stated, "He certainly cannot accept the Right Wing in New York, whose only ultimate satisfaction will come from deporting every Negro to Jersey, unless he has been taught to say 'Yessir' all over again," yet he also found himself questioning "the militant black left who swear whitey must eat turd before peace is here."[614]

Although he had never been to Israel, and had never been a Zionist, he was sympathetic to Israel's position. The black militant's virulent anti-Zionism and anti-Semitism reaction to Israel's victory during the Six-Day War offended him as did the black extremists' and left revolutionary organizations' denunciation of the Jews as the "imperialist aggressor" of the Arabs and other third world people. By 1972, the conflict had become so inflamed that the Anti-Defamation League (ADL), one of the major Jewish defense agencies, publicly accused the Far Left for its anti-Semitism, now surpassing the bigotry of the Far Right. Despite Mailer's ambiguous feelings toward his Jewish background, the black militant condemnation of Israel and the American Jew preoccupied him. In *The Fight,* he questions whether his loyalty to the Jews is consistent with his support of Mohammed Ali, a black Muslim.

Mailer's attitude to Black Power was extremely ambivalent. He found it "ambitious, beautiful, awesome, terrifying"[615]. From a positive viewpoint, he considered it as a form of black mysticism. Yet, he could not help but fear the violence of black militants. During the march on the Pentagon, which he relates in *The Armies of the Night,*

Mailer demonstrates his reluctance when he describes "the criminally-suggestive cool of Black Power in front of the snipers, the Molotov cocktails thrown from the roof tops"[616]. This ambiguity toward the Negro was exacerbated during the Six-Day War. By 1968, in *Armies of the Night,* he even came to question his sentiments with regard to the Negro, wondering whether there "Was a mad genius buried in every Negro? How fantastic they were at their best...how dim at their worst"[617]. By *Miami and the Siege of Chicago,* his feelings had become more hostile still. Early in the narrative, Mailer is forced to wait at a press conference for Ralph Abernathy. His irritation grows and he recognizes that, "he was getting tired of Negroes and their rights...He was weary to the bone of listening to Black cries of Black superiority in sex, Black superiority in beauty, Black superiority in war...He was so heartily sick of listening to the tyranny of soul music, so bored with Negroes triumphantly late for appointments, so depressed with Black inhumanity to Blacks in Biafra, so weary of being sounded in the subway by Black eyes, so despairing of the smell of booze and pot and used up hope in blood-shot eyes of Negroes bombed out at noon..."[618].

Mailer also alludes to the superficiality of his friendships with Negroes: "over the last ten years if he had fifty friendships with Negroes, sufficiently time to engage a part of his heart, then was it ten or even five of those fifty which had turned out well?"[619] In fact, James Baldwin was the Negro with whom Norman probably had the closest relationship, and it was Mailer, with his ambiguous treatment of his black friend, who was a disappointment to Baldwin. Despite his fascination with the Negro and his wish to be accepted in the black world, Negroes, with the exception of Cleaver, generally did not take Mailer seriously. In the same way that Baldwin's Negro jazz entourage in Paris did not find Mailer "hip". Flo Kennedy, the black lawyer and confidante of the Black Panthers, claimed that Mailer, "didn't know a goddam thing about blacks"; to which Mailer retorted that "to know one is to fuck one."[620]

During Mailer's political reportage in *Miami and the Siege of Chicago,* he was able, temporarily, to overcome his negative feelings toward the Negro and his cause. He was reluctant to side with the "insane Black militants", and to accept that "all Left Wing Blacks would be his polemical associates...the Lord protect him!"[621]. His reservations were lifted after his speech announcing his support of the movement was welcomed with warm applause and he decided to re-embrace Black Power. Mailer oscillated in much the same way in *The Fight*, which describes the fight between George Foreman and Mohammed Ali: "he would have been miserable at being able to prosper from such values. But his love affair with the Black soul, a sentimental orgy at its worst, had been given a drubbing through the seasons of Black Power. He no longer knew whether he loved blacks or secretly disliked them, which had too be the dirtiest secret in his American life."[622] He furthermore became conscious that "he had not only come to report on a fight but to look a little more closely into his own outsized feelings of love and—could it be?—sheer hate for the existence of Black on earth"[623]. Yet, when he returned to Zaire a month later and was greeted warmly by the Zairians in a manner similar to the way he was received by the American blacks at the Pentagon March, he once again revised his sentiments in their favor. Essentially, Mailer vacillated between emotionally embracing the Negro and intellectually rejecting him. Never insensitive to approval, when he felt he was being accepted by the blacks, his emotions tended to overrule, although less fervently than in the past. Thus, he continued, at a level, at least, to adopt his black brother, since he deeply empathized with him.

The second pivotal issue in Negro-Jewish relations was the 1968 school strike in the predominantly black Ocean Hill-Brownsville section of Brooklyn. As of 1967, the Afro-American Teacher's Association organized in 1964 had adopted a black-nationalist position with the rise of Black Power. It directed its anti-Semitic attacks against the Jews in general and the Jewish public school teacher in particular. By 1968, under the influence of the ATA in the Ocean Hill-Brownsville areas of Brooklyn, black militants began demanding community control of their schools, expelling teachers who were mainly white and Jewish and who had gained their jobs through passing the Civil

Service examinations. Black parents denounced the striking teachers as "Jew Pigs"[624].

Although Mailer had never tolerated anti-Semitism, he was systematically in favor of the Negroes controlling not only their own schools, but also their own neighborhoods, a program which was also part of his mayoral platform and which he expounds in *Existential Errands*: "I would look to encourage not merely new funding for businessmen who are Black, but Black schools with their own teachers and their own texts, Black solutions in Black housing where the opportunity might be given to rebuild one's own slum room... I would try to recognize that an area of a city where whites fear to go at night belongs by all existential—which is, to say natural—law to the Blacks, and would respect the fact, and so would encourage Black local self-government as in a separate city with a Black sanitation department run by themselves, a Black fire department, a funding for a Black concert hall, and most of all a Black police force responsible only to the city within our city and Black courts of justice for their own. There will be no peace short of the point where the Black man can measure his new superiorities and inferiorities against our own."[625]

Much of his mayoral campaign was aimed directly or indirectly at assisting the Negro, as many of the poor, the disenfranchised, the criminals, the prostitutes or junkies were black. His support of confiscatory taxes, massive welfare programs and other plans to redistribute wealth, job-training programs for the unemployed, the social rehabilitation of criminals, as well as the open admissions policy at City College in order to keep underprivileged youth away from crime were all directed at aiding the black underdog. With his usual imagination, he furthermore argued that the best way to curb juvenile delinquency was to create an artistic outlet for the ghetto youths' violence, creativity and sense of pageantry. He suggested organizing medieval jousting tournaments in Central Park where the Harlem gangs, removed from the streets, would concentrate on grooming their horses, designing their livery and learning to ride, to use the lance, and to oil their armor.

Many of the more conservative Jews were, however, against Mailer's program, believing that his extreme liberalism would ultimately disadvantage them. They questioned Mailer's plan to decentralize the government, a scheme which could only weaken their position in their neighborhoods. They were also strongly opposed to Mailer's open admissions policy because they felt that the greater enrollment of blacks would lower academic standards.

With Mailer's growing conservatism, by 1975 when *Tough Guys Don't Dance*, was published, its Negro character, Bolo Green, was no longer endowed with the same presence and sexuality as Shago in *An American Dream* or even D.J. in *Why Are We In Vietnam?*. His white hero, Tim Madden, no longer possesses the qualities which Mailer so admired in the white Negro. Although Patty Lareine, Tim Madden's wife, leaves him for "a black stud of her choice, a tall sullen beautifully put together dude who had been hanging around through the summer, ready to capitalize on that carnal affinity toward black men which lives in the hearts of certain blonds like lightning and thunder"[626]. However, unlike Shago, the "stud's" masculinity, given he "swung in both directions"[627] is more than questionable.

Although Madden seeks revenge, he does not have Rojack's courage, and is paralyzed by Bolo who "could be heavy, or he could be as quick as a basketball player, but he was always big. The size put him out of physical reach...I think it delighted her contempt for me that I was not man enough under such circumstances to load my pistol and do a down-home chase-off."[628] Mailer, however, continues to equate the Negro with sexuality, and illustrates this equation when Madden admits that, "Mr. Black... was just appropriating what I, too, would grab if I could fill his jockstrap and sweat properly in his black logic"[629]. Mailer continued, if to a lesser degree, to view the black as a glorified sex symbol. In *The Presidential Papers*, he had argued that: "Negroes are closer to sex than we are. By that I don't mean that every Negro's a great stud, that every Negro woman is capable of giving great sex, that those people just got rhythm... I think that any submerged class is going to be more accustomed to sexuality than a leisure class...You see, the upper classes in effect exchange sex for power. So they restrict themselves in their sexuality—whereas the submerged classes have to take their desires for power and plow them back into sex... Besides, the Negro has been forbidden any sort of intellectual occupation here for a couple of centuries. So he has to learn other ways of comprehending modern life."[630] Despite the fact that Madden was aware, like Rojack and D.J., that the way to conquer the black was to become black, Mailer's later hero was unable to assume a black identity like the earlier protagonists. He is intimidated by the Negro—"Do you feel a hint uncool around strange black dudes?"[631] he asks—and although he had "usually been able to picture [him]self as not wholly unmacho"[632]. Instead of attempting to avenge his wife's death, he tries to avoid Bolo. Finally, Bolo and Madden come to resemble each other. While Madden fails to become a white Negro, Bolo allows himself to be dominated by Patty and furthermore advises Madden to "keep the peace"[633]. By the publication of *Tough Guys Don't Dance,* neither the black character nor the white Negro were able to maintain the machismo of the author's earlier white and black protagonists.

By the time *The Executioner's Song* appeared, the Negro barely exists. Nevertheless, despite this evolution, Mailer remained true to his Jewish roots and thus sympathetic to the black, whom he continued to view as an underdog. In the novel, Dale Pierre is the lawyer by court appointment of a black convict, Gil Athay. The public is convinced that he is one of the hi-fi killers who have poured Draino down people's throats and stuck ballpoint pens in their ears. Certain of his client's innocence, Dale Pierre is persuaded that he has been convicted by the jury because he is black, a condition best avoided in the State of Utah where a Negro could not even become a priest in the Mormon Church.

With his growing conservatism, Mailer's ambivalence towards Black Power had turned to sheer rejection, while his earlier reservations about the Negro had evolved much of the time into pure condemnation. By 1991, he claimed that: "Then there were the blacks. The Black Power Movement of the sixties, intended to give blacks a more powerful sense of identity, had, in the absence of real social improvement, succeeded merely in moving whites and blacks even further away from each other. Encapsulated among themselves (in direct relation to how poor they were), the blacks were now divided between a bare majority who worked and a socially inassimilable minority who did not. Legions of black youth were marooned in hopelessness, rage at how the rich grew obscenely rich during the eighties, and self-pity. If there was a fair possibility that black people were more sensual than white people, then the corollary was that they suffered more from poverty. Sensual people who are poor can drown in self-pity as they dream of how much real pleasure they could enjoy if they had money."[634] Yet, despite Mailer's later criticism of Black Power and Negro self-pity, he still felt sympathy for the blacks and gave his support to Clinton, on account of his treatment of racial relationships. He believed that despite Clinton's political omissions, the political rapport between blacks and whites within the Democratic Party had improved. Furthermore, at the Dole convention, three percent of the delegates were black. In Chicago the figure was about nineteen percent. Blacks knew that they were the Democrats' best possibility for recapturing the House and the Senate.

Mailer's interest in the occult was another reason for his fascination with the black. He associated the Negro with the primitive and his highly developed intuitive, if not magical, powers. As early as *An American Dream,* Shago represents the instinctual life, which Mailer considered a gift bestowed upon the Negro. As suggested by the chapter entitled, "A Votive Prepared", Cooley describes Shago as "a kind of shaman, both priest and magician, who is instrumental in Rojack's initiation to the black universe. The author is influenced by homeopathic magic, the ancient principle according to which, "like produces like". Thus, from this esoteric standpoint, whites could best learn to be like blacks by symbolically becoming black. Homeopathy was the credence among primitive tribes that magical relationships exist between objects. Thus, primitives often wore the skin of an animal they wished to capture, in much the same way that Shago becomes his black mentor, when Rojack wears his robe. The initiate is tested for his strength and abilities. Thus, when Shago and Rojack wrestle, magic passes from the one to the other. This transmission is traditionally part of a puberty rite, yet in Stephen's case, it resembles a rite of sacred knowledge or marriage."[635] Through their physical confrontation, Stephen is reborn and armed with the necessary power to challenge his father-in-law, Barney Kelly.

Mailer's belief in the Negro's magical powers was further illustrated in his description of the Liston-Patterson fight, which he interprets as the telepathic victory of evil over good: Patterson is struck down by a psychic bolt of evil, a supernatural force. Mailer depicts the psychic energy surrounding the match in "Death—Ten Thousand Words a Minute": "Liston-in-the-ring was not just Sonny Liston; much more he was the nucleus of that force at Comiskey Park (and indeed from everywhere in the world from which such desire could reach) which wished him to win or hated him with an impotence that created force, to wit, hated him less than it feared him, and so betrayed its hate since the telepathic logic of the unconscious makes us give our strength to those we think to hate but favor despite ourselves. Just so, Patterson-in-the-ring was not Floyd Patterson sparring in his gym, but was instead a vehicle of all the will and all the particular love which truly wished him to win, as well as a target of all the hatred which was not impotent but determined to strike him down."[636]

Liston, the paragon of the black primitive, came to be associated not only with magic but with black magic: "Liston came from that world where a man with a dream was drunk in the gutter, and the best idealism was found in a rabbit's foot blessed by a one-eyed child. Liston was voodoo, Liston was magic, Liston was the pet of the witch doctor; ...Yes, Liston was the secret hero of every man who had ever given mouth to a final curse against the dispositions of the Lord and made a pact with Black Magic. Liston was Faust."[637] Between trips to Zaire for the Ali-Foreman fight, Mailer read the work, *Bantu Philosophy* by Father Tempels, a Dutch priest, and maintained that the instinctive philosophy of the African tribesmen resembled his own. Bantu philosophy viewed humans as forces, not beings. These forces inhabiting the individual came from all that was living and dead. Therefore, an individual was not only himself, but also the karma of past generations that existed within him. Thus the individual was a force of the dead.

In "Death", Mailer also alludes to Ali as "pugilism's master of the occult"[638], a powerful voice in the fearful and magical area between the living and the dead. The author also describes Ali's premonitory dream, in which Foreman's eye was cut. This actually did occur, but a week too soon. Ali furthermore not only acted out Foreman's victory, but also his own death so as to excite the invisible forces capable of helping him to win. Mailer supposed that Ali's qualms about the match were the result of a dream. The Zairians were very superstitious and firmly believed in magic. Mobutu was not only their dictator, he was also a fervent occultist, having a pygmy for his private witch doctor. Before the fight, the wealthy blacks in Kinshasa were consulting their medicine men and fetishists. George Plimpton even sought one for Mailer and himself.

Finally, the correlation between the Negro and the occult was also made by the author in *The Faith of Graffiti*. He considers the graffiti writing done with spray cans by black and Puerto Rican children in the Harlem subways as potent with psychic connotations: "names had grown all over walls—a jungle of ego creepers and tendrils had flowered through a series of psychic rainstorms, which passed the unwritten history over New York"[639].

Mailer's Jewish liberalism encouraged his empathy for the black, as both underdog and scapegoat, while his machismo made him romanticize his sexuality and primitivism, that Dionysian force so antithetical to the Apollonian values propounded by Jews, which he had always condemned. His creation of the white Negro was a means for him, and others of the counter-revolution of the 1950s and 1960s, to identify with the blacks and escape the constraints of their white, often Jewish, backgrounds. Mailer even admitted recently that his fantasy was to be born a black athlete in his next incarnation. Yet, the emergence of Black Power in the mid and late 1960s, with its militancy and its anti-Semitism, forced him to recognize the limitations of Mr. Black and to realize that, like other Jews, he had something to save while the blacks had never had anything to lose.

EPILOGUE

The Castle in the Forest, Mailer's last novel, appearing in 2007, is another testimonial that the author remained more than ever haunted by the specters of Nazism. While in his earlier writing, Mailer already described Hitler's atrocities in *Barbary Shore* and in *Oswald's Tale: An American Mystery*, now his narrator, Dieter, is an SS officer; he is, actually, part of an intelligence group directly under Heinrich Himmler, one of Nazi Germany's four most reputed butchers. Dieter, without a twinge of remorse, is the proud emissary of the Maestro, the Devil who once again acts in opposition to the Lord, the Dummkopf, the idiot, coined now as the D.K., in the habitual Maileresque tug of war between good and evil. Young Hitler, the novel's hero, or moreover anti-hero, is not surprisingly the Maestro's "most important client"[640], who Mailer struggles relentlessly to comprehend. In fact, the author states that he is "ready to speak of the obsession that revolved around Adolf Hitler. Yet what brings more of a dark cloud to one's mood than living with a question that will not return an answer. Even today, the first obsession remains Hitler. Where is the German who does not try to understand him? Yet where can you find one who is content with the answer?"[641]

This not withstanding, Mailer still probes into Hitler's childhood and early youth in an effort to enlighten himself and his readers with regards to the influence of the Führer's early life on his later political motivations and comportment. Mailer expounds on the fact that Adolf was the product of an incestuous union. His mother, Klara, and his father, Alois, were actually second cousins and in order to marry were even obliged to receive a Papal dispensation. As Mailer points out, incest can often lead to diverse forms of mental disorder or death. Was Hitler quickly not to find himself one of the two survivors of six siblings, whose mental state seemed more than precarious as he locked himself into his own narcissistic world, where, with the exception of his mother, he best communicated not with people but with the forest?

The incest pattern, as alluded to by Mailer, was also to be repeated by Hitler when later as a young man he becomes besotted by his niece, Geli Kaubal, who was soon found dead in the Führer's apartment on the Prinzegentenstrasse in Munich. Uncontestably, she had been shot but no one still knows whether her death was caused by murder or by suicide, nor to what extent her infatuated uncle was implicated.

Apart from being a product of inbreeding, Mailer also portrays Hitler, in fact, like himself, as the classic mother's boy, capable of all excesses, of the best and the worst. Having lost her first three children, Klara, Hitler's mother, was more than enraptured by the Führer's birth. Overnurtured and overprotected by his mother, Hitler was simultaneously at the mercy of a choleric father who by opposition he came to despise. Adolf, however, internalized his father's cruelty and wrath and, like Alois, soon came to abuse those family members weaker than himself, whether his younger siblings, Paula and Edmund, or even their dog, Luther. This early ruthlessness was, of course, later transferred into his barbaric treatment of the Jews throughout Europe. Similarly, whenever, Adolf found his parents involved in sexual relations, the repulsion and anger he felt again toward his father was once again later transposed into his virulent anti-Semitism. In fact, the only time that father and son seemed to bond was when the young Hitler was initiated into Alois' passion for apiculture. The bees, like the Jews, were reputed for their wealth. The other insects were thus jealous and six-year-old Hitler was already overjoyed when occasionally a colony of bees was gassed and the dead lined up in order to be counted. It is at this time that Alois further indoctrinates Adolf to the reality that "in nature there is no mercy for the weak."[642]

Mailer also addresses the issue of Alois' illegitimacy and the eternal question of whether or not the Hitlers were part Jewish. One of the most serious speculations regarding Hitler's Jewish origins comes, of course, from Hans Frank, the former Reich Minister of Justice and Governor General of Poland. While awaiting his death sentence in Nuremberg Prison, Frank affirmed in his book, *At the Gallows Foot: An Interpretation of Hitler and His Age*, that the Führer's paternal grandmother had definitely been impregnated by a nineteen-year-old Jewish boy for whose family she worked in Graz. The theory of Hitler's Jewish paternity was also maintained by Adolf's nephew, Patrick, who even wrote an article to that effect in the French newspaper, *Paris Soir*, earlier in 1939. Although Hitler's possible Jewishness remains an enigma, was it not from the beginning his Achilles heel? After the invasion of Austria in 1938, did he not a year later even evacuate and blast Döllersheim, his father's birthplace and the site of his grandmother's grave, in order to eradicate any potential trace?

Mailer also demonstrates that when Adolf, as a young boy, was not hiding in his mother's apron strings, he was playing war games in the forest with his comrades, when possible with younger ones who he could more easily dominate. Inevitably, always the leader and organizer, Hitler acted out the stories of Karl May and the tales of the Red Indians or as he later alludes to in *Mein Kampf*, the history of the Franco-prussian war, where the young Führer, along with his compatriots, basked in the glory of the German spiked helmets and the demise of the French troops; his mock war games became his major outlet for the frustrations he endured at home, while his early fantasies about war and heroism would later play a crucial role in his diabolic mission. As alluded to by Mailer, had Heinrich Treischke not announced that "God has given all Germans the earth for a potential home, and this assumes that there will come a time where there will be a leader of all the world, a leader to serve as the embodiment, the incarnation, the essence of a most mysterious power which will tie the people to the invisible majesty of the nation"[643] ? Later, at sixteen, after listening to Wagner's *Rienzi*, and having climbed to the summit of the Freinberg at midnight, was it not he, Adolf Hitler, who had the visionary recognition that he was to be this *Volkstribun*, this leader of the German people?

The young Führer's beginnings also elucidate the intrinsic link between his early nationalism and anti-Semitism. While his spare time was spent in war games and fantasies, his school, the "Realschule" at Linz was reputed for inoculating in its students a strongly German nationalist political view. Likewise, in the same school, the young Adolf was also first exposed to anti-Semitism, mainly through the prejudice of certain of his teachers. In fact, he is still remembered for having cursed one of the other schoolboys and denigrating him as a "filthy Jew". Had the young Hitler already imagined that the Jews would become the scapegoat of his Third Reich?

In the final analysis, Mailer deems that Adolf Hitler is "the most mysterious human being of the century". Ascertaining that "the world has an impoverished understanding of him"[644], the author attempts through fiction to re-create the Führer's early life in an effort to gain some insight into the impenetrable. Consequently, one quickly deduces, that the dictator's dysfunctional family forces him in boyhood to take flight into a magical world of fantasy and delusion which throughout his life he too often confused in a psychotic manner with reality. Furthermore, and according to Mailer, Hitler's quest to save Germany was also the result of his inflated sense of patriotism, which similar to other leaders created his country's ultimate downfall: "They now possess the mightiest of all social engines of psychic numbification-patriotism! That is still the most dependable instrument for guiding the masses, although it may be replaced by revealed religion. We love fundamentalists. Their faith offers us every promise of developing into the final weapon of mass destruction."[645] Adolf Hitler, "an overseer of death"[646] is the detested and delirious *châtelain* of the concentration camp, ironically coined by the author as "the castle in the forest", Hitler's "das waldschloss".

Mailer, ever plagued by the concentration camps and the gas chambers, concludes with resignation that, even today, that concerning the Holocaust there are still too many questions and no sufficient answers.

CONCLUSION

America bemoans its Jewish-American messiah, who died a sudden death at Mount Sinai Hospital November 10th, 2007, at the age of 84. Until the end, he viewed his role in American literature with regret. Like other authors of his generation, he believed that he had failed to achieve his goal: the writing of the prophetic novel, which could have changed America's destiny. This not withstanding, he still persisted, never completely disheartened, his life and work remaining inseparable until his demise.

Mailer was a complex and contradictory figure: both a successful, fully integrated American writer and a scandalous rebel. The manner in which he openly expressed his weaknesses and fantasies has always made him vulnerable to criticism. He remained the tormented exile, a nomad in an endless search of his identity… Anti-Semitism, blatant or covert, is at the heart of his literary work. The pain of his childhood and adolescence left him scarred with insecurity and rage, and nourished his literary ambitions. Consequently, even in old age, he remained haunted by the prejudice which clouded his youth. *The Castle in the Forest* reflects both his early nightmares as well as a need for personal and collective revenge. By writing about Germany's sadistic demagogue, Mailer re-awakens the readers' consciousness to the ultimate evil, perversity and barbarism engendered by Nazism toward the Jewish race.

By nature, Mailer was larger than life. This is why he always chose to see himself in the role of the American writer who transcended the limits and rules imposed by a community. Prior to his death, this *enfant terrible* of American literature humbly questioned the immortality of his writings: yet undoubtedly, to his great satisfaction, he at least remained among the major American and Jewish-American literary titans. As he recently stated, Mailer, however, found it difficult to assure the historical legacy of Judaism: "The pain of being a Jew is that you feel responsible for what other Jews do. To be Jewish, is to live with the echo of a thousand years of exclusion. I find it as difficult to defend my people as to criticize them. I am always ill at ease when I talk of Israel or the Jews."[647] Regardless, the author still felt compelled to write, *The Castle in the Forest*, an uncontestable declaration of the propound empathy, if also guilt, he felt toward his people; a statement too of his absolute horror of Hitler and the Nazi regime.

Furthermore, his ancestors had also bequeathed him the mission to contribute to a spiritual evolution, one on which he embarked either through his works on women, on blacks, or on politics. He was a precursor, a prophet, and never lost sight of his religious origins. His work as a whole, whether it be in his novels or essays, are tied to his roots. But there is no trace of nostalgia in this anchoring. On the contrary, its striking modernity sheds light on the present, enhancing our consciousness and responsibility. And this present is open to all, equal for all those who might be in search of a new ethic... Norman Mailer's fiction teaches America self-criticism.

In *The Naked and the Dead*, the author describes almost physiologically the one who "brought his spoon up, champed at the remote sweet pulp of the canned peach which mingled so imperfectly with the nervous bile in his throat, the hot sour turmoil of his stomach."[648] With the precision of his sensual, physical descriptive art, Mailer is also a precursor of body language. Subtly, his realism amplifies to the point of revealing those truths, which destroy our illusions. "Love of one's country's just fine, it's even a moral factor at the start of a war. But nothing is more uncertain than belligerence; the longer a war lasts, the less valuable it becomes. When a war has lasted a couple of years, only two things count: a superior material force and a low level of life."[649]

Mailer is an important novelist because he not only writes with his head, with his words, but with all that trembles beneath his flesh, translating the organic rumor of life perpetually labored by the visceral undercurrent of death. If he writes about the Second World

War, it is because he fought it, and to fight it, he insisted on being in the line of action. Thus in *The Naked and the Dead*, he was able to claim: "I'm not selling theories. I speak from experience."[650]

In order to translate the world's violence, Mailer's lucidity relies on the vitality and rigor of a style which seems to emanate directly from his senses. "[…] he could not have said at that moment where his hands ended and the machine-gun began; he was lost in a vast moil of noise out of which individual screams and shouts etched in his mind for an instant. He could never have counted the Japanese who charged across the river; he knew only that his finger was rigid on the trigger bar. He could not have loosened it. In those few moments, he felt no sense of danger. He just kept firing."[651] Here is one of the most powerful examples of the incredible energy of the English language, capturing the adventures and excesses of flesh and blood human beings, then sublimating them, transmuting them into fiction with virtuosity and a vengeful rage.

By now, his beliefs had become more moderate, yet he lost none of the edge of his former years and did not spare Bush his criticism of his conservative, imperialist strategy: "Dominate Iraq, dominate the Near East, then get China in a position to become Greece to our Rome."[652] In *Why Are We in the War?* he reiterates his condemnation of the Bush administration, while analyzing the relations between America and the Middle East. According to Mailer, September 11th became the Republicans' excuse for invading Iraq. Other than the imperialist and economic motivations, this war reflects a desire for vengeance against Arab terrorism. Disappointed at having failed to capture Bin Laden or put an end to Al Quaeda's activities, America has transformed Iraq into a scapegoat for the Middle East. The United States desperately clutches onto the notion of imperialism, because Mailer believed that insecurity and terrorism constitute the dark side of all empires. At the same time, he defends Israel's position, arguing that the Arabs, more provocative than ever, consider that the Jews are ultimately their best defense against the Palestinians. Mailer explains the Muslims' hatred of the United States in their fear of American imperialism imposing its values on the Arab world.

Despite his age, Mailer was still in contact with the twenty-first century. Although he might have congratulated America for preserving its freedom, in messianic fashion he still persisted in condemning its imperialism, its materialism and its apathy, all of which express the nation's decadence, and its risk of also becoming "a castle in the forest", virtually a concentration camp. As a visionary and prophet, he overtly expressed his Judaism and his writings fertilize the political reality of his country and his era. Undoubtedly, Mailer disturbs and ruffles us, but his work unleashes a redemptive emancipation.

Norman Mailer's muse, sometimes humane, sometimes monstrous, was the naked soul. Without complacency, he reveals our destinies, rendering through literature the shock of living and dying at the end of the second millennium and the dawn of the third.

ENDNOTES

Introduction

1   Carl Rollyson, *The Lives of Norman Mailer: A Biography*, 364.
2   *New York Times*, 22 January 2003, E10.
3   Ibid. E1.

Chapter I

4   Quoted in Charles E. Silberman, *A Certain People: American Jews and their Lives*, 73.
5   Abraham J. Karp, *A History of the Jews in America*, 278.
6   Charles Angoff and Meyer Levin, eds., *The Rise of Jewish Literature: An Anthology of Selections from the Major Novels*, 8.
7   Oscar Handlin, *The Uprooted*, 5.
8   Solomon F. Bloom, "The Saga of America's 'Russian' Jews", *Commentary* 1 n°4 (February 1946) 5.
9   Leslie Fiedler, "Genesis: The American-Jewish Novel Through the Twenties," *Midstream* 4 (Summer 1958) 23.
10   Abraham Cahan, *The Rise of David Levinsky*, 61.
11   David Martin Fine, "In the Beginning: American-Jewish Fiction, 1880-1930", *Handbook of American-Jewish Literature: An Analytic Guide to Topics, Themes, and Sources*, ed. Lewis Fried, 16.
12   Cahan, op. cit., 530.
13   Fine, op. cit., 30.
14   Leslie Fiedler, "The Jew in the American Novel", *Collected Essays of Leslie Fiedler*, 2 vols., 2: 76.
15   Ben Hecht, *A Jew in Love*, 45.
16   Norman Mailer, "Modes and Mutations: Quick Comments on the American Novel", *Commentary* 41 n°3 (March 1966) 37.
17   Henry James, "The American Scene", *Collected Travel Writings:*

Great Britain and America: English Hours, the American Scene, Other Travels, 465.

18   Theodore Dreiser, *Letters*, 3 vols., 2: 405

19   T.S. Eliot: "Gerontian", *Collected Poems 1909-1935*, 37.

20   Ezra Pound, "The Canto LXXIV", *The Pisan Cantos*, 439.

21   F. Scott Fitzgerald, *The Great Gatsby*, 69-70.

22   Lewis H. Lapham, *Money and Class in America*, 12.

23   Marcus Hansen, "The Third Generation in America: A Classic Essay in Immigrant History", *Commentary* 14, n°5 (November 1952) 494.

24   Nathan Glazer, "The Alienation of Modern Man; Some Diagnoses of the Malady", *Commentary* 3 n°4 (April 1947) 379.

25   David Pinsky, *The Generation of Noah Edon*, 203-204.

26   Meyer Levin, *The Old Bunch*, 169.

27   Will Herberg, *Protestant, Catholic and Jew*, 18.

28   Ludwig Lewisohn, *The Island Within*, 270-271.

29   Abraham Chapman, ed., *Jewish American Literature: An Anthology of Fiction, Poetry, Autobiography*, xxxviii.

30   Ibid. xxix.

31   Fiedler, "The Jew in the American Novel", 96.

32   Michael Gold, *Jews Without Money*, 41.

33   Ibid. 184.

34   Joseph Freeman, *An American Testament; A Narrative of Rebels and Romantics*, 8.

35   Allen Guttmann, "The Conversion of the Jews", *Wisconsin Studies in Contemporary Literature* 6 (Summer 1965) 171-172.

36   Allen Guttmann, *The Jewish Writer in America: Assimilation and the Crisis of Identity*, 138.

37   Gold, op. cit., 309.

38   Irving Howe, *The World of Our Fathers*, 607.

39   Stephen Birmingham, *Our Crowd*, 36.

40   Quoted in Joseph Gaer and Ben Siegel, *The Puritan Heritage: America's Roots in the Bible*, 26.

41   Norman Mailer, *The Naked and the Dead*, 162.

42   Jules Chametzy, et al., eds., *Jewish American Literature: A Norton Anthology*, 556.

43 Quoted in Harold U. Ribalow, "American Jewish Writers on Their Judaism", *Judaism* 3, n°4 (Fall 1954) 423.

44 Irving Malin and Edwin Stark, eds., *Breakthrough: A Treasury of Contemporary American-Jewish Literature*, 1.

45 Quoted in Daniel Walden, ed., *On Being Jewish: American Writers From Cahan to Bellow*, 24.

46 Ibid.

47 Chametzy, et al., op. cit., 917.

48 Hansen, op. cit., 7.

49 Pinsky, op. cit., 287.

50 Herberg, op. cit., 187.

51 Budd Schulberg, *What Makes Sammy Run?*, xi.

52 Nine Contemporary Jewish Novelists, "Why I Wrote a Jewish Novel", 21.

53 Judd L. Teller, *Strangers and Natives: An Evolution of the American Jew from 1921 to the Present*, 267.

54 William Dean Howells, "Editor's Easy Chair", *Harper's Monthly Magazine*, 130 (May 1915) 958.

55 Leslie Fiedler, "The Jew as Mythic American", *Ramparts* 2 n°2 (Autumn 1963) 43-44.

56 "Our Country and Our Culture: A Symposium", *Partisan Review* 19 (May-June 1952) 309.

57 Ibid. 283.

58 Alvin H. Rosenfeld, "The Progress of the American Novel", *Response* 7 n°1 (Spring 1973) 115.

59 Fiedler, "Styron's Choice", *Fiedler on the Roof: Essays on Literature and Jewish Identity*, 105.

60 Fiedler, "The Jew as Mythic American", 40.

61 Norman Podhoretz, "The Rise and Fall of the Jewish Novelist", *Jewish Life in America: Historical Perspectives*, 150.

62 Frederick R. Karl, *American Fictions, 1940-1980: A Comprehensive History and Critical Evaluation*, 7.

63 Philip Rahv, ed. Introduction, *A Malamud Reader*, vii.

64 Wolfgang Bernard Fleischmann, "The Contemporary 'Jewish Novel' in America", *Jarhbuch fur Amerikastudien* 12 (1967) 162.

65 Howe, op. cit., 596-597.
66 Chametzy, et al., op. cit., 749.
67 Ibid. 918.
68 Ibid. 915.
69 Ibid. 917.
70 Richard Fein, "Jewish Fiction in America", *Judaism* 24 (Fall 1975) 407.
71 J. Michael Lennon ed., *Conversations with Norman Mailer*, 357.
72 Fein, op. cit., 407.
73 Josephine Zardorsky Knopp, *The Trial of Judaism in Contemporary Jewish Writing*, 26.
74 Norman Mailer, Personal interview, 18 January 1991.
75 Donald Kaufmann, *The Countdown (The First Twenty Years)* 105, 108.
76 Diana Trilling, "The Moral Radicalism of Norman Mailer", *Norman Mailer: The Man and his Work*, 135.
77 Fiedler, "The Jew as Mythic American", 32.

Chapter II

78 Peter Manso, *Mailer*, 15.
79 J. Michael Lennon, ed. *Conversations with Norman Mailer*, 357.
80 Hilary Mills, *A Biography*, 71.
81 Norman Mailer, *Harlot's Ghost*, 527.
82 Alfred Kazin, *A Walker in the City*, 60.
83 Gwen Gibson Schwartz and Barbara Wyden, *The Jewish Wife*, 118.
84 Ibid.
85 Quoted in Adrienne Baker, *The Jewish Woman in Contemporary Society: Transitions and Traditions*, 124.
86 Ibid.
87 Gilbert Rosenthal, ed., *The Jewish Woman in a Changing World*, 38.
88 Avia Cantor, *Jewish Women / Jewish Men: The Legacy of Patriarchy in Jewish Life*, 210.
89 Manso, op. cit., 98.

ENDNOTES

90 Kazin, op. cit., 21-22.
91 Carl Rollyson, *The Lives of Norman Mailer: A Biography*, 7.
92 Mailer, *The Naked and the Dead*, 54.
93 Ibid.
94 Ibid. 482.
95 Mailer, *The Essential Mailer*, 212.
96 Ibid. 160.
97 Mailer, *Advertisements for Myself*, 160.
98 Ibid. 132.
99 Frederick Busch, "The Whale as Shaggy Dog: Melville and 'The Man Who Studied Yoga'" *Modern Fiction Studies*, 19, n°2 (Summer 1973) 195.
100 Mailer, *Cannibals and Christians*, 100.
101 Manso, op. cit., 25.
102 Norman Mailer, Personal interview, 19 January 1991.
103 Mills, op. cit., 55.
104 Isaac Bashevis Singer, *Love and Exile: A Memoir*, xx.
105 James Yaffee, *The American Jews: Portrait of a Split Personality*, 295.
106 Rollyson, op. cit., 2.
107 Carole Mallory, *Flash*, 66.
108 Ibid.
109 Dearborn, op. cit., 16.
110 Manso, op cit., 18-19.
111 Ibid.
112 Charles Rembar, Personal interview, 8 August 1995.
113 Rollyson, op. cit., 248.
114 Mailer, Conversation, 23 June 2002.
115 Manso, op. cit., 18.
116 Quoted in Yaffee, op. cit., 50.
117 James T. Farrell, *Studs Lonigan*, 99-100.
118 Mailer, *The Naked and the Dead*, 94.
119 Manso, op. cit., 25.
120 Rollyson, op. cit., 6.
121 Norman Mailer, "Maybe Next Year", *The Short Fiction of Norman Mailer*, 129-130.

122 Mark Zborowski and Elizabeth Herzog, *Life is with People: The Culture of the Shtetl*, 131.
123 Zena Blau Smith, "In Defense of the Jewish Mother", *Midstream* 13 (February 1967) 43.
124 Mailer, op.cit., 114.
125 Ibid. 45.
126 Manso, op. cit., 34.
127 Dearborn, op. cit., 10.
128 Germaine Greer, "My Mailer Problem", *Esquire* (September 1971) 92.
129 Mailer, *The Prisoner of Sex*, 12.
130 Mailer, *The Deer Park*, 115.
131 Norman Mailer, "The Time of Her Time", *Advertisements for Myself*, 446.
132 Rollyson, op. cit., 14.
133 Adele Mailer, *The Last Party: Scenes From my Life With Norman Mailer*, 283.
134 Matthew Besdine, 'Jewish Mothering", *The Jewish Spectator* (February 1970) 9.
135 Ibid.
136 Mailer, *The Prisoner of Sex*, 153.
137 Ibid.
138 Rollyson, op. cit., xii.
139 Mailer, *Advertisements for Myself,* 213.
140 Norman Mailer, "The Language of Men", *The Short Fiction of Norman Mailer*, 161.
141 Mills, op. cit., 19.
142 Adele Mailer, op. cit., 338.
143 Mailer, *The Naked and the Dead*, 484.
144 Ibid. 287.
145 Gold, op. cit., 158.
146 Quoted in Schwartz and Wyden, op. cit., 262.
147 Kazin, op. cit., 67.
148 Erica Jong, *Fear Of Flying*, 159.
149 Philip Roth, *Portnoy's Complaint*, 36-37.

150 Geoffrey Gorer, *The American Study in National Character*, 45.
151 Charlotte Baum, Paula Hyman and Sonia Michel, *The Jewish Woman in America*, 242-243.
152 Mailer, *Harlot's Ghost*, 114.
153 Beverly Bienstock, "The Changing Images of the American Mother", *Changing Images of the Family*, eds. Virginia Tufte and Barbara Myerhoff, 185.
154 Mailer, *Genius and Lust: A Journey Through the Major Writings of Henry Miller*, 93-94.
155 Mills, op. cit., 54.
156 Howard Silverstein, "Mailer's Quest for Manhood", 201.
157 Mailer, *Advertisements for Myself*, 152.
158 Norman Mailer, "An American Dream", *Esquire* 61 (April 1964) 148.
159 Mailer, *The Prisoner of Sex*, 154.
160 Carole Mallory, "Norman Mailer: The Power of Sex", *Ms* n°5 (February 1990) 82.
161 Norman Mailer, "The Homosexual Villain", *Advertisements for Myself*, 193.
162 Saul Bellow, *Mr. Sammler's Planet,* 186.
163 Mailer, *Advertisements for Myself*, 195.
164 Ibid. 194.
165 Norman Mailer, *The Idol and the Octopus: Political Writings on the Kennedy and Johnson Administrations*, 200.
166 Mailer, *Advertisements for Myself*, 193.
167 Norman Mailer, *The Presidential Papers*, 243.
168 Kate Millet, *Sexual Politics*, 327.
169 Mills, op. cit., 373.
170 Adele Mailer, op. cit., 349.
171 Dearborn, op. cit., 165.
172 Mailer, *Advertisements for Myself*, 432-433.
173 Mailer, *Cannibals and Christians*, 196.
174 Mailer, *The Presidential Papers*, 243.
175 Mailer, *A Portrait of Picasso as a Young Man*, 53.
176 Mailer, *The Deer Park*, 27.

177 Lennon, ed., op. cit., 164.
178 Ibid. 143.
179 Manso, op. cit., 304.
180 Mailer, *The Armies of the Night*, 93.
181 Ibid. 153.
182 Ernest Van Den Haag, *The Jewish Mystique*, 147.
183 Philip Roth, *My Life as a Man*, 182-183.
184 Saul Bellow, *The Dangling Man*, 9
185 Mary MacCarthy, "The Genial Host", *The Company She Keeps*, 150.
186 Guttmann, *The Jewish Writer in America: Assimilation and Crisis*, 154.
187 Kaufmann, op. cit., 102.
188 Mailer, *Advertisements for Myself*, 9.
189 Rollyson, op. cit., 12.
190 Manso, op. cit., 54.
191 Mailer, *The Armies of the Night*, 93.
192 Ibid. 26.
193 Rollyson, op. cit., 12.
194 Mailer, *The Naked and the Dead*, 336.
195 Myron S. Kauffmann, *Remember Me to God*, 188.
196 Mills, op. cit., 64.
197 Manso, op. cit., 62.
198 Rollyson, op. cit., 11.
199 Dearborn, op. cit., 19.
200 Rollyson, op. cit., 27.
201 Manso, op. cit., 179.
202 Rollyson, op. cit., 17.
203 Mills, op. cit., 64.
204 Mailer, *Advertisements for Myself*, 72.
205 Mailer, *Marilyn*, 30.
206 Ibid. 19.
207 Ibid. 119.
208 Mailer, *Harlot's Ghost*, 752.
209 Norman Mailer, "A Harlot High and Low", *Pieces*, 166.

ENDNOTES

210. Ibid. 160.
211. Saul Bellow, *Henderson the Rain King*, 191.
212. Bellow, *The Adventures of Augie March*, 485.
213. Leslie Fiedler, "Jewish Americans, Go Home!", *Waiting for the End*, 97.
214. Fiedler, "Going for the Ball", *Fiedler on the Roof: Essays on Literature and Jewish Identity*, 114-115.
215. Mailer, *Death for the Ladies (and other Disasters)*.
216. Kate Millet, *Sexual Politics*, 325.
217. Fiedler, "Going for the Ball", 112.
218. Fiedler, "Jewish Americans, Go Home!", 100.
219. Ibid. 102.
220. Adele Mailer, op. cit., 314.
221. Mailer, *Cannibals and Christians*, 25.
222. Mailer, *The Presidential Papers*, 184.
223. Norman Mailer, *Genius and Lust: a Journey Through the Major Writings of Henry Miller*, 104.
224. Mailer, *Cannibals and Christians*, 17, 25.
225. Norman Mailer, *Miami and the Siege of Chicago*, 35.
226. Lennon, ed., op. cit., 67.
227. Adele Mailer, op. cit., 255.
228. Norman Podhoretz, *Ex-Friends: Falling Out With Allen Ginsberg, Lionel and Diana Trilling, Lillian Hellman, Hannah Arendt, and Norman Mailer*, 217.
229. Dearborn, op. cit., 356.
230. Manson, op. cit., 602.
231. Rollyson, op. cit., 278.
232. Mailer, *Harlot's Ghost*, 693.
233. Dearborn, op. cit., 354.
234. Mailer, *The Armies of the Night*, 54.
235. Norman Mailer, *Tough Guys Don't Dance*, 18.
236. Mailer, *The Prisoner of Sex*, 164-165.
237. Mailer, *Harlot's Ghost*, 144.
238. Mailer, *Tough Guys Don't Dance*, 125.
239. Florence King, *WASP, Where Is Thy Sting?*, 84.

240 Mailer, *Cannibals and Christians*, 139.
241 Fiedler, "Going For the Ball", 111.
242 Rollyson, op. cit., 157.
243 Ibid. 158.
244 Ibid.
245 Ibid.
246 Norman Mailer, Personal interview, 18 January 1991.
247 Peter Shrag, *The Decline of the WASP*, 22.

Chapter III

248 Eva Figes, *Patriarchal Attitudes*, 41
249 Baum, Hyman, Michel, op. cit., 10.
250 Mary Antin, *The Promised Land*, 33.
251 Howe, op. cit., 267.
252 Roth, *My Life as a Man*, 118.
253 Carol Zonis Yee, "Why Aren't We Writing About Ourselves?", *Images Of Women In Fiction: Feminist Perspectives*, ed. Susan Koppelman, 132.
254 Leslie Fiedler, *Love and Death in the American Novel*, 36.
255 Joanna Russ, "What Can a heroine Do? Or Why Women Can't Write?", *Images of Women in Fiction: Feminist Perspectives*, ed. Susan Koppelman, 6.
256 Mailer, *An American Dream*, 36.
257 Mailer, *Marilyn*, 15.
258 Ibid. 100.
259 Ibid. 97.
260 Mailer, *An American Dream*, 173.
261 Norman Mailer, *Of a Fire on the Moon*, 7.
262 Buzz Farber, "Mailer on Marriage and Women", *Viva* (October 1973), 7.
263 Mailer, *The Naked and the Dead*, 186.
264 Ibid. 415-416.
265 Paul Carroll, "Interview With Norman Mailer", *Norman Mailer: The Man and His Work*, ed. Robert F. Lucid, 293.

266 Mailer, *The Naked and the Dead*, 487.
267 Mailer, *The Prisoner of Sex*, 485.
268 Frederic Jameson, "The Great American Hunter, or Ideological Content in the Novel", *College English* 34 (1972), 186.
269 Mailer, *The Prisoner of Sex*, 155.
270 Millet, *Sexual Politics*, 327.
271 Mailer, *The Naked and the Dead*, 416.
272 Mailer, *An American Dream*, 82.
273 Ibid. 100.
274 Mailer, *Advertisements For Myself*,
275 Mailer, *The Prisoner of Sex*, 47.
276 Ibid. 450.
277 Mailer, *The Presidential Papers*, 141.
278 Mailer, *Advertisements For Myself*, 449.
279 Ibid. 450.
280 Mailer, *An American Dream*, 45.
281 Mailer, *The Prisoner of Sex*, 23.
282 Nona Balakina, The Prophetic Vogue of the Anti-Heroine", *Southwest Review* (Spring 1962) 139.
283 Mailer, *The Deer Park*, 316-317.
284 Ibid. 198.
285 Ibid. 164.
286 Mailer, *The Naked and the Dead*, 332.
287 Mailer, *An American Dream*, 109.
288 Mailer, *The Deer Park*, 130.
289 Alfred Kazin, *Bright Book of Life: American Novelists and Storytellers, from Hemingway to Mailer*, 155.
290 Mailer, *An American Dream*, 136.
291 Ibid. 17.
292 Ibid. 27.
293 Ibid. 34.
294 Ibid. 23, 133.
295 Ibid. 216.
296 Ibid. 44.
297 Ibid. 17.

298 Ibid. 13.
299 Mailer, *The Deer Park*, 109.
300 Ibid. 285.
301 Ibid. 243.
302 Mailer, *Advertisements For Myself*, 447.
303 Ibid.
304 Ibid. 448.
305 Ibid.
306 Ibid.
307 Ibid. 449.
308 Mailer, *An American Dream*, 44.
309 Mailer, *The Prisoner of Sex*, 20.
310 Ibid. 28.
311 Ibid. 19.
312 Ibid. 13.
313 Ibid. 48-49.
314 Ibid. 12.
315 Lennon, ed., op. cit., 152.
316 Norman Mailer, *St. George and the Godfather*, 59.
317 Ibid.
318 Mailer, *The Presidential Papers*, 131.
319 Mailer, *Pontifications*, op cit., 100.
320 Mailer, *St. George and the Godfather*, 58.
321 Mailer, *An American Dream*, 44.
322 Adele Mailer, op cit., 282.
323 Norman Mailer, *The Time of Our Time*, 1129.
324 Mailer, *The Presidential Papers*, 143-144.
325 Dearborn, op cit., 293.
326 Diana Trilling, *We Must March My Darlings: A Critical Decade*, 201.
327 David Kenby, "The Contender", *The New Yorker* (20 April 1978), 70.
328 Susan Weidman Schneider, *Jewish and Female: Choices and Changes in Our Lives Today*, 504.
329 Mailer, *The Prisoner of Sex*, 21.

330 Mailer, *Cannibals and Christians*, 133.
331 Mary Ellmann, *Thinking About Women*, 46.
332 Dearborn, op. cit., 401.
333 Ibid.
334 Laura Adams, "Existential Aesthetics: An Interview With Norman Mailer", *Partisan Review* 42 (1975), 197.
335 Mailer, *The Prisoner of Sex*, 21.
336 Mailer, *Barbary Shore*, 171.
337 Mailer, *The Naked and the Dead*, 491.
338 Roth, *Portnoy's Complaint*, 153.
339 Mailer, *The Prisoner of Sex*, 64.
340 Mailer, *Of a Fire on the Moon*, 119.
341 Mailer, *The Armies of the Night*, 192.
342 Mailer, *Of a Fire on the Moon*, 464.
343 Farber, op. cit., 76.
344 Norman Mailer, *Why Are We in Vietnam?*, 126.
345 Cantor, op. cit., 216-219.
346 Mills, op. cit., 400.
347 Dearborn, op. cit., 198.
348 Rollyson, op. cit., 34.
349 Dearborn, op. cit., 39.
350 Schwartz, op. cit., 141.
351 Rollyson, op. cit., 63.
352 Dearborn, op. cit., 39.
353 Laura Cunningham, "Prisoners of Mailer:: Bea, Adele, Lady Jeanne, Beverly, Carol, et al.", *Cosmopolitan* (January 1963), 108.
354 Manso, op. cit., 334.
355 Rollyson, op. cit., 144-145.
356 Dearborn, op. cit., 89.
357 Manso, op. cit., 345.
358 Dearborn, op. cit., 174.
359 Rollyson, op. cit., 146.
360 Manso, op. cit., 346.
361 Roth, *Portnoy's Complaint*, 235.

362 Dearborn, op. cit., 222.
363 Ibid. 196.
364 Rollyson, op. cit., 177.
365 Ibid. 299.
366 Ibid. 302.
367 Ibid.
368 Mills, op. cit., 341.
369 Manso, op. cit., 570.
370 Ibid. 572.
371 Mills, op. cit., 417.
372 Rollyson, op. cit., 329.
373 *The New York Post*, 15 September 1995, 6.
374 Carole Mallory, *Flash*, 77.
375 Ibid. 64.
376 *The NewYork Post*, op. cit.
377 Millet, op. cit., 314.
378 Mailer, *Cannibals and Christians*, 199.
379 Lennon, ed., op. cit., 345.

Chapter IV

380 Mailer, *Advertisements for Myself*, 73.
381 Mailer, *The Armies of the Night*, 320.
382 Lennon, ed., op. cit., 295.
383 Mailer, *Advertisements for Myself*, 1.
384 T.B. Gilmore, "Fury of a Hebrew Prophet", *North American Review* 251 (November 1966) 43-44.
385 Rollyson, op. cit., 47.
386 *NewYork Times*, 7 May 1998, E1.
387 Mailer, *Cannibals and Christians*, 77.
388 Thornstein Veblen, "The Intellectual Pre-Eminence of Jews in Modern Europe", *Political Science Quarterly* 34 (March 1919) 38.
389 Isaac Rosenfeld, *An Age of Enormity: Life andWritings in the Forties and Fifties*, 69.

390 "Our Country and Our Culture: A Symposium", op. cit., 299.
391 Brian Paul Barry, "The Theologian and the Heretic: The Social and Political Thought of William Buckley Jr. And Norman Mailer" (Ph.D. dissertation, Syracuse Univ., 1974) 63.
392 Quoted in Irving Malin, *Jews and Americans*, 175.
393 Mailer, *Advertisements for Myself*, 324.
394 Mailer, *The Presidential Papers*, 4.
395 Quoted in Nigel Leigh, *Radical Fictions and the Novels of Norman Mailer*, 152.
396 Quoted in Louis Ruchames, "Jewish Radicalism in the United States", *The Ghetto and Beyond*, ed., 228-229.
397 James Toback, "Norman Mailer Today", *Commentary* 44, n°4 (October 1967) 68.
398 *Figaro*, 25 March 1998, 21.
399 Mills, op. cit., 168.
400 Ibid. 188.
401 Mailer, *Advertisements for Myself*, 306.
402 Ibid. 271.
403 Ibid. 325.
404 Ibid. 301.
405 Helen Weinberg, *The New Novel in America: The Kafkan Mode in Contemporary Fiction*, 126.
406 Ibid.
407 Martin Buber, *Good and Evil*, 91.
408 Mailer, *The Deer Park*, 356.
409 Mailer, *Cannibals and Christians*, 234.
410 Ibid. 235.
411 Kaufmann, op. cit., 131.
412 Mailer, *Advertisements for Myself*, 307.
413 Mailer, *An American Dream*, 203.
414 Mailer, *Advertisements for Myself*, 315.
415 Mailer, *An American Dream*, 38.
416 Quoted in Gersion Appel, *A Philisophy of Mitzvot*, 89.
417 Abraham Joshua Heschel, *God in Search of Man: A Philosophy of Judaism*, 307.

418 Mailer, *Advertisements for Myself*, 240.
419 Ibid. 313.
420 Mailer, *The Prisoner of Sex*, 117.
421 Mailer, *An American Dream*, 164.
422 Mailer, *Pontifications*, 106.
423 Mills, op. cit., 181.
424 Mailer, *Advertisements for Myself*, 312.
425 Mills, op. cit., 180.
426 Mailer, *Advertisements for Myself*, 309.
427 Manso, op. cit., 258.
428 Rollyson, op. cit., 114.
429 Ibid. 214.
430 Norman Mailer, "Responses and Reactions", *Commentary* 34, n°6 (December 1962) 505.
431 Ibid.
432 Ibid.
433 Ibid.
434 Dearborn, op. cit., 192.
435 Mailer, *The Presidential Papers*, 214.
436 Mailer, *Of a Fire on the Moon*, 468.
437 Aryeh Rubinstein, comp. *Hasidism*, 1.
438 Mailer, "Responses and Reactions", 505.
439 Mailer, *Cannibals and Christians*, 377.
440 Ibid. 215.
441 Mailer, *An American Dream*, 204.
442 Oriancia Fallaci, *The Egotists: Sixteen Surprising Interviews*, 4.
443 Norman Mailer, "Responses and Reactions", 504.
444 Heschel, op. cit., 341.
445 Mailer, *The Prisoner of Sex*, 137.
446 Quoted in Malin, op. cit., 13-103.
447 Mashey Maurice Bernstein, "The Individual as a Work of Art: Jewish and Puritan Values in the Fiction of Norman Mailer and Edward Lewis Wallant" (Ph.D. dissertation, Univ. Of California at Santa Barbara, 1977) 11.
448 Lennon, ed., op. cit., 14.

449 Elie Wiesel, "Jewish Values in the Post-Holocaust Future", *Judaism* XVI (Summer 1967) 281.
450 Elie Wiesel, *The Gates of the Forest*, 195.
451 Mailer, "Responses and Reactions", op. cit., 504.
452 Mailer, *The Naked and the Dead*, 206.
453 Mailer, *The Presidential Papers*, 193.
454 Ibid.
455 Ibid. 192.
456 Ibid.
457 Lennon, ed., op. cit., 357.
458 Mailer, *Of a Fire on the Moon*, 467-468.
459 Quoted in Louis Finkelstein, *The Jews: Their History, Culture and Religion*, 2 vols., 2: 936.
460 Mailer, *An American Dream*, 197.
461 Mailer, *The Gospel According to the Son*, 240.
462 Harold Bloom, "Sex, Creativity and God", *Norman Mailer*, 167-182.
463 Mailer, *An American Dream*, 9, 28.
464 Mailer, *Marilyn*, 242.
465 Joshua Trachenberg, *Jewish Magic and Superstition: A Study in Folk Religion*, 20, 67.
466 Mailer, *An American Dream*, 45.
467 Mailer, *Advertisements for Myself*, 309.
468 Louis M. Epstein, *Sex, Laws and Customs in Judaism*, 23.
469 Ibid. 146.
470 Mailer, *The Prisoner of Sex*, 189.
471 Mailer, *An American Dream*, 35.
472 Mailer, *Pontifications*, 54.
473 Norman Mailer, *Pieces*, 11.
474 Christopher Ricks, "Mailer's Primal Words", *Grand Street* 3 (Autumn 1983) 164.
475 Mailer, *An American Dream*, 98.
476 Ibid. 175.
477 Herbert Weiner, *9 ½ Mystics: The Cabala Today*, 204.
478 Irving Howe and Eliezer Greenberg, ed., *A Treasury: Yiddish Short Stories*, 9.

479 Mailer, *Pontifications*, 97.
480 Brock Brower, "Always the Contender", *Life*, 24 March 1965, 102.
481 Sam B. Girgus, "Song of Himself: Norman Mailer", *The New Covenant*, 143.
482 Mailer, *The Naked and the Dead*, 483.
483 Kaufmann, op. cit., 105.
484 Mailer, *Harlot's Ghost*, 76.
485 Ibid. 61.
486 Ibid. 528.
487 Toback, op. cit., 68.
488 Manso, op. cit., 471.
489 Mailer, *The Prisoner of Sex*, 183.

Chapter V

490 Leslie Fiedler, "The Jew in the American Novel", 2 vols, 2:112.
491 Mailer, *The Naked and the Dead*, 85.
492 Ibid. 84.
493 Mailer, *Advertisements For Myself*, 171.
494 Ibid. 175.
495 Mailer, "Responses and Reactions", 505.
496 Mailer, *Cannibals and Christians*, 43.
497 Ibid. 44.
498 Peter Manso, ed., *Running Against the Machine: The Mailer-Breslin Campaign*, 139.
499 Quoted in Stephen D. Isaacs, *Jews and American Politics*, 158.
500 Ernest Van Den Haag, *The Jewish Mystique*, 139.
501 Mailer, *Cannibals and Christians*, 3.
502 Jong, op. cit., 61.
503 Harold E. Quinley and Charles Y. Glock, *Anti-Semitism in America*, 36.
504 Van Den Haag, op. cit., 171-172
505 Kurt Lewin, *Resolving Social Conflicts: Field Theory in Social Science*, 137.

506 Mailer, *Advertisements For Myself*, 461.
507 Quoted in Nathan and Ruth Perlmutter, *The Real Anti-Semitism in America*, 188.
508 Karl Marx, "On the Jewish Question", *Karl Marx: Early Writings*, ed T.B. Bottomore, 34.
509 Isaacs, op. cit., 65.
510 Dearborn, op. cit., 396.
511 Mailer, *The Presidential Papers*, 129.
512 Dearborn, op. cit., 395.
513 Mailer, *Saint George and the Godfather*, 54.
514 Manso, op. cit., 226.
515 Mailer, *The Presidential Papers*, 11.
516 Mailer, *The Executioner's Song*, 953.
517 Carl Rollyson, op. cit., 316.
518 Ibid. 306.
519 Dearborn, op. cit., 361.
520 Arthur Herzberg, *The Jews in America: Four Centuries of an Uneasy Encounter: A History*, 201.
521 Mills, op. cit., 97.
522 Mark Shechner, *After the Revolution: Studies in the Contemporary American Imagination*, 161.
523 Mailer, *Barbary Shore*, 218.
524 Ibid. 277-278.
525 Ibid. 279.
526 Ibid. 282.
527 Ibid. 283.
528 Mailer, *Advertisements for Myself*, 359.
529 Ibid. 60.
530 Lennon, op. cit., 68.
531 Mailer, *The Armies of the Night*, 208.
532 Ibid. 47.
533 Mailer, *Miami and the Siege of Chicago*, 63.
534 Mailer, *St George and the Godfather*, 138.
535 Dearborn, op. cit., 271.
536 Manso, ed., op. cit., 11-12.

537　Ibid. 284.
538　Ibid. 126.
539　Ibid. 56.
540　Ibid. 227-228.
541　Dearborn, op. cit., 261.
542　Ibid. 271.
543　Mailer, *The Time of Our Time*, 1084.
544　Jean-Paul Sartre, *Anti-Semite and Jew*, 26.
545　Mailer, *Miami and the Siege of Chicago*, 53.

Chapter VI

546　William J. Weatherby, *Squaring Off: Mailer vs. Baldwin*, 63.
547　Ibid. 36.
548　Mailer, *The Naked and the Dead*, 69.
549　Ibid. 234.
550　Ibid. 73.
551　Ibid. 375.
552　Mailer, *Advertisements for Myself*, 303.
553　Fiedler, "Jewish Americans, Go Home!", 96.
554　Norman Mailer, *The Fight*, 132.
555　Ibid. 41.
556　Leslie Fiedler, "The Jig is Up!", *Waiting For the End*, 132.
557　Lenora Bersen, *The Negroes and the Jews*, 194.
558　Mailer, *Advertisements for Myself*, 301.
559　Ibid. 302-303.
560　Quoted in Stephen D. Isaacs, *Jews and American Politics*, 55.
561　James Baldwin, *Nobody Knows My Name: More Notes of a Native Son*, 217.
562　Mailer, *The Presidential Papers*, 187.
563　Ibid. 188.
564　Ibid. 189.
565　Ibid. 202.
566　Ibid. 203.

567 Ibid.
568 Ibid. 241.
568 Ibid. 240.
570 Ibid. 241.
571 Ibid. 266.
572 Mailer, *The Fight*, 72.
573 James Toback, "Norman Mailer Today", *Commentary* 44 n°4 (October 1967) 71.
574 Norman Podhoretz, "The Know-Nothing Bohemians", *Partisan Review* 25 (Spring 1958), 311.
575 Lennon, ed., op. cit., 121.
576 Mailer, *Advertisements for Myself*, 295.
577 Ibid. 296.
578 Manso, op. cit., 255.
579 Mailer, *Advertisements for Myself*, 330.
580 John Wenke, *Mailer's America*, 78.
581 John R. Cooley, *Savages and Naturals: Black Portraits by White Writers in Modern American Literature*, 78.
582 Baldwin, op. cit., 217.
583 Ibid. 220.
584 Ibid. 230.
585 Ibid. 228.
586 Weatherby, op. cit. 78.
587 Mailer, *The Presidential Papers*, 211.
588 Eldridge Cleaver; *Soul on Ice*, 98.
589 Ibid.
590 Ibid.
591 Ibid. 164.
592 Ibid.
593 Ibid. 111.
594 Mailer, *An American Dream*, 183.
595 Ibid. 180, 189-190.
596 Ibid. 190.
597 Ibid. 189.
598 Ibid. 191.

599 Ibid.
600 Cooley, op. cit., 153.
601 Mailer, *An American Dream*, 192.
602 Mailer, *Why Are We in Vietnam?*, 26-27.
603 Ibid. 161.
604 Ibid. 110.
605 Arnold Foster and Benjamin R. Epstein, *The New Anti-Semitism*, 176.
606 Norman Mailer, *The Idol and the Octopus: Political Writings on the Kennedy and Johnson Administration*, 125-126.
607 Norman Mailer, *Existential Errands*, 270.
608 Huey L. Perry and Ruth B. White, "Relationships Between Blacks and Whites", *Phylon* 47, n°1 (1986) 55-56.
609 Bladwin, op. cit., 68.
610 Quoted in Nathan and Ruth Anne Perlmutter, op. cit., 188.
611 Ernest Van Den Haag, op. cit. 103.
612 Mailer, *The Armies of the Night*, 118.
613 Ibid. 120.
614 Mailer, *Cannibals and Christians*, 61.
615 Mailer, *Existential Errands*, 267.
616 Mailer, *The Armies of the Night*, 250.
617 Ibid. 134.
618 Mailer, *Miami and the Siege of Chicago*, 51, 53.
619 Ibid. 52.
620 Weatherby, op. cit., 78.
621 Mailer, *Miami and the Siege of Chicago*, 214.
622 Mailer, *The Fight,* 35.
623 Ibid. 37.
624 Gerald S. Strober, *American Jews: Community in Crisis*, 123.
625 Mailer, *Existential Errands*, 267.
626 Mailer, *Tough Guys Don't Dance*, 26.
627 Ibid. 198.
628 Ibid. 26.
629 Ibid.
630 Mailer, *The Presidential Papers*, 255.

631 Mailer, *Tough Guys Don't Dance*, 47.
632 Ibid.
633 Ibid. 138.
634 Mailer, *The Time of Our Time*, 1086.
635 Cooley, op. cit., 150-151.
636 Mailer, *The Presidential Papers*, 255.
637 Ibid. 242.
638 Mailer, *The Fight*, 71.
639 Mailer, *The Faith of Graffiti*, 5.

Epilogue

640 Norman Mailer, *The Castle in the Forest*, 80.
641 Ibid. 9.
642 Ibid. 200.
643 Ibid. 446.
644 Ibid. 71-72.
645 Ibid. 405-406.
646 Ibid. 405.

Conclusion

647 Norman Mailer, *Why Are We At War?*, 93.
648 Mailer, *The Naked and the Dead*, 82.
649 Ibid.
650 Ibid.
651 Ibid. 152-153.
652 *New York Times*, 22 January, 2003.

GENERAL BIBLIOGRAPHY

Abbott, Jack Henry. *In the Belly of the Beast: Letters from Prison.* N.Y.: Random House, 1981.

Adams, Laura. "Existential Aesthetics: An Interview with Norman Mailer." 42 (1975): 197-214.

——. *Existential Battles: The Growth of Norman Mailer.* Athens: Ohio State Univ. Press, 1976.

——. *Norman Mailer: A Comprehensive Bibliography.* Metuchen, N.J.: Scarecrow, 1974.

——. *Will the Real Norman Mailer Please Stand Up?* Port Washington. N.Y.: Kennikat, 1974.

Aiken, Lisa. *To Be a Jewish Woman.* London and Northvale, N.J.: Jason Aronson, Inc., 1992.

Aldrich, Jr. *Old Money: The Mythology of America's Upper Class.* N.Y.: Alfred A. Knopf, 1988.

Alego, Ann M. *The Courtroom as Forum: Homicide Trials by Dreiser, Wright, Capote, and Mailer.* N.Y.: Peter Lang, 1996.

Alter, Robert. *After the Tradition; Essays on Modern Jewish Writing.* N.Y.: Dutton, 1969.

Angoff, Charles. *Journey to the Dawn.* N.Y.: Beechhurst Press, 1951.

——. *Memory of Autumn.* N.Y.: A.S. Barnes and Co., 1968.

Angoff, Charles and Levin, Meyer. eds. *The Rise of American Jewish Literature; An Anthology of Selections from the Major Novels.* N.Y.: Simon and Schuster, 1970.

Antin, Mary. *The Promised Land.* Princeton, N.J.: Princeton Univ. Press, 1969.

Appel, Gersion. *A Philosophy of Mizvot.* N.Y.: KTAV Publishing House, Inc., 1975.

Baker, Adrienne. *The Jewish Woman in Contemporary Society: Transitions and Traditions.* London: Macmillan Press, 1993.

Balakian, Nona. "The Prophetic Vogue of the Anti-Heroine." *Southwest Review* 47 (Spring 1962): 134-141.

Baldwin, James. *Nobody Knows My Name: More Notes of a Native Son.* N.Y.: The Dial Press, 1961.

Baum, Charlotte, Hyman, Paula and Michel, Sonia. *The Jewish Woman in America.* N.Y.: Dial Press, 1976.

Baumbach, Jonathan. *The Landscape of Nightmare: Studies in the Contemporary American Novel.* N.Y.: N.Y. Univ. Press, 1965.

Begiebing, Robert J. *Acts of Regeneration: Allegory and Archetype in the Works of Norman Mailer.* Columbia: Univ. of Missouri Press, 1980.

Bellow, Saul. *Henderson the Rain King.* London: Penguin Books, Ltd., 1966.

—. *Herzog.* N.Y.: Viking Press, 1964.

—. *The Adventures of Augie March.* London: Penguin Books, Ltd., 1996.

—. *Mr. Sammler's Planet.* London: Penguin Books, Ltd., 1985.

—. *The Dangling Man.* Weidenfeld and Nicolson, 1949.

Berson, Lenora E. *The Negroes and the Jews.* N.Y.: Random House, 1971.

Besdine, Matthew. "Jewish Mothering." *The Jewish Spectator* (February 1970): 7-10.

Bienstock, Beverly. "The Changing Image of the American Mother." *Changing Images of the Family*, eds. Virginia Tufte and Barbara Myerhoff. New Haven and London: Yale Univ. Press, 1979. 173-191.

Birmingham, Stephen. *Our Crowd.* London: Futura Publications, 1985.

Blankfort, Michael. *Behold the Fire: A Novel Based on Events that took Place Between 1914 and 1918 in London, Cairo, Constantinople, Jerusalem, and Some of the Villages of Palestine.* N.Y.: The New American Library, 1965.

—. *The Juggler.* Boston: Little, Brown, 1952.

Bloom, Solomon F. "The Saga of America's Russian Jews." *Commentary* 1 n°4 (February 1946): 1-7.

Bilik, Dorthy Seidman. *Immigrant-Survivors: Post-Holocaust Consciousness in Recent Jewish American Fiction*. Middletown, Conn.: Wesleyn Univ. Press, 1981.

Braudy, Leo. ed. *Norman Mailer: A Collection of Critical Essays*. Englewood Cliffs, N.J.: Prentice-Hall, 1972.

Breines, Paul. *Tough Jews: Political Fantasies and the Moral Dilemma of American Jewry*. N.Y.: Basic Books, 1990.

Brinig, Myron. *This Man is My Brother*. N.Y.: Farrar and Rinehart, 1932.

Brookhaiser, Richard. *The Way of the Wasp: How it Made America and How it Can Save It, So to Speak*. N.Y.: The Free Press, 1991.

Brossard, Chandler. *Who Walks in Darkness?* London: Lehman, 1952.

Brower, Brock. "Always the Contender." *Life*, 24 March 1965, 94-96, 98, 100, 102-115, 117.

Buber, Martin. *Good and Evil*. N.Y.: Charles Scribner's Sons, 1952.

—. *The Tales of the Hasidim, The Early Masters*. N.Y.: Schocken Books, 1947.

Bufithis, Philip H. *Norman Mailer*. N.Y.: Frederick Ungar, 1978.

Busch, Frederick. "The Whale as Shaggy Dog: Melville and The Man Who Studied Yoga." *Modern Fiction Studies*. 19 n°2 (Summer 1973): 193-206.

Cahan, Abraham. *The Rise of David Levinsky*. N.Y.: Harper and Row Bros., 1917.

Cantor, Aviva. *Jewish Women Jewish Men: The Legacy of Patriarchy in Jewish Life*. San Francisco: Harper, 1995.

Capote, Truman. *Breakfast at Tiffany's: A Short Novel*. N.Y.: The American Library, 1958.

—. *In Cold Blood: A True Account of a Multiple Murder and Its Consequences*. London: H. Hamilton, 1966.

Carroll, Paul. "Interview with Norman Mailer." *Norman Mailer: The Man and His Work*. ed. Robert F. Lucid. Boston: Little, Brown and Co., 1971. 259-295.

Chametzy, Jules. et al., eds. *Jewish American Literature: A Norton Anthology*. N.Y. and London: W.W. Norton and Co., 2001.

Chapman, Abraham. ed. *Jewish American Literature: An Anthology of*

Fiction, Poetry, Autobiography. N.Y.: New American Library, 1974.
Cleaver, Eldridge. *Soul on Ice.* N.Y.: McGraw-Hill Book Co., 1968.
Cohen, Bernard. *Sociological Changes in American Jewish Life as Reflected in Selected Jewish Literature.* Rutherford, Madison and Teaneck, Wisc.: Farleigh Dickinson Univ. Press, 1972.
Contemporary American Literature. 1945-1972. N.Y.: Ungar, 1973.
Cooley, John R. *Savages and Naturals: Black Portraits by White Writers in Modern American Literature.* Newark, N.J.: Univ. of Del. Press, 1982.
Cory, Donald Webster. *The Homosexual in America; A Subjective Approach.* N.Y.: Greenberg, 1951.
Cunningham, Laura. "Prisoners of Mailer: Bea, Adele, Lady Jeanne, Beverly, Carol, et al." *Cosmopolitan* (January 1963): 104-109.
Dahlberg, Edward. *Those Who Perish.* N.Y.: The John Co., 1934.
Dearborn, Mary V. *Mailer: A Biography.* Boston and N.Y.: Houghton Mifflin Co., 1999.
Denby, David. "The Contender." *New Yorker,* 20 April 1998, 60-66, 68-71.
Dinnerstein, Leonard. *Uneasy at Home: Anti-Semitism and the American Jewish Experience.* N.Y.: Columbia Univ. Press, 1987.
Drament, Carol. ed. *Jewish Marital Status.* Northvale, N.J.: Jason Aronson, Inc., 1989.
Dreiser, Theodore. *Letters,* 3 vols. Phil., Penn.: Univ. of Penn. Press, 1959.
Eckardt, A. Roy. *Black-Woman-Jew: Three Wars for Human Liberation.* Bloomington and Indianapolis: Ind. Univ. Press, 1989.
Ehrlich, Robert. *Norman Mailer: The Radical as Hipster.* Metuchen, N.J. and London: The Scarecrow Press, Inc., 1978.
Eliot, T.S. *Collected Poems 1909-1935.* N.Y.: Harcourt, Brace and Co., 1930.
Ellmann, Mary, *Thinking About Women.* N.Y.: Harcourt, Brace Jovanovitch, 1968.
Emerson, Ralph Walden. *Journals,* 10 vols. Boston: Centenary Edition, 1909-1914.
— . *The Sabbath.* N.Y.: Farrar, Straus and Young, 1952.

Epstein, Louis M. *Sex, Laws and Customs in Judaism*. N.Y.: Bloch Publishing Co., 1948.

Fallaci. *The Egotists: Sixteen Surprising Interviews*. Chicago: Henry Regnery Co., 1963.

Farber, Buzz. "Mailer on Marriage and Women." *Viva* (October 1973): 74-76, 144, 146, 148, 150, 152.

Farrell, James T. *Studs Lonigan*. N.Y.: The Modern Library, 1938.

Fein, Richard. "Jewish Fiction in America." *Judaism* 24 (Fall 1975): 406-415.

Fetterly, Judith. "An American Dream: Hula, Hula Said the Witches." *The Resisting Reader : A Feminist Approach to America*. Bloomington, Ind.: Indiana Univ. Press. 1978. 154-189, 197-198.

Fiedler, Leslie A. "Genesis: The American-Jewish Novel Throughout the Twenties." *Midstream* 4 (Summer 1958): 21-33.

——. "Going for the Long Ball." *Fiedler on the Roof: Essays on Literature and Jewish Identity*. Boston: David R. Godin, 1991. 111-115.

——. "Jewish-Americans, Go Home!" *Waiting for the End*. N.Y.: Stein and Day, 1968. 89-103.

——. *Love and Death in the American Novel*. N.Y.: Stein and Day, 1966.

——. "Master of Dreams." *Partisan Review* 34 n°3 (Summer 1967): 175-192.

——. "Negroes and Jews." *Fiedler Reader*. N.Y.: Stein and Day Publishers, 1977. 97-107.

——. "Styron's Choice." *Fiedler on the Roof: Essays on Literature and Jewish Identity*. Boston: David R. Godin, 1991. 103-110.

——. "The Breakthrough: The American Jewish Novelist and the Fictional Image of the Jew." *Midstream* 4 (Winter 1958): 15-35.

——. "The Jew as Mythic American." *Ramparts* 2 n°2 (Autumn 1963): 32-48.

——. "The Jew in the American Novel." *The Collected Essays of Leslie Fiedler*. 2 vols. N.Y.: Stein and Day, 1971. 2: 76.

——. "The Jig is Up!" *Waiting for the End*. N.Y.: Stein and Day, 1968. 118-137.

Figes, Eva. *Patriarchal Attitudes*, N.Y.: Stein and Day, 1970.

Fine, David Martin. "In the Beginning: American-Jewish Fiction,

1880-1930." *Handbook of American-Jewish Literature: An Analytic Guide to Topics, Themes, and Sources*. ed. Lewis Fried. N.Y., Westport, Conn. and London: Greenwood Press, 1988.15-34.

Finkelstein, Louis. *The Jews: Their History, Culture, and Religion*. 2 vols. N.Y.: Harper and Row, 1961.

Fitzgerald, F. Scott. *The Great Gatsby*. N.Y.: Charles Scribner's Sons, 1953.

Flaherty, Joe. *Managing Mailer*. N.Y.: Coward-McCann, 1970.

Fleischmann, Wolfgang Bernard. "The Contemporary Jewish Novel in America." *Jahrbuch fur Amerikastudien* 12 (1967): 159-166.

Foster, Arnold and Epstein, Benjamin R. *The New Anti-Semitism*. N.Y.: McGraw-Hill Book Co., 1974.

Freeman, Joseph. *An American Testament: A Narrative of Rebels and Romantics*. N.Y.: Farrar and Rinehart, 1936.

Freud, Sigmund. "Contributions to the Psychology of Love." *Collected Papers*. 4 vols. N.Y.: Basic Books, Inc., 1959. 4: 192-202.

Friedman, Bruce J. *A Mother's Kisses*. N.Y.: Simon and Schuster, 1964.

Fromm, Erich. *The Anatomy of Human Destructiveness*. N.Y., Chicago and San Francisco: Holt, Rinehart and Winston, 1973.

Fuchs, Lawrence II. *The Political Behaviour of American Jews*. Glencoe, Il.: The Free Press, 1956.

Gaer, Joseph and Siegel, Ben. *The Puritan Heritage: America's Roots in the Bible*. N.Y.: The New American Library, 1964.

Gerber, David A. ed. *Anti-Semitism in American History*. Urbana and Chicago: Univ. of Il. Press, 1986.

Gerson, Jessica. "Norman Mailer: Sex, Creativity and God." *Norman Mailer*. ed. Harold Bloom. N.Y.: Chelsea House, N.Y. 1986. 167-182.

Gilmore, T.B. "Fury of a Hebrew Prophet." *North American Review*. 251 (November 1966), 43-44.

Girgus, Sam. "Song of Himself: Norman Mailer." *The New Covenant*. Chapel Hill, N.C. and London: The Univ. of N.C. Press, 1984.

Glazer, Nathan. *American Judaism*. Chicago and London: The Univ. of Chicago Press, 1989.

— . "The Alienation of Modern Man: Some Diagnosis of the Malady." *Commentary* 3 n°4 (April 1947): 378-385.

Glenday, Michael D. *Norman Mailer*. N.Y.: St. Martin's, 1995.

Gold, Michael. *Jews Without Money*. N.Y.: Liveright, 1930.

Goldman, Ari L. *Being Jewish: The Spiritual and Cultural Practice of Judaism Today*. N.Y.: Simon and Schuster, 2000.

Gordon, Albert I. *Jews in Transition*. Minneapolis, Minn.: Univ. of Minn. Press, 1949.

Gordon, Andrew. *An American Dreamer: A Psychological Study of the Fiction of Norman Mailer*. Cranbury, N.J.: Associated Univ. Press, 1980.

Gordon, Graham. "The Naked and the Dead." *Literature and Psychology* n°3-4 (1969): 3-13.

Gorer, Geoffrey. *The American Study in National Character*. N.Y.: Norton, 1948.

Greenberg, Dan. *How to be a Jewish Mother: A Very Lovely Training Manual*. Los Angeles: Price, Stern, Sloan, 1964.

Greer, Germaine. "My Mailer Problem." *Esquire* (September 1971): 90-93, 214, 216.

— . *The Female Eunuch*. N.Y.: McGraw-Hill, 1971.

Gross, Theodore L. ed. *The Literature of American Jews*. N.Y.: The Free Press, 1973.

Gutman, Stanley T. *Mankind in Barbary: The Individual and Society in the Novels of Norman Mailer*. Hanover, N.H.: Univ. Press of New England, 1975.

Guttmann, Allen. "Jewish Radicals, Jewish Writers." *American Scholar* 32 (Autumn 1963): 563-575.

— . "The Conversion of the Jews." *Wisconsin Studies in Contemporary Literature* 6 (Summer 1965): 161-176.

— . *The Jewish Writer in America: Assimilation and the Crisis of Identity*. N.Y.: Oxford Univ. Press, 1971.

Hagar, Jennifer. "Beverly Bentley: A Life in the Theater of Our Times." *P'town Women* (1998): 40-46.

Hamill, Pete. *A Drinking Life*. Boston: Little, Brown, 1994.

Handlin, Oscar. *The Uprooted*. Boston: Little, Brown and Co., 1951.

Hansen, Marcus L. The *Problem of the Third Generation Immigrant*. Rock

Island, Il.: Augustana Historical Society, 1939.

Hansen, Marcus. "The Third Generation in America: A Classic Essay in Immigrant History". *Commentary* 3 n°4 (April 1947): 492-500.

Harap, Louis. *In the Mainstream: the Jewish Presence in Twentieth-Century American Literature, 1950's- 1980's*. Westport, Conn.: Greenwood Press, 1987.151-161.

Harper, Howard M. "Norman Mailer: A Revolution in the Consciousness of Our Time." *Desperate Faith: Study of Bellow, Salinger, Mailer, Baldwin and Updike*. Chapel Hill, Univ. of North Carolina Press, 1967. 96-136.

Hecht, Ben A. *A Jew in Love*. N.Y.: Covici. Fried Publishers, 1931.

Hemingway, Ernest. *The Hemingway Reader*. N.Y.: Scribner, 1953.

Herberg, Will. *Protestant, Catholic and Jew*. Garden City, N.J.: Doubleday and Co., 1960.

Hersey, John. *The Wall*. N.Y.: Knopf, 1950.

Hertzberg, Arthur. *The Jews in America: Four Centuries of an Uneasy Encounter: A History*. N.Y., London, Toronto, Sydney and Tokyo: Simon and Schuster, 1989.

Heschel, Abraham Joshua. *God in Search of Man; A Philosophy of Judaism*. Northvale, N.J. and London: Jason Avonson, 1987.

Hitler, Adolf. *Mein Kampf*. Trans. Ralph Manheim. Pimlico, London, 2005.

Hitler's Table Talk. 1941-1944. London, Weindenfeld and Nicholson, 1953.

Hobson, Laura Z. *Gentleman's Agreement*. N.Y.: Avon Books, 1968.

Howe, Irving and Greenberg, Eliezer. eds. *A Treasury: Yiddish Short Stories*. N.Y.: Schocken Books, 1973.

Howe, Irving. *The World of Our Fathers*. N.Y. and London: Harcourt Brace Jovanovich, 1976.

Howells, William Dean. "Editor's Easy Chair." *Harper's Monthly Magazine* 130 (May 1915): 958.

Isaacs, Stephen D. *Jews and American Politics*. Garden City, N.J.: Doubleday and Co., Inc. 1974.

James, Henry. "The American Scene." *Collected Travel Writings: Great*

Britain and America: English Hours, the American Scene, Other Travels. N.Y.: The Library of America, 1993. 351-736.

Janowsky, Oscar I. *The American Jew: A Reappraisal*. N.Y.: The Jewish Publication Society of America, 1964.

Jetzinger, Franz. *Hitler's Youth*. London: Hutchinson of London Press, 1958.

Jong, Erica. *Fear of Flying*. N.Y.: Rinehart and Winston, 1973.

Jordan, Winthrop D. *White Over Black: American Attitudes Toward the Negro 1550-1812*. N.Y.: Norton, 1977.

Karl, Frederick. *American Fictions, 1940-1980. A Comprehensive History and Critical Evaluation*. N.Y.: Harper and Row, 1983.

Karp, Abraham J. *A History of the American Jews in America*. Northvale, N.J.: Jason Aronson, 1997.

Kaufmann, Donald. *The Countdown (The First Twenty gears)*. Carbondale and Edwardsville, Il. Southern Il. Univ. Press, 1969.

Kaufmann, Myron S. *Remember Me to God*. N.Y. and Philadelphia: J.B. Lippincott and Co., 1957.

Kazin, Alfred. *A Walker in the City*. N.Y.: Harcourt, Brace and World, Inc., 1951.

Kazin, Alfred. *Bright Book of Life*. Boston: Little, Brown and Co., 1971.

Kiell, Norman. *The Psychodynamics of American Jewish Life: An Anthology*. N.Y.: Twayne Publishers, Inc., 1967.

King, Florence. *WASP, Where is Thy Sting?* N.Y.: Stein and Day, 1977.

Knopp, Josephine Zadorsky. *The Trial of Judaism in Contemporary Jewish Writing*. Urbana, Il.: Univ. of Il. Press, 1975.

Koltun, Elizabeth. ed. *The Jewish Woman: New Perspective*. N.Y.: Schocken Books, 1976.

Kraemer, David. ed. *The Jewish Family: Metaphor and Memory*. N.Y. and Oxford: Oxford Univ. Press, 1989.

Kubizek, August. *The Young Hitler I Knew*. Boston: Houghton Mifflin, 1954.

Landow, George P. *Elegant Jeremiahs: The Saga from Carlyle to Mailer*. N.Y.: Cornell Univ. Press, 1982.

Lapham, Lewis H. *Money and Class in America*. N.Y.: Weidenfeld and Nicolson, 1988.

Landis, Joseph C. "Jewish Vision and American Jewish Writers." *Jewish Heritage* 10 (Winter 1967-1968): 10-16.

Lant, Jeffrey. ed. *Our Harvard Reflections on College Life by Twenty-Two Distinguished Graduates.* N.Y.: Taplinger, 1982.

Leeds, Barry H. *The Structured Vision of Norman Mailer.* N.Y.: N.Y. Univ. Press, 1969.

Leigh, Nigel. *Radical Fictions and the Novels of Norman Mailer.* N.Y.: St. Martin's Press, 1990.

Lennon, J. Michael. ed. *Conversations with Norman Mailer.* Jackson, Miss. and London: Univ. Press of Miss., 1988.

——. *Critical Essays on Norman Mailer.* Boston: G.K. Hall, 1986.

Lewin, Kurt. *Resolving Social Conflicts: Field Theory in Social Science.* Washington, D.C.: American Psychological Association, 1997.

Levin, Meyer. *Citizens: A Novel.* N.Y.: Viking Press, 1940.

——. *The Old Bunch.* Secaucus, N.J.: Citadel Press, 1937.

Lewisohn, Ludwig. *The Island Within.* N.Y.: Harper and Bros., 1940.

Lucid, Robert. comp. *Norman Mailer; The Man and His Work.* Boston: Little, Brown, 1971.

Luska, Sidney [pseud.]. *Mrs. Peixanda.* N.Y.: Cassell and Co. Ltd., 1886.

McCarthy, Mary. *The Company She Keeps,* N.Y.: Harcourt, Brace, and World, Inc., 1942.

Mailer, Adele. *The Last Party: Scenes from My Life with Norman Mailer.* N.Y.: Barricade Books Inc., 1997.

Mailer, Norman. *A Transit to Narcissus.* N.Y.: Howard Fertig, 1978.

——. *Advertisements for Myself.* N.Y.: Henry Holt and Co., 1981.

——. *An American Dream.* N.Y.: Henry Holt and Co., 1965.

——. *Ancient Evenings.* Boston: Little, Brown, 1982.

——. *Barbary Shore.* N.Y. and Toronto: Rinehart and Co., Inc., 1951.

——. *Cannibals and Christians.* N.Y.: Dial Press, 1966.

——. *Death for the Ladies (and other Disasters).* N.Y.: G.P. Putnam's Sons, 1962.

——. *Existential Errands.* Bergenfield, N.J.: The New American Library, 1972.

—. *Genius and Lust: A Journey through the Major Writings of Henry Miller*. N.Y.: Gore Press, Inc., 1976.

—. *Harlot's Ghost*. N.Y.: Random House, 1991.

—. *Marilyn*. N.Y.: Grosset and Dunlop, Inc., 1973.

—. *Miami and the Siege of Chicago*. N.Y.: Donald I. Fine, 1986.

—. "Modes and Mutations: Quick Comments on the American Novel." *Commentary* 41 n°3 (March 1966): 37-40.

—. *Of a Fire on the Moon*. N.Y.: Grove Press, Inc., 1970.

—. *Of Women and Their Elegance*. N.Y.: Pinnacle Books, 1980.

—. "Only in America." *New York Times Review of Books*. 27 March 2003. 49-53.

—. *Oswald's Tale: An American Mystery*. N.Y.: Random House, 1995.

—. *Pieces*. Boston and Toronto: Little, Brown and Co., 1987.

—. *Pontifications*. ed. Michael Lennon. Boston and Toronto : Little, Brown and Co, 1982.

—. *Portrait of Picasso as a Young Man: An Interpretive Biography*. N.Y.: The Atlantic Monthly Press, 1995.

—. "Responses and Reactions." *Commentary* 34 n°6 (December 1962): 504-506.

—. *St. George and the Godfather*. N.Y.: New American Library, 1972.

—. "An American Dream." *Esquire* 61 (April 1964) 97-100, 146-148.

—. *The Armies of the Night: The Novel as History/History as a Novel*. N.Y.: New American Library, 1968.

—. *The Big Empty: dialogues on politics, sex, God, boxing, morality, myth, poker and bad conscience in America*. N.Y.: Nation Books, 2006.

—. *The Castle in the Forest*. N.Y.: Random House, 2007.

—. *The Deer Park*. N.Y. and London: Little, Brown and Co., 1997.

—. *The Deer Park: A Play*. N.Y.: Dial, 1967.

—. *The Essential Mailer*. London: New English Library, 1983.

—. *The Executioner's Song*. Boston and Toronto: Little, Brown and Co., 1979.

—. *The Faith of Graffiti*. N.Y.: Praeger Publishers, 1974.

—. *The Fight*. Boston and Toronto: Little, Brown and Co., 1975.

—. *The Gospel According to the Son*. N.Y.: Random House, 1997.

—. *The Idol and the Octopus: Political Writings on Kennedy and Johnson*. N.Y.: Dell Publishing Co., 1968.
—. *The Modest Gifts*. N.Y.: Random House, N.Y.: 2003.
—. *The Naked and the Dead*. Henry Holt and Co., 1988.
—. *The Presidential Papers*. N.Y.: G.P. Putnam's Sons, 1963.
—. *The Prisoner of Sex*. N.Y.: Donald I. Fine, Inc., 1985.
—. *The Short Fiction of Norman Mailer*. N.Y.: Pinnacle Books, 1967.
—. *The Spooky Art: Some Thoughts on Writing*. N.Y.: Random House, 2003.
—. *The Time of Our Time*. N.Y.: Random House, 1998.
—. *Tough Guys Don't Dance*. N.Y.: Random House, 1984.
—. "What I Think of Artistic Freedom." *Dissent* 2 n°2 (Spring 1955): 98, 192-193.
—. *Why Are We in Vietnam?* N.Y.: Holt, Rinehart and Winston, 1967.
Mailer, Norris Church. *Windchill Summer: A Novel*. N.Y.: Random House, 2000.
Malamud, Bernard. *The Assistant*. N.Y.: Farrar, Straus and Cudahy, 1957.
Malin, Irving and Stark, Edwin. eds. *Breakthrough: A Treasury of Contemporary American-Jewish Literature*. N.Y.: McGraw Hill, 1964.
Malin, Irving. ed. *Contemporary American Jewish Literature: Critical Essays*. Bloomington, Ind. and London: Ind. Univ. Press, 1973.
—. *Jews and Americans*. Carbondale and Edwardsville, Il.: Southern Il. Univ. Press, 1965.
Mallory, Carole. *Flash*. N.Y.: Poseidon Press, 1988.
—. "Norman Mailer: The Power of Sex." *Ms* n°5 (February 1990): 79-83, 146-148.
Manso, Peter. *Mailer*. N.Y.: Simon and Schuster, 1985.
—. ed. *Running Against the Machine: The Mailer-Breslin Campaign*. Garden City, N.J.: Doubleday and Co., Inc., 1974.
Marcus, Jacob R. *The American Jewish Woman: A Documentary History*. N.Y.: KATV Publishing House, 1981.
Marowitz, Sanford D. "Images of America in American-Jewish Fiction." *Handbook of American-Jewish Fiction: An Analytical*

Guide to Topics, Themes, and Sources. ed. Lewis Fried. N.Y., Westport, Conn. and London: Greenwood Press, 1988. 315-354.

Marx, Karl. "On the Jewish Question." *Karl Marx: Early Writings*. ed. T.B. Bottomore. N.Y.: McGraw-Hill, 1964.

Michener, James. *The Source: A Novel*. N.Y.: Random House, 1965.

Middlebrook, Jonathan. *Mailer and the Times of His Time*. San Francisco: Bay Books, 1976.

Miller, Arthur. *Focus*. N.Y.: Avon Books, 1968.

——. *The Death of a Salesman*. N.Y.: Viking Press, 1949.

Millet, Kate. *Sexual Politics*. Garden City, N.J.: Doubleday and Co., 1970.

Mills, Hilary. *Mailer: A Biography*. N.Y.: McGraw-Hill, 1984.

Mirsky, David. "The Jewish Tradition in American Literature." *Traditions of the American Jew*. ed. Stanley M. Wagner. N.Y.: Bloch Publishing, 1947. 956-964.

Moore, Deborah Dash. *At Home in America: Second Generation New York Jews*. N.Y.: Columbia Univ. Press, 1981.

Nine Contemporary Jewish Novelists. "Why I Wrote a Jewish Novel." *Congress Weekly* 18 n°13 (November 1951): 19-24.

Noah, Mordecai M. *The Fortress of Sorrento*. N.Y.: Published by D. Longworth, at the Dramatic Repository, Shakespeare Gallery, 1808.

Odets, Clifford. *Six Plays of Clifford Odets*. N.Y.: The Modem Library, 1939.

"Our Country and Our Culture: A Symposium." *Partisan Review* 19 (May-June 1952): 282-326.

Perlmutter, Nathan and Perlmutter, Ruth Ann. *The Real Anti-Semitism in America*. N.Y.: Arbor House, 1982.

Perry, Huey L. and White, Ruth B. "The Post-Civil Rights Transformation of the Relationship Between Blacks and Jews in the United States." *Pylon* 47 n°1 (1986): 51-61.

Pinsky, David. *The Generations of Noah Edon*. N.Y.: The Macaulay Co., 1931.

Plimpton, George. *Shadow Box*. N.Y.: Putnam's, 1977.

Podhoretz, Norman. *Ex-Friends: Falling Out with Allen Ginsberg, Lionel and Diana Trilling, Lillian Hellman, Hannah Arendt, and Norman Mailer.* N.Y.: Free Press, 1999.

——. *Making It.* N.Y.: Random House, 1967.

——. "The Know-Nothing Bohemians." *Partisan Review* 25 (Spring 1958); 305-318.

——. "The Rise and Fall of the Jewish Novelist." *Jewish Life in America: Historical Perspectives.* ed. Gladys Rosen. N.Y.: KTAV Publishing House, 1978. 141-150.

Pogrebin, Letty Cottin. "Anti-Semitism in the Woman's Movement." *Ms.* (June 1982): 45-48.

——. *Deborah, Golda, and Me: Being Female and Jewish in America.* N.Y.: Crown Publishers, Inc., 1991.

Poirier, Richard. *Norman Mailer.* N.Y.: The Viking Press, 1972.

Popkin, Zelda. *Quiet Street: A Novel.* Philadelphia: Lippincott, 1951.

Porter, Jack Nusan and Dreier, Peter. *Jewish Radicalism: A Selected Anthology.* N.Y.: Grove Press, 1973.

Pound, Ezra. *The Pisan Cantos.* N.Y.: New Direction Books, 1979.

Preston, Charles and Hamilton, Edward A. eds. *Mike Wallace Asks: Highlights from 46 Controversial Interviews.* N.Y.: Simon and Schuster, 1958.

Quest, David. *Sentenced to Death: the American Novel and Capital Punishment.* Jackson, Miss.: Univ. of Miss. Press, 1997.

Quinley, Harold E. and Glock, Charles Y. *Anti-Semitism in America.* N.Y. and London: The Free Press, 1979.

Radford, Jean. *Norman Mailer: A Critical Study.* London and Basingstoke: The Macmillan Press Ltd., 1975.

Rahv, Philip. ed. *A Malamud Reader.* N.Y.: Farrar, Straus and Giroux, 1967.

Reich, William. *The Sexual Revolution: Toward A Self-Governing Character Structure.* N.Y.: Noonday Press, 1962.

Ribalow, Harold U. "American Jewish Writers on Their Judaism." *Judaism* 3 n°4 (Fall 1954): 418-426.

Rich, Adrienne. *Of Woman Born: Motherhood as Experience and Institution.* N.Y.: Norton, 1976.

Ricks, Christopher. "Mailer's Primal Words." *Grand Street* 3 (Autumn 1983): 161-172.
Rideout, Walter B. *The Radical Novel in the United States, 1900-1954.* N.Y.: Hill and Wong, 1956.
Robertiello, M.D., Richard C. and Hoquet, Diana. *The Wasp Mystique.* N.Y.: Donald I. Fine, Inc., 1987.
Rollyson, Carl. *The Lives of Norman Mailer: A Biography.* N.Y.: Paragon House, 1991.
Rosenfeld, Alvin H. "The Progress of the American Novel." *Response* 7 n°1 (Spring 1973): 66-71.
Rosenfeld, Isaac. *An Age of Enormity: Life and Writings in the Forties and Fifties.* N.Y. and Cleveland: The World Publishing Co., 1962.
Rosenthal, Gilbert. ed. *The Jewish Family in a Changing World.* N.Y.: Thomas Yoseloff, 1971.
Rosenthal, Jean. "Norman Mailer: 'Je vis comme un espion vis-à-vis de moi'. " *Magazine Littéraire* (Février 1993): 96-103.
Roth, Henry. *Call it Sleep.* London: M. Joseph, 1934.
Roth, Philip. *Goodbye, Columbus and Five Short Stories.* Boston: Houghton Mifflin, 1959.
— . *My Life as a Man.* N.Y.: Holt, Rinehart and Winston, 1973.
— . *Portnoy's Complaint.* N.Y.: Random House, 1967.
— . *The Ghost Writer.* N.Y.: Farrar, Straus and Giroux, 1979.
Rubinstein, Aryeh comp. *Hasidism.* N.Y. and Paris: Leon Amiel, 1975.
Ruchames, Louis. "Jewish Radicalism in the United States." *The Ghetto and Beyond.* ed. Peter I. Rose. N.Y.: Random House, 1969.228-252.
Ruether, Rosemary Radford. ed. *Religion and Sexism: Images of Woman in the Jewish and Christian Traditions.* N.Y.: Simon and Schuster, 1974.
Russ, Joanna. "What Can a Heroine Do? Or Why Women Can't Write?" *Images of Women in Fiction: Feminist Perspectives.* ed. Susan Koppelman. Bowling Green, Ohio: Bowling Green Univ. Press, 1972.3-20.
Salzman, Jack with Back, Adina and Sorin, Gretchen Sullivan. eds.

Bridges and Boundaries: African Americans and American Jews. N.Y.: George Braziller, Inc., 1992.

Sartre, Jean-Paul. *Anti-Semite and Jew*. Trans. George F. Becker. N.Y.: Schocken Books, 1948.

Savona, Jeannette Laillou. *Le Juif dans le roman américain contemporain*. Ottawa: Didier, 1974.

Schaefer, Richard T. *Racial and Ethnic Groups*. Scott, Foresman and Co.: Glenview, Il., 1988.

Schaeffer, Susan Fromberg. *Anya; A Novel*. N.Y.: Macmillan, 1974.

Schneider, Isidor. *From the Kingdom of Necessity*. N.Y.: G.P. Putnam's Sons, 1935.

Schneider, Susan Weidman. *Jewish and Female: Choices and Changes in Our Lives Today*. N.Y.: Simon and Schuster, 1984.

Schrag, Peter. *The Decline of the Wasp*. N.Y.: Simon and Schuster, 1971.

Scholem, Gershom. *Major Trends in Jewish Mysticism*. N.Y.: Schocken Books, 1961.

Schulberg, Bud. *What Makes Sammy Run?* N.Y.: The Modem Library, 1952.

Schwartz, Gwen Gibson and Wyden, Barbara. *The Jewish Wife*. N.Y.: Peter H. Wyden, Inc., 1969.

Selznick, Gertrude J. *The Tenacity of Prejudice: Anti-Semitism in Contemporary America*. N.Y., Evanston, and London: Harper and Row Publishers, 1969.

Shapiro, Karl. "The Jewish Writer in America." *Defense of Ignorance*. N.Y.: Random House, 1960.

Shatzky, Joel and Taub, Michael. eds. *Contemporary Jewish-American Novelists*. Westport, Conn.: Greenwood Press, 1997.

Shaw, Irwin. *The Young Lions*. N.Y.: Modern Library, 1958.

Shechner, Mark. *After the Revolution: Studies in the Contemporary American Imagination*. Bloomington, Ind.: Ind. Univ. Press, 1987.

Silberman, Charles E. *A Certain People: American Jews and Their Lives Today*. N.Y.: Summit Books, 1985.

——. *American Modernity and Jewish Identity*. N.Y. and London: Tavistock Publications, 1983.

Silverstein, Howard. "Norman Mailer: The Family Romance and Oedipal Fantasy." *American Imago* 34 (Fall 1977): 277-286.

Singer, Isaac Bashevis. *Enemies, a Love Story*. N.Y.: Farrar, Straus and Giroux, 1972.

— . *Of a World That is No More*. N.Y.: Vanguard, 1970.

— . *Love and Exile: A Memoir*. Garden City, N.J.: Doubleday and Co., 1984.

Sklare, Marshall. *America's Jews*. N.Y.: Random House, 1971.

— . *The Jew in American Society*. N.Y.: Behrman House, 1974.

Smith, Bradley F. *Adolf Hitler: His Family, Childhood and Youth*. Stanford, Cal.: Hoover Institution Press (Stanford University), 1967.

Smith, Zena Blau. "In Defense of the Jewish Mother." *Midstream* 13 (February 1967): 42-49.

Solotaroff, Robert. *Down Mailer's Way*. Urbana, Il.: Univ. of Il. Press, 1974.

Sorkin, Adam. ed. *Politics and the Muse: Studies in the American Polities of Recent American Fiction*. Bowling Green, Ohio : Bowling Green State Univ. Popular Press, 1989.

Spilleu, Robert E. ed. et al. *Literary History of the United States*. N.Y.: Macmillan, 1973.

Steinert, Marlis. *Hitler*. Paris: Fayard, 1991.

Stern, Sydney Ladensohn. *Gloria Steinem : Her Passion, Politics, and Mystique*. N.Y. : Birch Lane, 1997.

Strober, Gerard S. *American Jews: Community in Crisis*. Garden City, N.J.: Doubleday and Co., 1974.

Teller, Judd L. *Strangers and Natives: An Evolution of the American Jew from 1921 to the Present*. N.Y.: Delacorte Press, 1968.

"The Playboy Panel: The Womanization of America." *Playboy* (June 1962): 43-50, 133-134, 136, 139-144.

Thomas, Claudine. *Norman Mailer: Le complexe d'Osiris*. Paris: Belin, 1997.

Toback, James. "Norman Mailer Today." *Commentary* 44 n°4 (October 1967): 68-76.

Torres, José, with Bee, Sugar. *Sting Like a Bee: The Muhammad Ali Story*. N.Y.: Abelard Schuman, 1971.

Trachenberg, Joshua. *Jewish Magic and Superstition: A Study in Folk Religion*. N.Y.: Atheneum, 1970.

Trilling, Diana. "The Moral Radicalism of Norman Mailer." *Norman Mailer: The Man and His Work*. ed. Robert F. Lucid. Boston and Toronto: Little, Brown, and Co. 1971. 108-136.

Trilling, Diana. *We Must March My Darlings: A Critical Decade*. N.Y. and London: Harcourt, Brace, Jovanovich, 1972.

"Under Forty: Symposium of American Literature and Younger Generation of American Jews." *Contemporary Jewish Record* 7 n°1 (1944): 3-36.

Updike, John. *Bech*. N.Y.: Knopf, 1970.

Van Den Haag, Ernest. *The Jewish Mystique*. N.Y.: Stein and Day, 1969.

Veblen, Thornstein. "The Intellectual Pre-Eminence of Jews in Modern Europe." *Political Science Quarterly* 34 (March 1919): 33-42.

Walden, Daniel. ed. *On Being Jewish: American Writers from Cahan to Bellow*. Greenwich, Conn.: Fawcett Publications, 1974.

Wallant, Edward Lewis. *The Pawnbrokers*. N.Y.: Harcourt, Brace and World, 1961.

Weatherby, William J. *Squaring Off: Mailer vs. Baldwin*. N.Y.: Mason/Charter, 1977.

Weidman, Jerome. *I Can Get it For You Wholesale*. N.Y.: Modern Library, 1959.

Weinberg, Helen. *The New Novel in America: The Kafkan in Contemporary Fiction*. N.Y.: Cornell Univ. Press, 1970.

Weiner, Herbert. *9 ½ Mystics: The Cabala Today*. N.Y.: Holt, Rinehart and Winston, 1969.

Welch, Susan and Ulrich, Fred. *The Political Life of American Jewish Women*. Fresh Meadows, N.Y.: Biblio Press, 1984.

Wenke, John. *Mailer's America*. Hanover, Mass.: Univ. Press of New England, 1987.

West, Nathaniel. *Miss Lonelyhearts*. London: Picador, 1983.

——. *The Day of the Locust*. N.Y.: Random House, 1935.

——. *The Jew in American Politics*. New Rochelle, N.J.: Arlington House, 1968.

Whitmer, Peter O. *Aquarius Revisited: Seven Who Created the Sixties Counterculture that Changed America*. N.Y.: Macmillan, 1987.
Wiesel, Elie. "Jewish Values in the Post-Holocaust Future." *Judaism* 16 (Summer 1967): 266-299.
——. *The Gates of the Forest*. N.Y.: Holt, Rinehart and Winston, 1966.
Wisse, Ruth R. *The Schlemiel as Modern Hero*. Chicago: Univ. of Chicago Press, 1971.
Wouk, Herman. *Marjorie Morningstar*. N.Y.: Doubleday, 1955.
Yaffee, James. *The American Jews: Portrait of a Split Personality*. N.Y.: Random House, 1968.
Yee, Carol Zonis. "Why Aren't We Writing About Ourselves?" *Images of Women in Fiction: Feminist Perspectives*. ed. Susan Koppelman, Bowling Green, Ohio : Bowling Green Univ. Press, 1972. 116-130.
Yezierska, Anzia. *Hungry Hearts*. Boston and N.Y.: Houghton Mifflin Co., 1920.
Zborowski, Mark and Herzog, Elizabeth. *Life with the People: The Culture of the Shtetl*. N.Y.: Schocken Books, 1952.

Newspaper Articles

New York Times, 7 May 1998, E41.
New York Times, 22 January 2003. E1, E9 and E10.
Figaro, 25 March 1998, 21.
"Mailer's Ex-Lover Writes it Down." *New York Post*. 15 September 1995, 6.

Unpublished manuscripts

Mailer, Norman. *No Percentage*. June-September, 1941.

Conversations and interviews

Mailer, Norman. Conversation. 23 June 2002.
Mailer, Norman. Personal interview. 19 January 1991.
Rembar, Charles. Personal interview. 8 August 1995.

Conferences

Mailer, Norman. "James Jones in America." Lecture at the 12th Annual Symposium of the James Jones Literary Society, American Univ. of Paris. 22 June 2002.

University studies on Mailer

Barry, Brian. "The Theologian and the Heretic: The Social and Political Thought of William Buckley, Jr. and Norman Mailer." Ph.D. diss., Syracuse Univ., 1974.

Bernstein, Mashey Maurice. "The Individual as a Work of Art: Jewish and Puritan Values in the Fiction of Norman Mailer and Edward Lewis Wallant." Ph.D. diss., Univ. of California at Santa Barbara, 1977.

Meyer, Adam. "Co-operation and Conflict: Cross-Ethnicity in Contemporary Jewish-American and Afro-American Literatures." Ph.D. diss. Vanderbilt Univ., 1991.

Paklar, Sarla Gajanan. "The Other Country of Love: Man-Woman Relationships in the Fiction of Roth, Mailer and Malamud." M.A. thesis. Univ. of Baroda, 1989.

Quart, Barbara. "The Treatment of Women in the Work of Three Contemporary Jewish-American Writers: Mailer, Bellow, Roth." Ph.D. diss. N.Y. Univ., 1979.

Silverstein, Howard. "Mailer's Quest for Manhood." Ph.D. diss. N.Y. Univ., 1972.

ABOUT THE AUTHOR

Gwendolyn Chabrier graduated magna cum laude from New York University with a BA and MA in American literature. She began her Doctoral studies at Harvard, which were completed in France, and she holds a Doctorat d'Etat with highest honors from the Université de Paris IV-Sorbonne. Ms. Chabrier has been a professor of literature at New York University, the University of Rouen, and the Sorbonne. She has also been a literary scout for Les Editions Lebaud in Paris.

Dr Chabrier is the author of two previous literary monographs, *William Faulkner: la saga de la famille sudiste* (Paris 1988), and *Faulkner's Families: a Southern Saga* (NY 1993) as well as a novel, *An Asian Destiny* (Bangkok 2006).

www.ingramcontent.com/pod-product-compliance
Lightning Source LLC
Chambersburg PA
CBHW020329170426
43200CB00006B/326